insight

Upper-Intermediate Student's Book

Jayne Wildman
Fiona Beddall

Reading and vocabulary Challenges

1 SPEAKING Discuss the quotes. Do you agree or disagree with them? Which quote do you like the most? Justify your answers.

1 'Being challenged in life is inevitable, being defeated is optional.' (Roger Crawford)

2 'Attitude is a little thing that makes a big difference.' (Winston Churchill)

3 'Challenges are what make life interesting; overcoming them is what makes life meaningful.' (Joshua J. Marine)

4 'The only disability in life is a bad attitude.' (Scott Hamilton)

2 Read the article. What challenges did Amar face? What was his attitude towards them?

STRATEGY

Critical thinking: questioning the author

While you read, think about what the author means and how they have presented the information. Ask yourself questions about:

■ the author's intention and reasons for writing.

■ why they have told the story or written the article in a certain way.

This will develop your critical thinking skills and help you to check understanding and to remember what you have read.

3 Read the strategy. Answer questions 1–3 as you read paragraphs A and B of *The only way is forward*.

1 What is the author focusing on in these paragraphs? What point is he / she trying to make?

2 Why do you think the author quotes Amar? What impression do you have of him?

3 Does the author explain why Amar has experienced these problems? Why / why not?

4 Read paragraph C of the article. What key information does the author give us? Why does he / she tell us this now?

5 Read the article again and answer the questions.

In which paragraph A–G does the author:

1 point out the practical skills a Traveleyes guide needs?

2 describe Amar's early success and a change in his objectives?

3 describe how people perceive or experience a place in different ways?

4 explain why certain things weren't easy for Amar?

5 sum up Amar's character and achievements?

6 illustrate the benefits that tours can have for local communities?

7 describe a disappointment very early in Amar's life?

THE ONLY WAY IS FORWARD

A Like most sixteen-year-old teenagers, Amar Latif loved riding his bike. He'd often fall off, but undeterred he'd always get right back on. Then one day, after yet another accident, his parents decided that enough was enough, and sold it. It was his first major setback in life, but he managed to get over it. 'You are constantly told the world is your oyster,' said Amar later, 'but it didn't feel like my oyster ... you've [just] got to get out of that way of thinking.' This positive attitude helped Amar later. After successfully completing his degree, he travelled across Canada and North America with his friends. Travel was Amar's passion, but it soon became clear that he would have to overcome significant obstacles to do it. This was his second major blow. 'There were two ways forward,' he said. 'I could just accept that I was not able to travel. Or I'd need to change something. I chose the second option.'

B On his return home, Amar started a career in finance where his perfectionism and constant efforts to do his best led to success and promotion. Then, after nine years he gave up his job to pursue his real passion, setting up an innovative travel company called Traveleyes. Amar had always loved to travel, but since his trip to America, he'd been painfully aware of how difficult it was for people like him.

Vocabulary: describing qualities; synonyms; words with *self-*; word analysis; purpose and result
Grammar: tense revision; past perfect and past perfect continuous

Speaking: choosing a winner of a local hero award
Writing: an article

1A

C The reason was his eyesight. At the age of four, Amar was diagnosed with a rare degenerative eye condition. By sixteen, his eyesight had deteriorated so much that he couldn't ride his bike. Today, Amar is blind – and Traveleyes organizes holidays for visually-impaired people.

D Amar's idea for his company is revolutionary, based on a ground-breaking concept that partners blind travellers with sighted ones. Sighted guides are offered a discounted holiday in return for acting as 'eyes' for blind travellers. As a guide, they are constantly expected to notice and describe the world around them and to think about how best to transfer the details of the places and sights to their blind companions. It requires commitment and staying power, as well as patience and perseverance in the face of new challenges – and they need to get on with their partner, too. But despite these demands, sighted guides find the holidays both inspirational and educational. They challenge people's perception of 'disability' and illustrate the importance of social inclusion.

E This sense of community brings out the best in human nature, encouraging tolerance, compassion (a concern for others), and good humour. Sighted guides also take home an understanding of how a blind person experiences the world. 'Some things are more intense as a blind person,' explains Amar. 'When you're walking along cobbled streets, hearing church bells in the distance. Feeling the spray of Niagara Falls on your face when you're on the *Maid of the Mist* boat.' What might first be perceived as a hindrance turns out to be an unexpected benefit and most guides return home with more vivid and richer memories of what they've experienced.

F But this change of perception isn't limited to travellers. In countries such as the Gambia and Cuba, holidays often include a visit to a local blind school. Travellers take time to interact with the children and their teachers, sharing knowledge and talking about their own life experiences. It provides the children with role models and gives them optimism and more confidence in their own abilities. 'A lot [of the blind travellers] have great jobs back home, running their own businesses, accountants, lawyers, that sort of thing,' says Amar. 'So that changes [the kids'] perceptions ... It can give them hope, that they can do this as well.'

G Amar has come a long way since he fell off his bike all those years ago. His enthusiasm, ingenuity and ability to reinvent himself have made his story an inspirational tale. Single-mindedness and focusing on his passion have helped him conquer adversity and realize his dreams. 'Life is short, with or without sight,' he says. 'And you've got to get out there and do what you can. This isn't a dress rehearsal. You can't stop life. You can't rewind it. The only way is forward.'

6 SPEAKING Discuss the questions.

1 Would you consider being a guide on a Traveleyes holiday? Why / why not?

2 What things influence our perception of places? What things do you usually notice when you visit somewhere for the first time?

V Describing qualities

7 Find words in the article for definitions 1–8. Then rank the qualities in order of importance. Justify your answers.

1 a desire to do something as well as you possibly can (B)
2 dedication to an activity (D)
3 continuing on a course of action despite difficulties (D)
4 ability to accept something different (E)
5 sympathy for the suffering of others (E)
6 hopefulness and confidence about the future (F)
7 the ability to invent new things and being original (G)
8 focusing on and determination to achieve only one aim (G)

8 Complete the sentences with the words in exercise 7. There are three words that you do not need.

1 'You need a more positive outlook on life. A little .... will help you to deal with your problems more effectively.'

2 It was his amazing ...., involving hundreds of experiments – many of which failed – that enabled Edison to invent the light bulb.

3 He was quite a cold person and lacked .... He didn't understand other people or how they felt.

4 Her .... to her music was extraordinary. She practised for hours every evening after school.

5 She spent a long time on her science project. It was an example of her .... – everything had to be exactly right.

V insight Synonyms

9 Complete the lists of synonyms with the highlighted words in the article. Check any words that you do not know in a dictionary and write any common collocations.

1 a problem: ...., ..., ...

2 to successfully deal with a problem: ...., ..., ...

3 new, never done before: ...., ..., ...

4 an advantage: ....

10 SPEAKING What sort of challenges have you faced in your life? How have you dealt with them? Choose two challenges, describe them, say how you reacted and explain what the outcome was. Use the synonyms in exercise 9.

Vocabulary bank | Ways of looking page 134

---

1 ◉ 1.01 SPEAKING Study the list below and choose the three most important things for teens today. Justify your answers. Then listen to the radio programme. Have your ideas changed? Compare your ideas.

■ money ■ happiness ■ possessions ■ community life
■ helping others ■ having lots of free time
■ not working too hard

Tense revision

2 ◉ 1.01 Put sentences 1–10 in the correct order. Then listen and check. Identify the highlighted tenses and explain why they have been used.

1 Charities like We Day are turning 'me' into 'we' one hashtag at a time.

2 As a small child, he had worked twelve-hour days on handmade carpets, so he knew the misery suffered by child workers.

3 The story was about Iqbal, a Pakistani child, whose parents had sold him into forced labour.

4 That's why Craig had created Free the Children and twelve years later, he also founded We Day with his brother Marc.

5 Every year, We Day organizes special six-hour events or parties around the country.

6 Eventually, Iqbal escaped and joined an organization that fought for children's rights.

7 Recently, it's been growing in popularity – it has 3.3 million followers on Facebook.

8 Craig Kielburger was reading a newspaper when he came across an interesting article. ı

9 Since We Day began (in 2007), school children have given over 6 million hours of service.

10 'I've always believed there are plenty of hard-working, selfless teens out there.'

3 Identify the tenses in these pairs of sentences and explain why they have been used.

1 a Craig Kielburger has been supporting children's rights for years.
   b Craig Kielburger has believed in children's rights for years.

2 a Our school has taken part in most of the We Day events.
   b Our school took part in a We Day event last year.

3 a We have been collecting money for We Day all term.
   b We have collected £250 for We Day today.

4 a When we got to the fundraising party, Craig had already given a speech.
   b When we got to the fundraising party, Craig gave a speech.

5 a While the concert was finishing, we took some more photos.
   b When the concert finished, we took some more photos.

6 a At the moment, she's updating her Facebook account.
   b She's always updating her Facebook account!

Reference and practice 1.1   Workbook page 109

4 Complete the text with the correct form of the verbs in brackets.

A voice for the voiceless

Thirteen-year-old Kesz Valdez **1**.................... (smile) as he receives his award. Today is a big day as he **2**.................... (just / win) the International Children's Peace Prize for helping street children in the Philippines.

However, life **3**.................... (always / not be) kind to Kesz. When he was just two years old, his father **4**.................... (force) him to work in the Cavite City dump. Life was so bad that when he was four, he **5**.................... (run away) from home and began living on the streets. Then, a few years later, an accident happened. While he **6**.................... (look for) food in a rubbish dump one night, he **7**.................... (fall) into a pile of burning rubbish and severely injured his arm.

Things couldn't get any worse for Kesz, but fortunately, his luck started to change. A community worker called Harnin Manalaysay **8**.................... him.................... (take in), **9**.................... (look after) him and treated his wounds. Kesz **10**.................... (never / know) such kindness before, and the experience changed his life.

He wanted to help other street children in the same way, so, with his guardian's help, Kesz **11**.................... (found) an organization called Championing Community Children. Kesz and his friends **12**.................... (visit) underprivileged communities and talking to children about their rights for eight years now. They **13**.................... (give out) 'Hope Gifts' to more than 5,000 children, which include hygiene products, clothing and toys. Since 2006, Kesz **14**.................... (become) a new voice for the voiceless. 'I want children in the streets to get the same chance I had,' he says. 'My motto is: we can change the world one heart at a time.'

5 Make questions about Kesz's life. Then ask and answer in pairs.

1 Why / Kesz / smile / at the moment
2 Where / he / work / when he was two
3 Why / he / run away / from home
4 What / he / look for / when the accident happened
5 Who / look after / him afterwards
6 What / Kesz / never / experience / before
7 What effect / this / have on him
8 What / Kesz's organization / achieve / since it was founded

6 **SPEAKING** Discuss the questions.

1 Think about your local community. What challenges are there, e.g. poverty, environmental issues, crime, education, unemployment, housing?
2 In what ways could an individual help to solve these problems? Can you give examples of people who have tried to make a difference locally or globally?

DVD extra   Oxfam

1 🔊 **1.02 SPEAKING** Listen to the first part of a news story and discuss the questions.

1 Where did the story take place?
2 Who was there? What were they doing?
3 What happened next? What do you think each person on the platform did next?

2 🔊 **1.03** Listen to the rest of the news story and compare your ideas. Did the ending surprise you? Why / why not?

3 🔊 **1.04 SPEAKING** Why do you think some people help in life-threatening situations? Why do others stand back and do nothing? Listen to the radio discussion and compare your ideas.

4 🔊 **1.04** Listen again. Are the sentences true (T) or false (F)?

1 The speakers agree that Wesley was irresponsible.
2 During the bank robbery, people panicked when they saw the gun.
3 Our first reaction to danger is to acknowledge the threat.
4 Stress hormones help us to think faster.
5 The bank customer reacted quickly to protect himself.
6 Heroes usually feel in control of their lives.
7 They have greater levels of stress hormones.
8 They interact more with their local community.
9 Not many people are truly heroic.

V insight **Words with *self-***

5 Study the words from the recording. What does *self* mean in all these words? Check the meanings of any words you do not know in a dictionary. Then complete the text.

■ self-interest ■ self-defence ■ self-control ■ selflessness ■ self-assurance ■ self-obsession ■ self-preservation ■ self-sacrifice

When we talk about heroes, we imagine people who are fearless, have little concern for their own ¹................ in the face of danger, who rarely act out of ²................ , serving instead the interests of others. We don't usually associate such ³................ with 'selfish' teenagers, who are often called the 'me' generation because of their ⁴................ . If they do something brave, they are probably protecting themselves and acting in ⁵................ . However, despite the bad press, there are plenty of teens who do the right thing.

When it comes to ⁶................ , or putting yourself at risk for others, it's hard to beat fourteen-year-old Marcus Urgate. Marcus, from Oregon, saved an eight-year-old boy from a fire in a neighbour's house. The quick-thinking teen was calm and showed ⁷................ in the face of extreme danger, climbing up to the second floor, breaking the window and guiding the boy out.

In another incident in Florida, a group of teenagers were on their way to a prom when a van in front of them crashed. The teenagers immediately stopped and ran to the aid of the family trapped in the van, freeing the adults and children inside. They acted quickly, believing they could make a difference in a life-and-death situation. Their courage and ⁸................ helped to save seven lives.

Choosing the winner of a local hero award

6 **SPEAKING** Study the qualities below. Decide on the ones which you think a hero has. Then rank them in order of importance. Justify your choices.

■ selflessness ■ compassion ■ bravery ■ materialism ■ self-interest ■ optimism ■ single-mindedness ■ perfectionism

7 ◉ **1.05** A school committee is deciding on the winner of a local hero award. Study the list of candidates below, then listen to the committee discussing the options. Who do they choose and why?

B

A

A famous sports star who gave free tickets to underprivileged children to watch a football match.

A pilot who safely landed a plane in trouble, saving the lives of all the passengers.

C

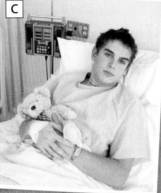

D

A teenage carer who looked after her disabled father at home while studying for exams at school.

A young person suffering from a terminal illness, who raised money for other children with the same condition.

E

A young boy who donated his kidney to save his brother.

8 ◉ **1.05** Listen again and tick the phrases that the students use. Then match all of them to categories A–C.

■ My view is that … . ■ Are you saying that … ? ■ Can you just explain that again? ■ For me … . ■ What do you mean exactly? ■ I understand that point of view. ■ I see where you're coming from.

A Giving an opinion
B Acknowledging an opinion
C Asking for clarification

9 ◉ **1.06** Listen to a similar discussion. Put the phrases in the order that you hear them. Then match all of them to categories A–C in exercise 8. Which person did the girl choose and why?

■ The point is that … . ■ I think we need to consider … . ■ Could you explain what you mean? ■ That makes sense to me. ■ I appreciate what you're saying … .

10 **SPEAKING** Work in small groups and decide who deserves the award. Choose from the people in exercise 7 or use people from your local area. Who would you vote for? Who would you not vote for? Give reasons for your choices using the phrases in exercises 8 and 9.

1 SPEAKING Rank the things below in order of importance in your life. If you had to make a choice and support just one of them, which would you choose? Then read the extract from an autobiography. What was important to the writer?

- ■ a political movement ■ education ■ family
- ■ fight against poverty ■ fight against discrimination
- ■ solution to an environmental issue ■ career

2 The extract is from a book *Long Walk to Freedom* by Nelson Mandela. Read the extract again and discuss the questions.

1 Why was Mandela's impression of time different from other people's?
2 What did Mandela realize when he saw his mother and children?
3 Why did he have mixed emotions when he saw his mother?
4 What impression of the authorities does Mandela give in the second paragraph?
5 What family tradition was Mandela forced to break?
6 How did it make him reflect on his life choices? What regrets did he have?
7 What is the 'struggle' he refers to? How did his family initially react to his commitment to this 'struggle'?
8 What conclusion does he come to about the life choices he made?

V insight **Word analysis**

3 Answer the questions, referring closely to the extract.

1 Which two adjectives does the writer use to describe 'change'? What is the difference between these two adjectives? (A)
2 Which adjective describes a transformation that is extreme or unusual, and therefore attracts attention? Why does the writer use it to describe his mother's appearance? (A)
3 Which word refers to a period of time between one event and another? (C)
4 Which word means *to look tired and ill*? What does it describe? (D)
5 Which phrase does the writer use instead of *a lot*? What does it refer to? (F)
6 Which word means *helpful*? What does the writer refer to when he uses this word? (F)
7 Which word does the writer use for a confusing problem or a question that is difficult to solve? What problem did the writer have? (G)
8 Which word means *to be punished for something*? How was the writer's family punished? (G)

This extract is from an autobiography called *Long Walk to Freedom* by the former President of South Africa, Nelson Mandela. In the book, Mandela describes his early life and later fight against the South African apartheid regime. He first became involved with the African National Congress (ANC) in 1942, supporting non-violent protest. [1]By 1962, he had been working for the party for more than twenty years. He started to realize that armed struggle was the only way forward and began to use guerrilla tactics. He was arrested in 1963 for political offences and sentenced to life imprisonment. In this passage he describes his time at Robben Island, a maximum security prison for political prisoners. [2]At this point in his life, he had been living in a small prison cell for many years.

From Robben Island: the Dark Years

A Time may seem to stand still for those of us in prison, but it did not halt for those outside. I was reminded of this when I was visited by my mother in the spring of 1968. I had not seen her since the end of
5 the Rivonia Trial. Change is gradual and incremental, and when one lives in the midst of one's family, one rarely notices differences in them. But when one doesn't see one's family for many years at a time, the transformation can be striking. My mother suddenly
10 seemed very old.

B She had journeyed all the way from the Transkei, accompanied by my son Makgatho, my daughter Makaziwe, and my sister Mabel. Because I had four visitors and they had come a great distance, the
15 authorities extended the visiting time from a half an hour to forty-five minutes.

C I had not seen my son and daughter since before the trial and they had become adults in the interim, growing up without me. I looked at them with
20 amazement and pride. But though they had grown up, I am afraid I still treated them more or less as the children they had been when I went to prison. They may have changed, but I hadn't.

D My mother had lost a great deal of weight, which
25 concerned me. Her face appeared haggard. Only my sister Mabel seemed unchanged. While it was a great pleasure to see all of them and to discuss family issues, I was uneasy about my mother's health.

E Several weeks later, after returning from the quarry,
30 I was told to go to the Head Office to collect a telegram. It was from Makgatho, informing me that my mother had died of a heart attack. I immediately made a

Past perfect and past perfect continuous

4 Study the underlined sentences in the extract and answer the questions.

a In sentence 3, which highlighted event happened first?

b Which two sentences emphasize the duration of an activity?

c Which three time expressions below cannot be used with the past perfect continuous tense?
■ for ■ since ■ already ■ by the time ■ after ■ yet ■ an hour / day / week before ■ never ■ just ■ still

Reference and practice 1.2	Workbook page 110

5 Complete the text with the correct form of the verbs in brackets. Use the past simple, past perfect or past perfect continuous. If both the past perfect simple and continuous are possible, explain the difference in meaning.

request to the commanding officer to be permitted to attend her funeral in the Transkei, which he turned down. 'Mandela,' he said, 'while I know you are a man 35 of your word and would not try to escape, I cannot trust your own people, and we fear that they would try to kidnap you.' It added to my grief that I was not able to bury my mother, which was my responsibility as her eldest child and only son. 40

F Over the next few months I thought about her a great deal. Her life had been far from easy. ³I had been able to support her when I was practicing as an attorney, but once I went to prison, I was unable to help her. I had never been as attentive as I should have been. 45

G A mother's death causes a man to look back on and evaluate his own life. Her difficulties, her poverty, made me question once again whether I had taken the right path. That was always the conundrum: Had I made the right choice in putting the people's welfare even before 50 that of my own family? For a long time, my mother had not understood my commitment to the struggle. My family had not asked for or even wanted to be involved in the struggle, but my involvement penalized them.

H But I came back to the same answer. In South 55 Africa, it is hard for a man to ignore the needs of the people, even at the expense of his own family. I had made my choice, and in the end, she had supported it. But that did not lessen the sadness I felt at not being able to make her life more comfortable, or the 60 pain of not being able to lay her to rest.

On 11 February 1990, the world's press gathered outside a prison in South Africa. Many ¹ .... (camp) there for days, waiting for an event that would change the history of their nation. Inside, an old man was pacing back and forth, and then he ² .... (look) impatiently at his watch. It was almost 3.30 p.m., but he ³ .... (wait) for this moment for a long time and was getting restless. His people ⁴ .... (fight) for his release for twenty-seven years and he did not want to keep them waiting, but his car still ⁵ .... (not come). At 4 p.m., the car finally ⁶ .... (arrive), but a quarter of a mile from the prison gate, it ⁷ .... (slow down) and the old man and his wife got out. Then, as they ⁸ .... (walk) towards the gate, a huge crowd of people started cheering. The old man felt alarmed – he had not expected such a scene and he ⁹ .... (never / experience) anything like it before. Then, he smiled and ¹⁰ .... (raise) his right fist in a victory salute. The crowd roared. Nelson Mandela was free.

6 SPEAKING Discuss the questions.

1 What qualities would you expect a leader to have? How do Mandela's actions illustrate these qualities?

2 Think of another leader. What qualities do they have? Do you admire them? Why / why not?

Vocabulary bank	Qualities of a hero page 134

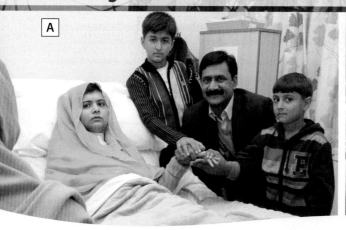

1 SPEAKING Look at the photos from a person's life. Describe what is happening.
What do you think is the connection between the events in the photos?

STRATEGY

The writing process

When you are writing, remember this five-stage process. It will help you to improve your work:

1 prewriting
2 drafting
3 editing and revising
4 rewriting
5 publishing (or creating the finished work)

2 Read the strategy. Then match the elements below to stages 1–5 in the strategy.

■ incorporating changes ■ writing the final draft ■ self-correction ■ publishing a blog post
■ peer-correction ■ brainstorming ■ planning ■ emailing to the teacher ■ writing the first draft

3 Read the article topic below. Work in groups of four and brainstorm ideas that you could use. Then read the article and compare your ideas. Were your answers in exercise 1 correct?

> A recent newspaper article claimed that teenagers today have few teenage role models. Write an article in response to this for your school's online magazine. Give an example of a teenager who inspires you or who is your role model.

4 Read the article plan. Did the writer follow the plan?

> Paragraph 1: Who is your teenage role model?
> Paragraph 2: Why is the teenager inspirational?
> Paragraph 3: Mention events in his / her life to support this.
> Paragraph 4: Sum up and mention the teenager's achievements.

V Purpose and result

5 Study the highlighted phrases in the article. Then complete the categories below.

    1 purpose: in order that, ..., ..., ..., ...
    2 result: as a result, ..., ..., ..., ...

6 Rewrite the sentences using the words in brackets.

    1 The school didn't close because Malala's father owned it. (so)
    2 She studied hard because she wanted to become a doctor. (so that)
    3 People were upset when Malala was hurt and sent her flowers. (so … that)
    4 After the shooting, more people supported Malala's cause. (as a consequence)
    5 There was a lot of publicity and Malala became an international celebrity. (such … that)
    6 She was taken to a hospital in England to recover. (in order to)
    7 As there were still threats against Malala, she stayed in England. (so)

No teen role models?

I read an article about teenagers yesterday that claimed there are no teen role models. It was such a shock that I have decided to prove the writer wrong. In my opinion, there are plenty of inspiring teens out there and Malala Yousafzai is just one of them.

A few years ago, in a small town in north-west Pakistan, a group of teenage girls were on their way to school. They were sitting on the school bus, when suddenly an armed man jumped on. 'Who is Malala?' he shouted, then he fired his gun. Malala was seriously injured.

At the time, in north-west Pakistan, the Taliban* was winning a war against the government. The Taliban didn't believe in educating girls and destroyed many schools in order to make it impossible for them to learn. However, students at Malala's school were determined to learn, so the school stayed open, and eleven-year-old Malala became their spokesperson. In 2008, she gave a speech to the national press, then wrote a blog for the BBC so as to raise awareness of their problems. The blog was so popular that Malala became a well-known supporter of children's rights, and that's why she was attacked.

Malala is an amazing role model because she risked her life so that other girls could learn. Today, Malala has won peace awards and has spoken in support of children's rights at the United Nations. As a consequence, she has inspired other girls to continue their fight for education. 'Books and pens ... are our most powerful weapons,' she says. 'Education is the only solution. Education first.'

* Taliban = a fundamentalist Islamic political movement

WRITING GUIDE

■ **Task** Write your own response to the article topic in exercise 3.

■ **Ideas** Choose a teenage role model and make notes about:
  ■ key events in their life.
  ■ their personality and character.

■ **Plan** Follow the plan:

Paragraph 1: Write an introduction and give a clear statement of your opinion.

Paragraph 2: Introduce your teenage role model. You could start with the main event in their life.

Paragraph 3: Recount their life story to show how they arrived at the main event.

Paragraph 4: Sum up why they are a role model. You could include their positive qualities.

■ **Write** Write your article. Use the paragraph plan and the strategy to help you.

■ **Check** Check the following points:
  ■ Have you responded to the opinion in the task?
  ■ Have you included arguments that support your opinion?
  ■ Have you checked grammar, vocabulary, spelling and punctuation?

1 Work in pairs. Study the list of reasons for using a dictionary when learning a foreign language. Do you use a dictionary in these situations?

1 to check the meaning of an unknown word
2 to check the spelling of a word
3 to check the meaning of a word in your own language
4 to check the meaning of a fixed phrase
5 to find all the phrasal verbs with a particular verb
6 to find a synonym or an antonym of a word
7 to find what other words go with a particular word
8 to find out how to say a word

STRATEGY

Choosing the right dictionary

There are many types of dictionaries. It is important to know what information you can find in each type and to choose the dictionary which matches your needs. The most common types of dictionaries are:

a monolingual dictionaries
b bilingual dictionaries
c thesauruses
d collocations dictionaries
e dictionaries of phrasal verbs
f dictionaries of idioms
g pronunciation dictionaries

2 Read the strategy above. Which dictionary a–g would you use to find information 1–8 in exercise 1?

3 Match each dictionary entry 1–6 to a dictionary a–g in the strategy.

1

> **kidnap** /ˈkɪdnæp/ verb [T] (**kidnapping**; **kidnapped**) to take sb away by force and demand money for their safe return: *The child was kidnapped and £50 000 ransom was demanded for her release.* ▶ **porywać, uprowadzać** *(dla okupu)* ➔ look at **hijack**
> ■ **kidnapper** noun [C] ▶ **porywacz/ka** | **kidnapping** noun [C,U] ▶ **porwanie, uprowadzenie** *(dla okupu)* ➔ note at **crime**

2

> **guerrilla** *noun*
> ADJ. **armed** | **urban** ◇ *Urban ~s detonated a car bomb in front of the company's headquarters.* | **communist, right-wing, separatist**
> GUERRILLA + NOUN **army, band, force, group, movement, organization, unit** | **commander, fighter, leader** | **activity, attack, campaign, offensive, raid, resistance, struggle, war, warfare** ◇ *Ten years of ~ resistance followed the occupation.* | **tactics**

3

> **prison** *noun*
>
> **prison · jail · camp · detention centre · penitentiary · jailhouse · correctional facility**
> These are all words for a building where people are kept and prevented from leaving.
>
> PATTERNS AND COLLOCATIONS
> ▸ **in** prison / jail
> ▸ **in a** prison / jail / camp / detention centre / penitentiary / jailhouse / correctional facility
> ▸ a **local** prison / jail / correctional facility
> ▸ a **juvenile** prison / jail / detention centre / correctional facility
> ▸ a **women's** prison / jail / correctional facility
> ▸ to **go to** / **be sent to** / **be released from** / **get out of** prison / jail
> ▸ a prison / jail **sentence** / **term**

4

> **con·un·drum** /kəˈnʌndrəm/ *noun* **1** a confusing problem or question that is very difficult to solve **2** a question, usually involving a trick with words, that you ask for fun ꜱʏɴ **riddle**

5

> **be a man/woman of his/her ˈword**
> be a person who always does what he/she has promised to do: *If he said he'd help you, he will — he's a man of his word.*

6

> ᴦ**turn sb/sth ˈdown** to reject or refuse sb/sth: *Why did Clare turn down your invitation?* ◇ *He asked her to marry him, but she turned him down.* ◇ *They turned down my offer of help.* ◇ *She turned the job down because it paid too little.* ◇ *My book was turned down by eight publishers.*
> ᴏʙᴊ **offer, application, invitation, request, job, proposal** ꜱʏɴ **reject sb/sth**
> ◆ v + adv + n ◆ v + n/pron + adv

4 Use the correct dictionary to find information 1–6.

1 a translation of *perseverance* in your own language
2 an explanation of *ingenuity* in English
3 common expressions with *fate* and *destiny*
4 synonyms of the word *overcome*
5 different meanings of the particle *on*
6 adjectives commonly used with the word *challenge*

STRATEGY

Using synonyms correctly

A thesaurus will provide several different synonyms for the same word, but it isn't common for them to have the exact same meaning. Check the definition of each synonym carefully. It is also important to check the connotations of words. Synonyms may have the same general meaning, but they often have different connotations. For example, one synonym can be more formal than another.

5 Read the strategy above. Then study the thesaurus entries for three synonyms of the word *child* and answer the questions.

1 Which words are informal? Which word is formal?
2 Which word has a negative connotation?

> *babies and is easily treated.* See also **baby** ➔ SON
> **kid** [C] (*informal, especially spoken*) a child: *He's only a kid. You can't expect him to understand what's going on.* ◇ *A bunch of kids were hanging around outside.* See also **kid** ➔ SON

> **infant** /ˈɪnfənt/ [C] (*formal or technical*) a baby or very young child: *We studied newborn infants up to two months old.* ◇ *The country has an appallingly high infant mortality rate.* ❶ In the British and Australian education systems **infant** is also the word for a child at school between the ages of four and seven: *The majority of infant teachers are women.* ◇ *I've known her since we were in the infants* (= at infant school).

> ➔ ADULT
> **brat** [C] (*informal, disapproving*) a person, especially a child, who behaves badly: *He's a spoilt little brat!*

6 Complete the sentences with the correct synonym of *child*.

1 I really don't like my cousin. He behaves like a .... !
2 This part of the hospital is for babies and ....
3 Please don't be a .... ! Sit down and be quiet.
4 All the .... around here are crazy about skateboarding at the moment.
5 The older children go home at 3.30 p.m., but the .... finish school at 2.45 p.m.
6 I'm not surprised she looks tired – she's got six .... !

Dictionary entries from *Oxford Wordpower słownik angielsko-polski polsko-angielski*; *Oxford Collocations Dictionary for students of English* 2ᵉ; *Oxford Learner's Thesaurus*; *Oxford Advanced Learner's Dictionary* 8ᵉ; *Oxford Idioms Dictionary for learners of English* 2ᵉ; *Oxford Phrasal Verbs Dictionary for learners of English*.

Vocabulary

1 Choose the correct answers.

Christy Brown was an Irish writer who was born almost completely paralyzed, and his parents treated him with love and **¹optimism / compassion**. Through his mother's **²tolerance / single-mindedness**, Christy learned how to read. His own **³perseverance / perfectionism** enabled him to learn to write with his left foot. He started writing an account of his life, and his **⁴ingenuity / optimism** never failed as he was certain that one day it would be published. Writing required 100% **⁵commitment / tolerance**, because progress was slow. His own **⁶compassion / perfectionism** meant that he rewrote each page many times before he was satisfied. But by the time Christy Brown was 22 years old, his autobiography *My Left Foot* had been published.

Marks .... / 6

2 Choose the odd one out.

1 a hindrance / an obstacle / a benefit
2 groundbreaking / perfectionism / innovative
3 blow / conquer / overcome
4 advantage / benefit / defeat
5 blow / conquer / problem

Marks .... / 5

3 Complete the sentences with a word with *self-*.

1 You should never use violence, even in ....
2 People who act out of .... rarely support charities.
3 He didn't go back into the burning house; some sense of .... stopped him.
4 Mother Teresa showed great .... in dedicating her life to the poor.
5 Surgeons have to have .... during operations and be confident in what they're doing.
6 Teenagers usually lose their .... and start thinking about others when they get older.
7 You need a lot of .... as you'll be working long hours, away from home and without any pay.

Marks .... / 7

4 Complete the sentences with the words below. There is one word that you do not need.

■ attentive ■ conundrum ■ gradual ■ haggard
■ incremental ■ interim ■ striking

1 Recovery from a back injury is usually ....
2 She looked .... after the night shift.
3 He bears a .... resemblance to his father.
4 Some students do voluntary work in the ...., between school and university.
5 Good doctors are always .... to the needs of their patients.
6 She faced a .... because she didn't know if she should go abroad or stay and look after her parents.

Marks .... / 6

Grammar

5 Complete the text with the correct forms of the verbs in brackets.

It's Saturday afternoon, and Maria Ndiaye ¹.......................... (sit) in the shade of a tree, reading. Maria ².......................... (read) a lot, but there isn't any ink in her books. Instead, she ³.......................... (pass) her fingers over a series of raised dots. Maria ⁴.......................... (be) blind since birth, and she ⁵.......................... (read) braille for nearly ten years now. Braille is the system that blind and visually-impaired people ⁶.......................... (use) to read and write. It is named after its inventor, the Frenchman Louis Braille. Braille became blind as a child when he ⁷.......................... (play) with a tool in his father's workshop and it hit him in the eye. Despite his disability, he ⁸.......................... (attend) the local school, but it was while he ⁹.......................... (study) in Paris that he developed his new system. He ¹⁰.......................... (hear) of a system called 'night writing' devised by Captain Charles Barbier of the French army. Night writing was a code of dots and dashes, which ¹¹.......................... (allow) soldiers to read in the dark. Braille ¹².......................... (simplify) Barbier's system into columns containing six dots. Nearly two centuries later, the braille system ¹³.......................... (remain) an invaluable tool for people who have lost their sight, like Maria Ndiaye.

Marks .... / 13

6 Choose the correct answers.

1 A lifeboat **rescued / had rescued / had been rescuing** the man after he was swept off a rock by a freak wave.
2 They didn't call an ambulance because somebody **already called / had already called / had already been calling** one.
3 I fainted because I **stood up / had stood up / had been standing up** all day.
4 We were shocked because we **never witnessed / had never witnessed / had never been witnessing** an accident before.
5 The boys were given a reward because they **returned / had returned / had been returning** the woman's bag.
6 The river flooded because it **rained / had rained / had been raining** for so long.
7 The judge **sentenced / had sentenced / had been sentencing** him to three weeks of community service for vandalizing the bus shelter.
8 The sick child was relieved to be admitted to hospital because she **waited / had waited / had been waiting** for this treatment for a long time.

Marks .... / 8

Total .... / 45

2 The world around us

Reading and vocabulary Real education

1 SPEAKING Look at the photos and discuss the questions. Then read the article and compare your ideas.

1 How would you describe the environment? What do you think life is like for teenagers there? What might they do in their free time?

2 How does this compare to your local environment?

2 Read the article again and choose the correct answers.

1 Why did Wagner miss class?
   a Because the weather was unpredictable.
   b To go fishing with a relative.
   c Because he had to stay at home and help his family.
   d To get away from the village.

2 Why isn't Wagner going to college?
   a A degree would be difficult to do.
   b He's already a good scientist.
   c He doesn't mind earning less money.
   d He has to look after his brother and sisters.

3 A large number of students on St. Lawrence Island
   a would like to attend college.
   b complete their high school education.
   c don't go hunting with their families.
   d believe in the benefits of education.

4 Jobs in the community
   a are mostly in the fishing trade.
   b are quite hard to find.
   c are often well-paid.
   d often demand degrees.

5 Local people are worried about
   a the community being isolated.
   b the island population decreasing.
   c losing a sense of community.
   d young people forgetting their traditions.

6 Many people think that the community needs
   a to have less autonomy.
   b to give up some traditions.
   c to have a different type of education.
   d to take their children out of school.

3 SPEAKING Answer the questions.

1 Is there anything unexpected in the opening paragraph? What is its purpose?

2 What is the point of the story about the fish (paragraph I)? What lesson did the speaker learn?

DVD extra An English education

Making school meaningful

by Sarah Garland

A Wagner Iworrigan, a seventeen-year-old high school senior on St. Lawrence Island in Alaska, knows a lot about biology, meteorology and maths. He's an expert at telling whether a walrus is too sick to eat, if the weather is likely to turn dangerous, and the best angle for throwing a harpoon at a bowhead whale.

B On a recent unseasonably warm day last autumn, he missed class to join his uncle on their boat. With nets and hooks, they motored through the choppy grey waves of the Bering Sea until the lights of their village, Savoonga, seemed further away than the stars above. They hoped to catch a plump seal to feed the rest of the family: Wagner's two younger sisters, a younger brother, four cousins and a grandfather. All ten of them share a three-bedroom house.

C Wagner might make a good scientist, but he's not planning on going to college. He feels a responsibility for his siblings – his mother died and his father lives in another village – and college is 'so far from home'. He's also unclear about what he would do with a degree: 'We don't have a lot of jobs here,' he says. After graduating, he plans to become a commercial fisherman to 'make some good money' at one of the most dangerous jobs in the US.

D Many St. Lawrence students say they want to go to college but half of them drop out of high school, and only two per cent graduate from college. The benefits of a degree are not obvious for people living on this remote island. Families have a subsistence lifestyle, hunting walruses, seals and whales in the spring, and gathering berries in the summer. The largest employer is the school system; otherwise, there are only a handful of jobs in fishing, oil and the airlines that connect the island to the mainland. There isn't much demand for anything else and more than a quarter of adults are unemployed.

Vocabulary: word analysis; nouns + prepositions; antonyms: urban regeneration; adjective suffixes: -*able* and -*ible*

Grammar: future tenses; future continuous, future perfect, future perfect continuous; future time clauses

Speaking: deciding on a new community project

Writing: describing a place for a travel blog

2A

E Many people feel that the educational programs are too stifling, not allowing students to go beyond the curriculum, with little connection to the real world. 'We want our children to achieve academically, but we need to be able to design programs that deal with the challenges they face day-to-day,' said one teacher. Those challenges are profound with no easy solutions: what is the relevance of school to kids who spend much of their time hunting and gathering berries?

F Families also worry that sending children away to study in Higher Education could endanger the Yupik language and culture. Already, the younger generation is losing its fluency and grasp of skills like sewing, walrus-ivory carving and fish-cutting. Respect for the old ways and knowledge of traditions are disappearing. Can the community send more students to university without sacrificing its desire to preserve Native culture and language?

G The Yupik Eskimos have inhabited St. Lawrence Island continuously for the last 2,000 years. Today two villages remain with a population of just 1,400. People there are used to the harsh landscape and climate – in the summer, meadows of grassy tundra stretch from snow-capped ridges to the stony shorelines, but in winter the sun disappears, there is a lot of snow, and polar bears arrive on ice floes. Leaving the island is not an option, as a ticket on a bush plane costs $400, a week's earnings for many islanders. The sense of community is strong. When a whale is killed, the houses and school empty as everyone races to the beach to take a share of the meat. As Wagner put it, 'We're all one big family because we're so isolated.'

H But the old ways are inevitably changing. The children drink soda and eat macaroni-and-cheese in addition to the traditional diet of fish, sea mammals

and berries. They ride snow machines instead of walking. And in the evening, they prefer playing video games and watching satellite television to listening to their elders tell stories.

I Unsurprisingly, locals are protective of their independence and their heritage. They recognize the value of 'education', but feel that the definition is too narrow. 'I think about when my grandmother taught me to cut fish,' remembers one resident. 'It wasn't do it once and I'll give you a grade. It was hours of practice until you get it right ... . There's a distinction between an education and school. Education is what Native people have been doing for their children since the beginning of time. School has been what has been imposed on people from outside,' she adds. 'We need to get in the business of education again.'

4 Answer the questions, referring closely to the article.

1 Which word describes the location of the island? How does this affect students' attitudes to education? (D)

2 Which phrase sums up the way of life on the island? What examples does the author give? (D)

3 Which word implies a criticism of the educational system? (E)

4 Which word describes the challenges the community faces? Will these challenges be easily overcome? (E)

5 Which verb emphasizes the threat to native culture if young people go to college? (F)

6 Which word describes the landscape and climate? What examples does the author give? (G)

7 Which word implies that changes are unavoidable? (H)

V insight Nouns + prepositions

5 Study the highlighted words in the article and explain their meaning. Then use them to complete the text. There is one word that you do not need.

Seventeen-year-old Theo Drummond is an expert on sea birds; he's also a student at a small school in the Orkney Islands off the coast of North Scotland. At the moment, he's writing an article about the birds for their online magazine, *Word of the Wild*. He's one of a ¹............... students who are preparing the latest issue. 'Working on the magazine gives students a ²............... computer skills, as well as encouraging ³............... their local environment,' explains teacher John Greenaway, who has ⁴............... for the running of the project and sees the real ⁵............... connecting academic work to day-to-day life. Meanwhile, eighteen-year-old Kelly Blair is busy photographing an unusual specimen of lobster. It was found by her fisherman father. 'Many families work in fishing, so there's a ⁶............... projects that involve these activities,' says Kelly.

'It's important to teach students about the outside world, but it's also important to show ⁷............... local ways of life and help reinforce our ⁸............... community,' continues John. 'It helps to keep students engaged and it helps them to learn – that's what matters most.'

6 SPEAKING Work in pairs. Discuss the questions.

1 Does school prepare you for day-to-day challenges? If not, what changes would you make to the school curriculum to do so?

2 Does school prepare you for your future life?

3 Is there a difference between school and education? What is the distinction?

4 Should Wagner go to college? Discuss arguments for and against.

Vocabulary bank	The natural world and outer space page 135

1 🔊 **1.07 SPEAKING Look at the photos and discuss the questions. Then listen to an interview and compare your ideas. Which job are they talking about?**

1 Where are the people? What are they doing? Describe their jobs.

2 What might be the challenges of working in these environments?

2 🔊 **1.07 Listen again. Are the sentences true (T) or false (F)?**

1 The forecast says it'll probably be rainy and cold.

2 Brad sees clouds in the distance and thinks it's going to snow.

3 The afternoon flight might be a little late.

4 Brad is delivering food and letters to McCarthy later.

5 Planes fly to the town just once a day.

6 He is going to take a scenic route today.

7 He hopes he'll see some snow on the flight.

8 During the conversation, Brad says he'll give the interviewer a tour.

Future tenses

3 Study the sentences in exercise 2 again and answer the questions.

Which sentence(s):

a talk about future plans and arrangements?

b talk about future predictions (two sentences)? Which sentence is based on evidence?

c talk about scheduled events or a timetable?

d are uncertain future predictions (two sentences)?

e refer to future intentions?

f refer to a decision or an offer at the moment of speaking?

g refer to a future hope or wish?

Reference and practice 2.1	Workbook page 111

4 Study the alternative future tenses in the sentences below. Explain the difference in meaning, if any.

1 I *'m meeting / 'm going to meet* some friends at the airport later this evening.
2 The weather forecast is good for this afternoon, so I *'ll probably do / 'm doing* the tour.
3 The next plane *leaves / might leave* at five o'clock. There's usually one every hour, but it depends on the weather.
4 Do you think you *'ll fly / might fly* the same routes next year?
5 There's heavy snow tonight, so I *might call / 'm going to call* some friends and stay in McCarthy.
6 'Hey, the baggage door is open outside.' 'Don't worry. I *'ll close / 'm going to close* it now.'
7 Oh, no! They've already boarded the plane. It *'s going to leave / 's leaving*.

Future continuous, future perfect and future perfect continuous

5 Read the extract from another interview for *Life on the edge*. What is the job? Match the underlined phrases 1–5 to descriptions a–d below. Which phrases are in the future continuous, future perfect or future perfect continuous?

Interviewer How long have you been a ....?
Logan Well, next month ¹I'll have been working as a .... for exactly eight years.
Interviewer I understand that Kilauea in Hawaii is your next destination. ²What will you be doing there?
Logan On Monday, ³we'll be hiking across the island, looking for the best locations. Then, according to the schedule, on Tuesday morning, we ⁴will be shooting. By the time we leave, ⁵we'll hopefully have captured some amazing images. And survived!

a an activity in progress at a certain time in the future
b an activity in the future that is fixed or decided
c an activity that will be completed in the future (two phrases) – which phrase focuses on duration?
d asking politely about someone's plans for the near future

Reference and practice 2.2   Workbook page 111

6 Complete the text with the correct form of the verbs in brackets. Use the future continuous, future perfect or future perfect continuous.

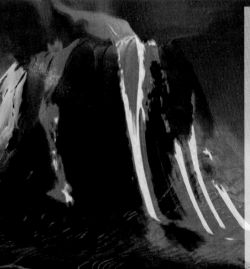

By tomorrow eveneing, Logan Jones and Pete Sawyer ¹............................ (prepare) to go to Big Island in Hawaii. In the morning, they ²............................ (probably / pack) their swimsuits and camping gear and they ³............................ (check) their camera equipment. Logan and Pete aren't ordinary tourists and they ⁴............................ (not stay) at a beach resort. Instead, they'll be exploring the remote Hawaii Volcanoes National Park. By the end of their stay, they ⁵............................ (take) enough photos for their next exhibition. Logan and Pete are volcano photographers.

For two days, the photographers ⁶............................ (camp) on the edge of an active volcano, waiting for the best moment to take their photos. They ⁷............................ (also / swim) in the choppy sea, in 110°F water, for close-ups of 'lava surf'. By the time they leave the island, they ⁸............................ (probably / risk) their lives on many occasions, but for Logan and Pete, it's worth it. 'This time next week, we ⁹............................ (work) together for five years, so this trip is special,' says Pete. 'We know the risks and have a profound respect for the volcanoes. We also have knowledge of lava movement, the wind and the ocean. Once this trip is done, we ¹⁰............................ (visit) Kilauea more than ten times. She's like an old friend to us!'

7 **SPEAKING** Work in pairs. Write questions using the future continuous, future perfect or future perfect continuous. Then choose a dangerous job from the list below or imagine one of your own. Take it in turns to interview each other.

■ war correspondent ■ crab fisherman ■ lion trainer ■ prison security guard ■ bicycle courier

1 What / do / this time tomorrow ?
2 Where / work / this time tomorrow ?
3 How long / work as a … / by this time next month?
4 How many / … / by this time next week ?
5 still work as / this time next year? Why / why not ?

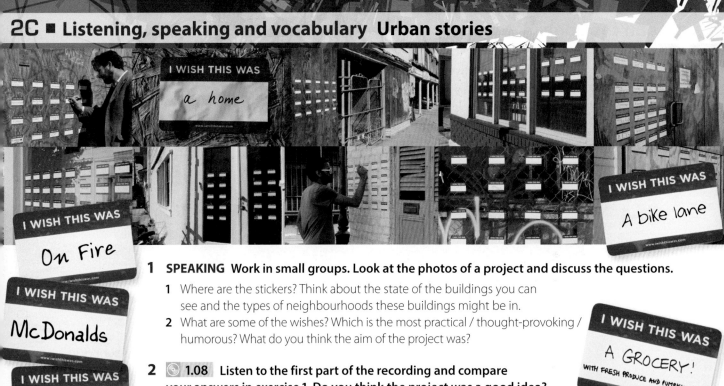

1 **SPEAKING** Work in small groups. Look at the photos of a project and discuss the questions.

1 Where are the stickers? Think about the state of the buildings you can see and the types of neighbourhoods these buildings might be in.

2 What are some of the wishes? Which is the most practical / thought-provoking / humorous? What do you think the aim of the project was?

2 🔘 **1.08** Listen to the first part of the recording and compare your answers in exercise 1. Do you think the project was a good idea? Are there empty buildings in your area? What could they be turned into?

STRATEGY

Active listening (1)

People recall about 50% of what they hear immediately after listening and only 25% two days later. To be a more active listener, follow the SIER hierarchy:

■ **Sensing:** focusing on the content
■ **Interpreting:** understanding the argument
■ **Evaluating:** judging the argument
■ **Responding:** formulating an opinion about the argument

Listening critically means evaluating and judging information, rather than simply listening.

3 🔘 **1.09** Listen to a radio discussion and answer the questions.

1 What is the discussion about? (sensing)
2 What are the main arguments? (interpreting)
3 Do they make sense to you? (evaluating)
4 What is your opinion? (responding)

---

4 🔘 **1.09** Listen again and answer the questions.

1 According to the interviewer, how were neighbours in the past different from neighbours today?
2 What two things might unite neighbours today?
3 What does the Neighborland website allow people to do?
4 What practical things have people proposed?
5 What's the point of the more 'fun' proposals?
6 How can suggestions be realized?
7 What is the 21st century known as?
8 How will websites like Neighborland help?

V insight Antonyms: urban regeneration

5 Complete the table with the words from the two recordings. Use a dictionary to help you.

■ neglected
■ run down
■ worthwhile
■ abandoned
■ wasteful
■ thriving
■ attractive

positive adjectives	negative adjectives
cared for	1 ....
inhabited	2 ....
3	declining
4	unappealing
efficient	5 ....
6	pointless
renovated	7 ....

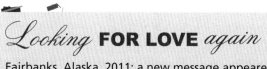

Looking FOR LOVE *again*

Fairbanks, Alaska, 2011: a new message appeared high on the side of an old high-rise building in the centre of the city. The message read 'Looking for love again'. At street-level below, chalkboards were fixed to the walls for people to write down memories of the building's past and dreams for its future. The ¹*deserted* tower block was the Polaris Building, previously a(n) ²*appealing* apartment complex, then a hotel, which had ³*successful* shops and restaurants, but now a space that had been empty for more than a decade.

This eye-catching project was focusing on a ⁴*forgotten* place and asking how we could make it something ⁵*useful* again. It provided a way for citizens to influence its future and almost everyone wanted the building ⁶*repaired* and restored, rather than demolished. Ideas for its new life ranged from creating a theatre and performing arts school, or developing a recreational centre, including a roller rink, to creating a huge, highly ⁷*economical* greenhouse to produce cheaper local food. Everyone wanted to recreate the dynamic space of the past – a focal point for the local community. Today, the building is still for sale. What will it be in the future?

6 Read the text about another project by Candy Chang. Replace the words in italics with a synonym in exercise 5.

7 SPEAKING Work in small groups and discuss the opinions. Do you agree or disagree? Give reasons for your answers.

   1 'Communities are less sociable and open than they used to be. Residents don't often come together as a community. They don't even speak to each other in the street.'

   2 'Public space is where life happens – it's important because it brings people together and this gives the community an identity.'

Vocabulary bank	Urban landscape page 135

Deciding on a new community project

8 SPEAKING Work in pairs. Discuss three things that you would like to be a ten-minute walk from your home. Give reasons for your choices.

9 🔊 **1.10** Listen to students at a school meeting discussing the needs of their local community. What ideas do they mention?

10 🔊 **1.10** Listen again and complete the phrases from the recording.

A Introducing requirements	**C Desirable requirements**
My main ¹............................ is	I think that's a '⁴............................-to-have'.
It's important to draw attention to	We could ⁵............................ (a park).
B Essential requirements	**D Evaluating requirements**
What we ²............................ need is	I'm not ⁶............................ by (the sports club) ... .
For me it's a must.	I think the last idea is the best.
(A sports centre) would be a big ³.............................	

11 🔊 **1.11** Listen to another discussion and tick the phrases that you hear. Then match all of them to categories A–D in exercise 10. Which idea did all three speakers like?

   ■ That should be the / a priority (in this area). ■ It's important to highlight neglected ... .
   ■ It's essential / crucial to ... . ■ It might be an idea to have ... .
   ■ That could be useful for some people. ■ It's probably not that useful or practical.

12 SPEAKING Work in groups. Follow the instructions.

You have received a grant from the local government to spend on an innovative community project that would improve the quality of everyday life. Decide on a project. Think about:
   ■ the purpose of the project.
   ■ the types of people who might benefit from it.
   ■ how it will improve everyday life.
   ■ whether it will have long-term or short-term benefits.

1 SPEAKING Discuss the questions. Then read an article about the early Australian Aborigines and answer the same questions. What kinds of similarities or differences are there?

1 When you travel, how do you find your way around?

2 Do you use manmade or natural landmarks, for example, a park or a river?

3 Do you use memories attached to a place, for example, somewhere you went as a child?

2 Complete the article with sentences A–F. There is one sentence that you do not need.

A They believed that the earth and its animals were there for the benefit of human beings.

B As more people arrived and more land was taken, Aboriginal culture became increasingly threatened.

C The journeys of these beings were recorded in song, describing the first pathways or songlines.

D They showed people where to find a water hole, where there was a river and where they could hunt.

E It's a way of life that predates the Ice Age, beginning around 70,000 years ago, with more than 2,000 generations since then.

F Their reaction was ruthless: many were killed or put into camps where missionaries 're-educated' them.

3 SPEAKING Think about famous natural or manmade landmarks in your country. Are there any stories or myths related to them?

V | insight Adjective suffixes: *-able* and *-ible*

4 Study the highlighted adjectives in the article. Answer questions 1–3, to help you work out when we use the suffixes *-able* and *-ible*.

If you remove the suffix, which words:

1 are still complete words, or complete if you add an *-e*?

2 end in a hard *c* or *g*?

3 are not complete words?

Be careful! There are exceptions, for example:
accessible, flexible, irresistible, sensible.

SONGLINES

Journalist Gina Baxter learns about songlines and Dreamtime in the Australian outback.

'We don't mind using GPS,' says Baamba, our Aboriginal guide, looking out across the wilderness which belongs
5 to his tribe, the Adnyamathanha people. The red ground ahead is covered with scrub brush and gum trees, all the way to the distant Flinders mountain range, and although it's early, it's already thirty degrees in the shade. It's difficult terrain, but Baamba is a sensible guide: he
10 always carries a satellite phone in his backpack in case of emergencies. His ancestors, however, relied on songs.

The early Australian Aborigines made the land navigable through songs, dance and paintings. The songs described pathways or 'songlines', which provided an oral 'map' of
15 the land. ¹.................... Generations of Aborigines followed these pathways, leaving legible marks and etchings on rocks and trees to help future travellers. 'But the songs describe more than a pathway,' explains Baamba. 'They also tell stories about the 'creator beings' who shaped the
20 earth in Dreamtime.'

According to Aboriginal creation myths, Dreamtime marked the beginning of the world, when giant beings, part human, part animal, came down from the sky, from across the sea and from deep in the earth. These giant beings travelled 25 across the land, making rivers and mountain ranges; then they disappeared back into the landscape, in places which became sacred sites. ² .... 'The Adnyamathanha people sing songs that tell the story of Akurra, the rainbow serpent,' continues Baamba. 'During Dreamtime, he created 30 the Flinders mountain range. We'll see the cave paintings later at Arkaroo Rock.'

Arkaroo Rock is one of many sacred sites mentioned in the songs and stories about the land. These stories show the considerable attachment the first Australians had to 35 their environment, how they saw themselves as part of nature rather than masters of it, and how their way of life resulted in a profound and valuable knowledge of their land. ³ .... It was a way of life that was safe from invasion and influence ... until 1788.

40 When the Europeans arrived in 1788, they had a different attitude to the land. ⁴ .... They also believed that if land wasn't farmed, then it didn't belong to anyone. At first, Aborigines didn't understand this attitude, so their first contact was amicable, even friendly. However, conflicts 45 soon arose as new settlers took away the Aboriginal hunting grounds and divided them up into farms and ranches. ⁵ .... Some tribes were not allowed to travel from one place to another, while others were relocated into special camps. Sadly, this destroyed their ancient way of life, and 50 many Aboriginal songlines were lost. Today, people like Baamba are trying to restore this heritage and preserve it.

ªIt's late now and Baamba is waiting outside Arkaroo Rock until we've finished exploring. ᵇInside, we're admiring the beautiful cave paintings, but as soon as we've taken some 55 photos, we leave. ᶜDark clouds are visible on the horizon and if we stay any longer, we'll be caught in a storm. ᵈBy the time we reach camp, the rain will be here,' says Baamba. ᵉ'We'll have problems getting back unless we leave now.' He's right, of course – there are already flashes of lightning, and 60 thunder is audible in the distance. As we drive away, the wind whistles through the gum trees, and we can almost hear the voices of those first Australians, singing the songs of their ancestors, and following the songlines.

5 Complete the words with -able or -ible.

1 It's incred......................... that Aboriginal culture is the oldest continuing culture on Earth.
2 Many tribes are elig........................ for compensation after an unaccept........................ loss of tribal lands.
3 The marks and etchings in the Wollemi cave were incomprehens........................ .
4 The Papunya Tula artists paint fashion........................ and collect........................ Aboriginal art.
5 Parts of the outback are harsh and inaccess........................ . It's not advis........................ to travel there on your own.
6 If you know where to look, you'll find lots of ed........................ insects in the outback. They may taste horr........................, but they'll help you to survive.
7 Most snakes in the outback aren't dangerous; their bites are usually treat........................ .

Future time clauses

6 Study sentences a–e in the last paragraph of the article and answer the questions.

1 Which tenses are used after the underlined time clauses?
2 Which underlined phrase means *if not*?
3 Which one means *up to a specific time*?
4 Which three phrases tell us that one event will be completed before another?
5 Which of these three phrases says something happens immediately after?
6 Which of the phrases below can be used instead of *if*?
- as long as ■ suppose / supposing ■ before ■ after
- in case ■ when

Reference and practice 2.3 | Workbook page 112

7 Rewrite the sentences using the words in brackets.

1 Baamba won't do the tour if he doesn't have a GPS system. (unless)
2 We'll tell people where we're going because we might get lost. (in case)
3 You'll enter the outback, then you'll lose your phone signal. (as soon as)
4 Take a satellite phone; then you'll be perfectly safe. (as long as)
5 We still might get lost – then what will we do? (supposing)
6 Stay close to the car; then a helicopter will see you. (until)
7 Hopefully it won't be too late when they find you. (by the time)

8 SPEAKING Work in pairs. Talk about your hopes and plans for the future using the prompts below.

1 By the time I've finished school ... .
2 As long as I save enough money ... .
3 Before / After I leave home ... .
4 Until I get my own job ... .
5 Unless I study hard ... .
6 As soon as I have the time ... .

1 SPEAKING Work in pairs. Look at extracts A–D about Sydney, Australia, and answer the questions. Then read the extracts and check your answers.

1 Where do you think the extracts are from?
2 Who do you think they are written for?
3 What do you think each extract will include?

STRATEGY

Recognizing style

When you first read a text, think about its style. The style of the text will give you clues about where it is from and who it was written for. Pay attention to:

- structure and length
- sentences and linking words
- grammar and vocabulary
- punctuation
- extra features (for example, highlighted words or numbered references)

2 Read the strategy. Answer the questions for extracts A–D. Then decide which extracts are formal and which are informal. Which features usually belong to a more formal style?

1 Does it use headings or subheadings? Is there clear paragraphing?
2 Are the sentences and linking words simple, or long and complex?
3 Are there examples of the passive or reported speech? Are there any personal pronouns? Does it use imperatives?
4 Are there examples of idiomatic or colloquial language, phrasal verbs or abbreviations?
5 Are there contractions or full forms? Are exclamation marks or capital letters used for emphasis?

A

1.1 Geography

Sydney, Australia, is located in a coastal basin bordered by the Pacific Ocean to the east and the Blue Mountain range to the west. As a result of this location, it has more than seventy natural harbours and ocean beaches, including the well-known Bondi Beach.

1.2 Demographics

Sydney is an extremely diverse city, with an enormous number of ethnic and cultural groups. Of the 4.6 million people that live there, … .

B

Summer at the House

Experience the Opera House – a vibrant arts centre and one of the most recognizable buildings in the world.

- Come and take part in *Summer at the House*, a seasonal festival with some utterly awesome events.
- Discover the history and magic of this extraordinary World Heritage site.
- Don't miss *The Illusionists* – an absolutely spellbinding magic show with some of the boldest tricks ever!

C

🔍 Sydney Opera House

'Well worth a visit'

★★★★☆ 12th June

Really enjoyed the Opera House tour with our very knowledgeable guide! (Although my 9-yr-old son complained it was a little bit tedious and not particularly kid-friendly!) But I'd still give it a big 'thumbs up' – ESPECIALLY the ballet rehearsal! The weather was pretty disappointing (yes, it DOES rain in Sydney), but we still took great photos ☺ – it's a totally overwhelming place!

Was this review helpful? Yes ‹ 3

D

'We are now approaching Sydney airport,' announced the flight attendant over the Tannoy. 'Please fasten your seatbelts.' The holiday was a fairly last-minute trip to get away from it all and recharge my batteries. I'd heard that Sydney was an ideal destination and first impressions didn't disappoint. In the distance, I could see the Opera House looking quite magnificent in the afternoon sun. But I didn't know then what was about to happen. This last-minute trip would change my life forever.

Modifying adverbs with gradable and non-gradable adjectives

3 Study the highlighted adjectives in the extracts. Which are positive, negative or neutral?

4 Study the information about gradable and non-gradable adjectives and answer the questions.

> Gradable adjectives describe qualities that you can measure, e.g. *disappointing*: We use grading adverbs with these adjectives, e.g. *very / a bit disappointing*.
> Non-gradable adjectives describe qualities that are absolute or extreme, e.g. *enormous*. We use non-grading adverbs with these adjectives, e.g. *utterly / absolutely enormous*.
> **Be careful:** the adverbs *quite*, *really*, *pretty* and *fairly* can be used with both types of adjectives.

    1 Which of the highlighted adjectives are: (1) gradable, (2) non-gradable?
    2 Which of the underlined adverbs are: (1) grading, (2) non-grading?

Reference and practice 2.4   Workbook page 112

5 Read the travel blog entry and choose the best answers. Which adjectives are non-gradable?

A SMALL TOWN IN A BIG COUNTRY

After a(n) [1]**utterly / very** exhausting journey, I arrived in Oodnadatta at around one o'clock. It was baking hot and there were flies – lots of them – but the first thing I noticed was a large pink roadhouse which looked [2]**completely / particularly** inviting after a long trek through the desert. The town itself is tiny, [3]**very / fairly** quiet and [4]**pretty / absolutely** ordinary, but then first impressions can sometimes be deceptive, and Oodnadatta had a lot more to offer than I initially thought.

My first stop was the roadhouse, run by the [5]**extremely / completely** knowledgeable Lynnie. I ordered some lunch and had an Oodnaburger, which was [6]**a little bit / totally** delicious. In fact, many people stop off at the roadhouse on their way to Alice Springs and, as I soon found out, these travellers often have interesting stories to tell. But the town has more to offer than travellers' tales: a short walk from the roadhouse is an [7]**absolutely / extremely** fascinating station museum, originally part of the transcontinental railway. Oodnadatta is also a starting point for outback camel safaris and, for those with some cash, sightseeing flights with [8]**very / quite** magnificent views of the Painted Desert.

All in all, Oodnadatta was a(n) [9]**really / utterly** interesting stop-off, and offered some unusual things to do. But for those who simply want a bit of peace and quiet, Oodnadatta could be the place for you, too.

6 Read the travel blog entry again and answer the questions.

    1 Is the style of the travel blog formal, informal or neutral? Give examples to support your answer.
    2 How would you describe the writer's first impression? Which adjectives tell you this?
    3 Which activities did the writer try?
    4 How did the writer's first impressions change?

WRITING GUIDE

- **Task** Write a travel blog entry about a place you have visited or a place in your local area that you enjoyed.

- **Ideas** Brainstorm ideas for your description. Make notes about:
  1 the first impressions you had of the place. What things did you notice?
  2 what you think about the place. What are the benefits and drawbacks of visiting it?
  3 what type of things a visitor can see and do there.

- **Plan** Follow the plan:
  Paragraph 1: Describe your first impressions of the place: the landscape, the weather, what visitors are likely to notice.

  Paragraph 2: Describe what people can see and do, and recommend excursions.
  Paragraph 3: Sum up the main features of the place and what makes it an interesting destination.

- **Write** Write your description. Use the paragraph plan to help you.

- **Check** Check the following points:
  - Is your style consistent?
  - Does your description use gradable and non-gradable adjectives?
  - Have you checked grammar, vocabulary, spelling and punctuation?

Vocabulary insight 2 Using suffixes to build complex words

1 Read the extract. Study the highlighted words and identify the root words, prefixes and suffixes. How do the prefixes and suffixes change the meanings of the root words?

> Arkaroo Rock is one of many sacred sites mentioned in the songs and stories about the land. These stories show the considerable attachment the first Australians had to their environment, how they saw themselves as part of nature rather than masters of it, and how their way of life resulted in a profound and valuable knowledge of their land. It's a way of life that predates the Ice Age, beginning around 70,000 years ago, with more than 2,000 generations since then.

STRATEGY

Adjective suffixes

Knowing the meanings of some of the most common suffixes will help you to guess the meaning of any new words that you come across. It will also help you to build new, more complex words.

2 Read the strategy above. Then study the examples in the table. Complete the table with the correct meanings a–f of the suffixes.

suffix	examples	meaning
-able / -ible	navigable, reversible	....
-al	educational, traditional	....
-ed	inhabited, renovated	....
-ful	successful, wasteful	....
-ish	puppyish, English	....
-less	worthless, fearless	....

a full of, having a particular quality
b without
c related to
d having, being in a particular state
e can be done
f sort of (like), fairly, inhabitant of, language of

3 Complete the sentences with the correct form of the words below. Use the suffixes in the table in exercise 2.

■ change ■ child ■ collect ■ home ■ rest ■ politics
■ Sweden ■ worry

1 When something is entirely calm and relaxing, it is ....
2 A person from Sweden is ....
3 Something that is related to the subject of politics is ....
4 Something that people can collect is ....
5 A person who has no home is ....
6 When someone behaves like a child, they are ....
7 When you're in a state of worry, you are ....
8 Something that can change from one thing into another is ....

STRATEGY

Multiple suffixes

In English, it is common to use multiple suffixes with the same root word to build more complex words. The suffix can affect both meaning and part of speech.

4 Read the strategy above. Then look at the word *unseasonably* on line 7 in the article on page 16. What is the root word? How many suffixes has it got? What part of speech does each suffix form?

5 Study the dictionary entries and answer the questions.

1 Which suffixes do we use to form different words from *urban*?
2 What parts of speech are they?
3 How do the suffixes change the meaning of the word *urban*?

> **urban** 0━ /ˈɜːbən; NAmE ˈɜːrbən/ adj. [usually before noun]
> **1** 0━ connected with a town or city: *damage to both urban and rural environments* ◇ *urban areas* ◇ *urban life* ◇ *urban development* (= the process of building towns and cities or making them larger) ◇ *urban renewal/regeneration* (= the process of improving the buildings, etc. in the poor parts of a town or city) ◇ *efforts to control urban sprawl* (= the spread of city buildings into the countryside) ◗ compare RURAL **2** connected with types of music such as RHYTHM AND BLUES and REGGAE that are played by black musicians: *today's urban music scene* ◇ *urban radio shows*

> **ur·ban·ized** (BrE also **-ised**) /ˈɜːbənaɪzd; NAmE ˈɜːrb-/ adj. **1** (of an area, a country, etc.) having a lot of towns, streets, factories, etc. rather than countryside **2** (of people) living and working in towns and cities rather than in the country: *an increasingly urbanized society* ▸ **ur·ban·iza·tion**, **-isa·tion** /ˌɜːbənaɪˈzeɪʃn; NAmE ˌɜːrbənəˈz-/ noun [U]

6 Choose the correct answers.

1 Many parts of the country are becoming more **urban / urbanized / urbanization**, as people move away from the countryside.
2 The process of **urban / urbanized / urbanization** is destroying some beautiful countryside, but providing more jobs and amenities for people.
3 The **urban / urbanized / urbanization** population of Latin America has now reached approximately 74%.
4 The twenty-first century has seen a massive growth in the development of **urban / urbanized / urbanization** farms as people want to know more about where their food comes from.
5 South Asia is one of the least **urban / urbanized / urbanization** areas in the world.
6 There is a clear link between the level of **urban / urbanized / urbanization** in a country and its economic development.

7 Use multiple suffixes to make new words from the root words below. Check your answers in a dictionary. Then write an example sentence for each word.

■ commercial ■ industrial ■ priority ■ social ■ special

Dictionary entries from *Oxford Advanced Learner's Dictionary* 8ᵉ, Oxford University Press 2010.

Vocabulary

1 Complete the sentences with the words below and the correct prepositions.

■ benefits ■ demand ■ handful ■ relevance ■ respect ■ responsibility

1 Most people think that the .... educating children lies with the parents.

2 In the colder months, there is always a greater .... electricity.

3 Only a .... teenagers know how to cook these days.

4 In the past, people had more .... their elders.

5 What are the .... attending a single-sex school?

6 The .... some university degrees is questionable.

Marks .... / 6

2 Complete the text with the words below.

■ harsh ■ inevitably ■ profound ■ remote ■ stifling ■ subsistence

The reindeer farmers of Siberia are nomadic and they face a number of **¹** .... challenges every day. The biggest are the **²** .... weather conditions. The farmers lead a **³** .... lifestyle, so they live on what they farm or hunt. Educating their children is also a problem. In the past, the children only had a **⁴** .... chance of attending school because their families were always moving. **⁵** ...., something had to be done about this. Today, there are special nomadic schools that follow the reindeers' migration routes. The children avoid the **⁶** .... atmosphere of a conventional classroom, but they still manage to get an education.

Marks .... / 6

3 Write the antonyms of the words below.

1 cared for ....
2 inhabited ....
3 thriving ....
4 attractive ....
5 worthwhile ....
6 efficient ....
7 renovated ....

Marks .... / 7

4 Complete the text with the correct adjective forms of the words in brackets.

Zhang Jiawan village in the Badagong Mountains of South East China is only **¹** .... (access) to the fittest. The maps are far from **²** .... (comprehend), so it's easy to get lost. The children in the village use a more practical route to get to the school in the valley below every day. There are ladders fixed to the side of the cliffs which are not **³** .... (vision) from a distance. The journey to school would not be **⁴** .... (accept) to most parents, but children as young as five do it twice a day. They show **⁵** .... (consider) courage, but they say it's **⁶** .... (advise) not to look down during the climb.

Marks .... / 6

Grammar

5 Complete the sentences. Use the present simple, present continuous, *might*, *will* or *be going to*.

1 a He intends to return before it gets dark.
  b He ....

2 a We really want to see some polar bears.
  b Hopefully, we ....

3 a The departure time of our train is 10.30.
  b Our train ....

4 a She's arranged to do a bungee jump next week.
  b She ....

5 a That car is in danger of crashing. It's out of control.
  b That car ....

6 a Shall I get you a glass of water?
  b I ....

Marks .... / 6

6 Complete the dialogue. Use the future perfect, future perfect continuous or future continuous tense.

Joe Next Friday **¹** .... (we / finish) our exams at last! When **²** .... (you / go) to Switzerland?

Dan **³** .... (I / fly) to Zurich on 1ˢᵗ August to meet my Swiss friend. Then, **⁴** .... (we / travel) by train to an adventure camp in the Alps. Hopefully, **⁵** .... (we / arrive) by 9 p.m.

Joe Which sports **⁶** .... (you / do) while you're there?

Dan White-water rafting and mountain biking.

Joe Great! You'll be able to practise your German, too.

Dan That's right. By the time I get home, **⁷** .... (I / speak) German for two weeks.

Marks .... / 7

7 Complete the text with a word in A and the correct form of a verb in B.

A ■ as long as ■ as soon as ■ by the time ■ in case ■ supposing ■ unless ■ until

B ■ come ■ decide ■ follow ■ return ■ say ■ spot ■ tell

Early morning safari
Please read carefully

1 You will be completely safe .... you .... the instructions of your guide.

2 Keep the windows up .... some animals .... to investigate your car.

3 .... you .... some wildlife, keep quiet and don't move around.

4 Do not leave the vehicle .... your guide .... it is safe to do so.

5 Keep your seat belt on .... the vehicle .... to a stop.

6 Get back into the vehicle .... your guide .... you to.

7 Hopefully, you'll have seen some wonderful wildlife .... you .... to the hotel.

Marks .... / 7

Total .... / 45

Listening

1 🕐 **1.12** **Listen to a radio presentation about storm chasing. Are the sentences true (T) or false (F)?**

1 Tornado Alley is located roughly in the middle section of the USA. ....

2 Tornadoes occur in the area because two different airstreams meet there. ....

3 The best tour companies are the ones with the greatest experience and the most modern equipment. ....

4 Tour guests never know where they are going when they leave their hotels. ....

5 Most tours aim to chase a storm before lunch. ....

6 More often than not, tour guests miss out on seeing a tornado. ....

7 Tour guests have to pay for their own flights to the start of the tour. ....

8 All meals are included in the price of the tour. ....

Speaking

A

B

C

2 **Work in pairs. Choose one photo each and describe it to each other. Then decide which phenomenon poses the biggest threat to people and justify your choice.**

3 **Work in pairs. Imagine you are judging a photo competition called *Forces of nature*. Decide which of the photos in exercise 2 should win the competition. Discuss the things below.**

- requirements the photo needs to meet to be selected
- reasons why you chose this photo and rejected the other photos

Top three mysterious places

A Situated on the north coast of Northern Ireland, the **Giant's Causeway** is an area of approximately 40,000 interlocking basalt columns. Volcanic activity 60 million years ago created these rugged symmetrical rock
5 formations, which look like stepping stones leading into the sea. Most of the columns are hexagonal, although there are some with four, five, seven or eight sides. The tallest are about 12 metres high, and the solidified lava in the cliffs is about 28 metres thick in places. The feature plays a major
10 part in Ireland's heritage and some prefer the colourful stories behind it to the geological explanation. According to legend, the causeway was built by an Irish giant called Finn MacCool, so that he could meet his rival the Scottish giant Benandonner and defeat him in battle. Whichever
15 explanation you prefer, the Giant's Causeway is regarded as one of the natural wonders of the United Kingdom and it was declared a World Heritage Site by UNESCO in 1986.

B The **Richat Structure** in central Mauritania is a geological feature first spotted by astronauts on early
20 space missions. Otherwise called the Eye of Africa, the formation is a series of concentric circles of alternating layers of sedimentary, metamorphic and igneous rocks which covers a diameter of about 48 kilometres in the Maur Adrar Desert of Africa's Western Sahara. Originally,
25 scientists thought that the impression was a crater caused by a meteorite hitting the Earth. But now it is believed to be the remains of a volcanic dome which has been worn away by erosion. Over time, desert weather has caused the volcano to gradually shed layers, resulting in the
30 structure's remarkable flatness. Despite the remoteness and hostility of the area, it is a favourite for 4×4 driving enthusiasts, who welcome the challenge of the barren landscape. There are companies offering organized helicopter tours, and surprisingly, there is a hotel smack
35 in the middle of the structure, which offers adequate accommodation to tired tourists.

Reading

4 **Read the article and answer the questions. Some questions may have more than one answer.**

Which place (A, B or C):
1 is internationally recognized? ....
2 has several different names? ....
3 may be appreciated best from the air? ....
4 transforms according to the time of year? ....
5 is explained in different ways? ....
6 may not be explored by visitors? ....

Grammar and vocabulary

5 **Complete the text with one word in each gap.**

China's State Council, the country's highest administrative authority, ¹............... recently approved a plan to build a new metropolis on the outskirts of Lanzhou. The project hopes to deal with demands ²............... a solution to the area's environmental problems. The area suffers from serious air pollution and frequent water shortages, and ³............... something is done soon, the inhabitants may start abandoning the area. However, there are a ⁴............... deal of obstacles to get ⁵............... before the new town can be built. Lanzhou is situated in a mountainous area in north-western China, and seven hundred mountains ⁶............... have to be flattened for the new development. In ⁷............... there are any doubts about the project, a promotional video showing the end result can be seen on the Lanzhou New Area website. If everything goes according to plan, the residents will ⁸............... working in a brand new oil refinery and an extra airport will ⁹............... opened in the area ¹⁰............... the time the project is finished.

C Known as Kliluk to the natives of the Okanagan Valley, the **Spotted Lake** in British Columbia, Canada is a sacred and culturally significant site. To outsiders, it looks more like a giant painter's palette than a body of water. 40 Its vibrant colours are due to the high concentration of numerous different minerals in the lake, including sodium, calcium and magnesium sulphate. The water changes colour throughout the year and therefore is beautiful to look at in any season. In the summer, most 45 of the water evaporates, leaving behind large 'spots' of minerals. Depending on the mineral composition left behind, the spots will be of white, pale yellow, blue or green colour. Around and between the spots, the magnesium sulphate hardens to form natural walkways. 50 The site is owned by the First Nations – the Aboriginal people of Canada – who value the lake for its therapeutic powers. It is not open to the public, but it can easily be seen from Highway 3, which runs past the lake.

Writing

6 **Write an article for a travel magazine about a mysterious place you have visited. Include the information below.**

▪ your first impressions of the place
▪ a past event related to the place
▪ your opinion of the place
▪ a recommendation of the place

3 Things that matter

Reading and vocabulary Hoarders

1 SPEAKING Why do we keep things we do not use or need? Which of the reasons do you agree with? Why?

1 'It's mine. Why should I give it away?'
2 'I don't like throwing things out – it's a waste.'
3 'You never know, I might use it in the future.'
4 'It has sentimental value.'
5 'I haven't got time to sort out that stuff.'
6 'I hoard things, but I have the space, so why not?'

2 Read the article. Which reasons in exercise 1 are mentioned? What other reasons does it mention?

STRATEGY

Detecting purpose and point of view

When you read a non-fiction text, think carefully about the writer's purpose and point of view.

1 Decide on the main purpose. Is it to inform and teach (are there facts and quotes)? Or is it to persuade and influence? It may be trying to do several things.
2 Decide on the writer's point of view. Is the language neutral or does it praise or criticize? How does the writer want us to react?

---

3 Read the strategy. Read sentences 1–3 and decide on the article's main purpose. Then study the words in italics and decide on the point of view.

1 … *unfortunately* our modern consumer culture *actively* encourages us to accumulate.
2 … when the average American family moves house, an *incredible* eight tonnes of belongings moves with them.
3 … people are naturally resistant to change and prefer things the way they are; the end result is *loads* of clutter, taking up *valuable* space.

4 Read the article again. Are the sentences true (T) or false (F)? Correct the false ones.

1 Susie is patient with her mother, despite the hoarding.
2 The writer says that most people have a similar impulse to hoard.
3 One reason people stopped being nomads is because they had too much stuff to transport.
4 Elaine is sympathetic towards her mother and her hoarding.
5 Advertisements encourage people to be happy with their lives.
6 People like things in their lives to remain the same.
7 Sharon is emotionally attached to some of her things.

5 SPEAKING Work in pairs. Discuss the questions.

1 What role do adverts and mass media play when it comes to owning and keeping things?
2 What advice does Elaine give her mum? What advice would you give her?

The stuff in our lives

Elaine and Susie Beaupit live in a large house with a white picket fence in a typical New Jersey suburb. They enjoy shopping, texting their friends and watching sitcoms on cable TV. Being
5 sisters, they also argue a lot! In fact, Elaine and Susie appear to be normal American teenagers, although appearances can be deceptive. The truth is that everyday life for the sisters is far from normal: things which we might take for granted,
10 like cooking a meal or ¹picking out an outfit, are incredibly difficult for the girls. Why? Because their mum, Sharon, is a compulsive hoarder. 'We spend most of our time in a small area in the living room, just in front of the TV,' complains
15 Susie. 'Mum's stuff has ²spread out everywhere. It's taken over our lives.'

In Sharon's house, every room is crammed with piles of records and CDs, mountains of laundry and stacks of magazines. The kitchen is impossible
20 to use, so meals are cooked in a microwave in the garage and dishes are washed in the shower. Compulsive hoarding can be an extreme condition and this family has ³run out of space. But while it's true that most of us would never hoard to
25 this extent, the fact is that many of us buy more things than we need and, once we have them, we're reluctant to throw them away.

Vocabulary: synonyms; phrasal verbs with *out*; adjectives describing objects; compounds with participles
Grammar: articles; determiners; verb patterns

Speaking: selecting things to exhibit
Writing: a story

3A

According to anthropologists, people have been collecting stuff for centuries. About 15,000 years
30 ago, primitive communities began to lose their nomadic ways and rely on stored food, resulting in a change in our material culture. Permanent homes were built as people amassed more objects, and these things soon became impossible to carry
35 around. The loss of nomadic ways was not just thanks to agriculture, but also to the number of possessions people had.

Back in New Jersey, Elaine is feeling increasingly frustrated by her mother's junk as she searches for
40 a place to do her homework. In the end, she uses a heap of laundry as a temporary desk. 'After a while you just put up with it,' she sighs. 'You start thinking it's normal.' In some ways it is normal, because unfortunately our modern consumer
45 culture actively encourages us to accumulate. Advertisements convince us that we can't live without certain products and imply that these things can change our lives. It's very difficult to resist this culture, to ⁴opt out and buy less. In the
50 USA, the amount of stuff people own has doubled since 1947 and, according to a recent study, when the average American family moves house, an incredible eight tonnes of belongings moves with them.

So why is it so difficult to get rid of things? One 55 explanation is that people are naturally resistant to change and prefer things the way they are; the end result is loads of clutter, taking up valuable space. Psychologists also talk about the 'endowment effect', or the way we attach more value to things 60 once we own them. For example, you might not use your old MP3 player, but it still has 'value' because it belongs to you. Ownership is as important as usefulness. But as Elaine says, 'Mum needs to ask herself: if I didn't have it, would I go out and buy 65 it? If the answer is 'no', then she should bin it.'

'Sentimental value' is another reason for not junking things. Many of the objects we keep have connections to a place, an event or a person in our past, such as birthday cards from a grandparent 70 or an old football shirt from an important match. These objects, like Sharon's record collection, have emotional currency, which is why we never ⁵throw them out.

Luckily, Elaine and Susie's story has a happy ending. 75 Sharon has finally got help with her hoarding and has slowly started to ⁶clear out their home. 'She had to,' says Elaine, 'or our family would have fallen apart.' It's been a few months, but the girls are ⁷helping out and things are gradually getting 80 better. 'When I walk through the house now, I can find the things I need ... . They're not hidden by junk any more,' smiles Elaine. 'The next stage is to invite my friends round,' she adds. 'I'm really looking forward to that. I just hope they don't 85 bring much stuff.'

V insight **Synonyms**

6 Complete the lists of synonyms with the highlighted words in the article. Check any words you do not know in a dictionary and write any common collocations.

1 loads of: .... , ... , ... ,
....
2 things: .... , ... , ... ,
.... , ...
3 rubbish: .... , ...
4 throw out: .... , ... , ...
5 hoard: .... , ...

7 **SPEAKING** Look at the photos in the article. Use the words in exercise 6 to describe them.

V insight **Phrasal verbs with *out***

8 Study phrasal verbs 1–7 in the article. Match them to the meanings of *out* a–f.

a choosing pick out
b removing
c disappearing, using completely
d uncontained
e stopping being involved
f supporting, intending to support

9 Complete the text with the correct form of the phrasal verbs below. Then match them to meanings a–f in exercise 8.

■ sort out ■ drop out of ■ spill out of ■ take out
■ wear out ■ reach out to

'Like most of my friends, I had too much stuff,' explains seventeen-year-old Kayte Green, 'but I did something about it.' Kayte is a teenage minimalist. She writes a blog that ¹.................. other teens who want to simplify their lives.

A year ago Kayte decided to ².................. consumer culture. 'I started with my clothes,' explained Kayte. 'Jeans and T-shirts ³.................. my wardrobe and onto the floor, so I ⁴.................. everything .... and put it into boxes. I put clothes back as I used them, and then after a few weeks, I gave away the stuff that was still in boxes.'

'It was hard to ⁵.................. what to keep and what to junk,' she adds, 'but if something had sentimental value, I'd ask myself: Does it really bring back memories or just collect dust?'

Today, Kayte's room is transformed. 'It's great without the clutter,' she says. 'And I've saved money too, because I wear clothes until they are ⁶..................! I don't worry about having the latest fashions any more, and I don't feel guilty about letting things go.'

10 **SPEAKING** Work in pairs. Answer the questions.

1 What do you think about Kayte's ideas?
2 What other ways of reducing the amount of stuff we have can you think of?

Vocabulary bank British vs American English page 136

1 ◉ **1.13** **SPEAKING** Listen to two dialogues. For each dialogue identify where the speakers are, the problem and the solutions. Then work in pairs and answer the questions.

1 What things do most people leave behind on holiday? Agree on a list of the top three items.
2 Have you ever left anything behind on holiday? What was it? What did you do?

Articles

2 Read the text and choose the correct articles. What types of things do people usually leave behind on holiday?

Don't forget your toothbrush …

Over 70% of travellers return from their holidays, unpack their bags and find something is missing. In hotel and hostel rooms across the world, ¹**the / –** people have left toothbrushes, false teeth and even funeral urns! ²**The / –** rich forget things like Ferrari car keys or expensive jewellery; however, most of us just leave toiletries or mobile phone chargers. But perhaps ³**the / –** strangest item ever forgotten was found in a hotel in Portugal.

Maria Carmen Fernandez is ⁴**– / a** maid at a hotel in the Algarve. She usually cleans around twenty-five rooms ⁵**the / a** day and she often finds lost property. One day, she came across a fish in a bathtub and had the fright of her life. Why? Because ⁶**the / a** fish was a fully-grown shark! A guest at the hotel had caught it on a fishing trip and then left it behind. Luckily, ⁷**the / an** animal survived and the hotel returned it to its natural habitat.

So what causes this wave of ⁸**the / –** forgetfulness? Many people are in a hurry to leave; others bring too much stuff in the first place, so it's not surprising that things are forgotten. As a wise man once said: 'He who would travel happily must travel light.'

3 Match examples 1–8 in the text to rules a–h.

We use *a / an* when:
a we say what someone's job is.
b the meaning is *each* or *per*.

We use *the* when:
c we talk about a person or thing that was mentioned before.
d it is obvious what we are talking about.
e there is only one person or thing (for example, *the sun*), or with superlatives.
f an adjective refers to a group of people who share a characteristic.

We use no article when:
g we talk about something in general or before general plural nouns.
h we use abstract nouns.

Reference and practice 3.1 Workbook page 113

4 SPEAKING Look at the photo and answer the questions. Then read the text and compare your ideas.

1 What things have been left on the beach?
2 What impact might they have on the environment?
3 Can you think of any solutions to this problem?

One step at a time

Do you pack flip-flops when you go on holiday? Probably. In fact, hardly any people have never worn flip-flops and many of us go through several pairs every year. But once the holiday's over, where do they go? Some flip-flops end up in rubbish dumps, but far too many of them float out to sea.

A few years ago, marine biologist Julie Church was working in Kenya when she saw some children making toys out of old flip-flops. It gave her the idea to start a business which could create jobs for local people and which would clean up much of the coastline. Because of ocean currents, rubbish on Kenya's beaches comes from places as far away as Indonesia and a lot of the things washed up are plastic, including flip-flops. People on the beach collect these flip-flops, then sell them to Julie's company, UniquEco, where workers wash them and use a little glue to fix together the different parts. Almost none of the material is wasted, so almost all of the flip-flops are made into something else – everything from earrings to elephant sculptures!

However, critics say there is little point in collecting the footwear – there may be few flip-flops on the beach now, but there is still a lot of other rubbish. Julie replies that she's taking it one step at a time. There's far too much pollution everywhere, she argues, 'so whatever we're doing is better than doing nothing because the amount of rubbish is only going to get worse.'

Determiners

5 Study the highlighted determiners in the text and put them into the correct category. Then decide which can be used with both uncountable and plural countable nouns. Use the Grammar reference section in the Workbook to help you.

1 With uncountable nouns we use: ....
2 With plural countable nouns we use: ....

6 Complete the chart with the determiners below.

▪ far too much / many, almost all ▪ several ▪ (a) little, (a) few ▪ almost none ▪ some
▪ many, much, a lot of ▪ hardly any

0%   100%
none ¹............... ²............... ³ several ⁴............... ⁵............... ⁶............... ⁷............... all / every

7 Replace the words in italics with *not much / not many* or *some*.

1 He needs *a few* flip-flops to finish his sculpture.
2 It was raining, so *few* volunteers turned up for the beach clean.
3 We could do with *a little* help in the shop. It's quite busy today.
4 There's *little* rubbish on the beach at the moment. It's not too dirty.

Reference and practice 3.2 | Workbook page 113

8 SPEAKING Choose the correct answers. Then work in pairs, choose one opinion and discuss it. Do you agree or disagree with it? Why?

1 'We can recycle **much / almost all** of the products we buy. That's great, but what **few / a few** people realize is that it's not about recycling, it's about reducing consumption.'
2 'There are far **too many / too much** adverts on TV and they persuade us to acquire **much / a lot of** things we don't need. Get rid of the adverts and we won't produce so **much / many** rubbish!'
3 'A **few / Few** of my neighbours recycle, so why should I? There's **little / a little** point in doing it if no one else does it.'

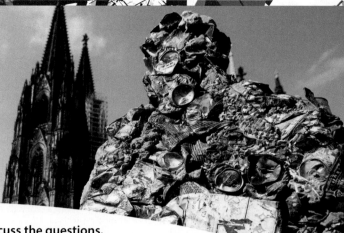

1 **SPEAKING** Look at the photos and discuss the questions.

1 What is an environmental artist? What do they do?

2 In what ways can environmental art influence us? Do you think it's effective?

3 'We produce trash, are born from trash and will turn back into trash.' What does the speaker mean? Do you agree? Why / why not?

2 ◎ **1.14** Listen to a radio interview about the artist HA Schult and compare your ideas.

3 ◎ **1.14** Listen again. Are the sentences true (T) or false (F)?

1 Hundreds of people worked with Schult on *Trash People*.

2 Each trash person was made from the same materials.

3 His main aim was to show how we can recycle rubbish into beautiful art.

4 According to Schult, the trash people symbolize modern people.

5 The presenter finds Schult's work unimpressive.

6 Artists have used rubbish to highlight environmental problems since the early 20th century.

7 James says that artists like Schult think they can help us to change our habits.

V Adjectives describing objects

4 Study phrases 1–7 from the interview. Then match the highlighted adjectives to categories a–i below.

1 Arms and legs made from rusty aluminium cans, ...

2 ... bodies made up of dated, decaying plastic keyboards ...

3 ... smooth, transparent car headlights becoming broad, triangular shoulders.

4 ... controversial German artist HA Schult ...

5 ... using all sorts of junk, from crushed aluminium cans to tangled copper wire ...

6 ... ripped packaging for a mouth ...

7 ... he created a huge, winding paper river in New York ...

a type or purpose	**d** age	**g** shape
b material	**e** colour	**h** opinion
c size	**f** origin or nationality	**i** other qualities

5 Match the adjectives below to categories a–i in exercise 4. Use a dictionary to help you. Then put the categories in the order they appear before a noun, depending on which type of adjective comes first.

■ witty ■ contemporary ■ delicate ■ troubling ■ tiny ■ stunning ■ silk ■ Indian ■ colourful ■ bronze ■ rectangular ■ wooden ■ antique ■ abstract

6 Complete the sentences with the adjectives in brackets in the correct order.

1 Slinkachu makes .... urban art. (troubling, contemporary, tiny)

2 There's a .... statue outside the museum. (bronze, controversial)

3 There was a(n) .... mural on the side of the office block. (abstract, rectangular, stunning)

4 The auction house sold a(n) .... carving. (wooden, antique, Chinese)

5 The library has a collection of .... paintings. (delicate, Indian, silk)

6 The artist Banksy is famous for .... graffiti. (witty, colourful)

7 SPEAKING Work in small groups. Look at the photo and discuss the questions.

1 Describe the photo. What is the object normally used for? What has the artist transformed it into?

2 What do you think about the artwork and how do you think the artist wants us to react?

3 Decide on a title for the artwork and explain why you chose it.

Selecting things to exhibit

8 SPEAKING Work in pairs. You are going to listen to people choosing objects to display at a local museum. Look at the photos. Where do you think the museum is located?

Environment   Culture   History

9 🔊 **1.15 Listen to the discussion and check your ideas. Which objects did the people select and why?**

10 🔊 **1.15 Listen to the first part of the discussion again and complete the phrases from the discussion. Then complete A–D with the headings below.**

■ Rejecting suggestions ■ Stating aims ■ Making suggestions ■ Approving suggestions

A ....
Our main [1] .... is to ... .
One of our main goals involves ... .

B ....
We could have something from ... .
We [2] .... want to have a ... , as well.
How about having ... ?

C ....
That [3] .... like a really good idea.
That [4] .... be the best place for it.
... will help [5] .... that.
OK, you've [6] .... me!

D ....
I'm not [7] .... this is the right place.
Maybe, although ... – don't you [8] .... ?
Perhaps we should think again.

11 🔊 **1.16 Listen to another discussion and tick the phrases that you hear. Then match all of them to categories A–D in exercise 10. Which display case are the students talking about?**

■ I don't think that's the best choice. ■ We're not going to see eye-to-eye on this one!
■ Let's look at ... . ■ That might be the solution. ■ I think that's an excellent point.
■ We could focus more on ... . ■ Well, I'm not convinced. ■ The aim is to concentrate on ... .

12 SPEAKING Work in pairs. Follow the instructions below.

■ Choose three objects to display at a museum exhibition about your local community, one for each of the following display cases: environment, culture and history.

■ Define your 'community': is it your local area, your town, your street?

■ Then choose each object carefully. Think about the following points.
  • Its purpose: what does it tell us about everyday life?
  • Its story: does it relate to an important past, present or future event?
  • Its appearance: is it interesting to look at?

1 SPEAKING Work in pairs. Discuss the questions. Then read the article and compare your ideas.

1 What things should national museums have in them?

2 What do you understand by the term 'encyclopaedic museum'? Do you know any?

2 Read the article again. Match paragraphs A–E to summaries 1–6. There is one summary that you do not need.

1 Examining pros and cons of encyclopaedic museums.

2 Speculating about how objects were acquired, and if they should be returned.

3 Describing an object which was a war trophy, and why it is unlikely to be given back.

4 Describing an object which was given away by one government, then asked to be returned by another.

5 Giving advice on which objects to view in the museum.

6 Exploring the purpose of museums, and a definition of an encyclopaedic museum.

V insight Compounds with participles

3 Study the highlighted words in the article. What types of compounds are they?

well-earned – *adjective / adverb + present / past participle*
self-defeating – *noun + present / past participle*

4 Complete the sentences using the words below.

■ highly ■ heart (×2) ■ thought ■ well ■ much
■ mind ■ fast

1 The ....-anticipated exhibition had some ....-known Egyptian exhibits.

2 Some of the stories behind the photographs at the Magnum exhibition were ....-provoking. Others were simply ....breaking.

3 The nation made a ....felt plea for the return of its cultural heritage. A ....-respected museum had prepared a room to house the statues.

4 The Science Fair was ....-paced and impressive. The exhibits displayed lots of .... -blowing solutions to environmental problems.

5 SPEAKING Describe an exhibition or museum you have attended using compound adjectives.

Verb patterns

6 Match the verbs in 1–5 to the patterns that follow them, a–e. Then check your answers in the text.

1 get, inspire

2 imagine, consider, suggest, recommend

3 afford, need, prefer

4 try, go on, remember, forget, stop, regret

5 let, make

a + -*ing*

b + object + infinitive with *to*

c + object + infinitive without *to*

d + infinitive with *to*

e + -*ing* or infinitive with *to* with a change in meaning

SAVED OR STOLEN?

A 'Telling history through things is what museums are all about,' explains Neil MacGregor, director of the British Museum. He should know, as the museum is one of the oldest and largest in the world. It also has a well-earned reputation as an 'encyclopaedic' museum, with a global story told through eight million objects. Inside, a wide-ranging collection includes everything from prehistoric pottery to precious hand made jewellery from India and Ming dynasty vases from China. The museum helps us to understand how events that happened at different times and in different places were connected, and how they influenced each other. Indeed, this was the vision of its founder, Sir Hans Sloane, who tried setting up cross-cultural comparisons in his original collection in 1753.

B As you walk around the British Museum today, it's clear that Sloane's broad-minded vision is very much alive and well. What's less clear is how the museum acquired many of the objects on display and whether they should remain there. Some have a well-documented history, but others were added during Britain's colonial period, so it's possible they were stolen from famous archaeological sites or acquired as trophies of war. Imagine having an important national monument from your country kept permanently in another country. How would you feel? Would you try to get the country to return it? It's not surprising that many countries have gone on to ask for their treasures back. However, where they should be kept is a question that is still fiercely debated.

C The Rosetta Stone is a well-known exhibit that illustrates this problem. Carved in 196 BC, the stone shows a pharaoh's decree in ancient hieroglyphics, Demotic and classical Greek, and was the key to unlocking the language of the ancient Egyptians. It was first discovered in 1799 near the town of el-Rashid (Rosetta) by soldiers in Napoleon's army, but on Napoleon's defeat in 1801, it became the property of the British. Many of the museum's treasures were acquired in a similar way, but unsurprisingly, the British Museum is reluctant to let the Rosetta Stone go. It argues that more people see the Stone in London than they would in Cairo, the location is more secure and the exhibit is a critical part of its global collection. The Egyptian government has other ideas and is trying to persuade the museum to return it. They claim that it's important for their nation's history and identity, and that many Egyptians can't afford to go to London to see it. But the British museum won't let the Rosetta Stone go, even as a loan, as they fear it won't be returned.

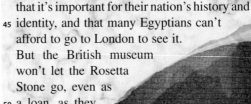

D The Elgin Marbles is another famous and controversial exhibit. Taken from the Parthenon temple in 1802 by Lord Elgin, the sculptures are considered a crucial part of Greek ⁵⁵ history – so much so that the Greek government, supported by UNESCO, has repeatedly asked for the marbles to be returned. According to the Greeks, Lord Elgin 'looted' the sculptures as well as seriously damaging the monument; however, the British claim that Elgin had the permission ⁶⁰ of the Ottoman authorities* to remove them. It wasn't until 1822 during the Greek War of Independence that the Acropolis was handed over to the Greeks, but by then the English Parliament had approved Elgin's acquisition. No one can make the museum give back the marbles; ⁶⁵ however, the Greek government will go on campaigning for their return until they are back in Athens.

E The British Museum is a place dedicated to international understanding, and the advantages of an encyclopaedic museum are clear to see: 'We need to ⁷⁰ explore common ground, how people perceive their relationship to each other ... and (to) see human history as an ongoing joint project,' explains MacGregor. But this attempt to bring different cultures together has been self-defeating, ultimately having the opposite effect: ⁷⁵ taking treasures from other countries has resulted in never-ending international rows. So as you admire the breathtaking objects on display at the museum, think about their legacy. Remember to ask yourself: Does the end justify the means? Is taking an object for a museum ⁸⁰ that different from theft? And shouldn't important objects be exhibited where they were originally made?

* At the time Athens had been a part of the Ottoman Empire for some 350 years.

7 Complete the sentences with the correct infinitive or *-ing* form of the verbs in brackets. What is the difference in meaning in each pair of sentences?

1 a Remember .... (read) the guidebook before you visit the museum.
b I remember .... (read) about the Mummy of Hornedjitef on the museum website.
2 a The guide stopped .... (talk) about the Rock Crystal Skull in front of the exhibit.
b The guide stopped .... (talk) about the Rock Crystal Skull and moved on to the next exhibit.
3 a If you want to see if you would enjoy being a guide, try .... (take) your friends around the museum.
b I tried .... (take) my friends on a tour around the museum, but nobody wanted to go.
4 a I forgot .... (see) the Elgin Marbles.
b I'll never forget .... (see) the Elgin Marbles.
5 a We regret .... (inform) you that the exhibition has been cancelled.
b I regret .... (inform) him about the exhibition.
6 a The guide first told us about Ice Age tools and then went on .... (describe) Ice Age art.
b The guide went on .... (describe) Ice Age art for two hours.

| Reference and practice 3.3 | Workbook page 114 |

8 Complete the text with the correct form of the verbs in brackets.

Once inside the museum, most people prefer
¹..................... (go) with the crowds to famous exhibits, such as the Rosetta Stone. They forget ².....................
(explore) the less popular, but equally interesting displays. In fact, MacGregor suggests ³.....................
(visit) these lesser-known objects first – so stop
⁴..................... (look) at a 5th century Sudanese cup or an Aboriginal bark shield. He also recommends
⁵..................... (focus) on just one object. For example, think about whose hands fashioned the cup and why. For just a moment, imagine ⁶..................... (be) that person – it might inspire you ⁷..................... (think) about the object in a new way and help you ⁸.....................
(realize) we are not that different. They were probably similar to you – they just lived in a different time.

9 SPEAKING Work in pairs. Discuss the questions.

1 Can you think of examples of 'national treasures' from:
- other countries that are displayed in museums in your country?
- your country that are displayed in museums abroad?
2 Should they be returned? Why / why not?

| Vocabulary bank | Objects in a museum page 136 |

| DVD extra | Museums |

1 SPEAKING Answer the questions.

1 Have you ever lost something while travelling? When did you lose it? Where were you going? Did you get it back?

2 What effect did losing the object have on your day?

2 Read parts 1 and 2 of *Lost and found*. What was lost? What effect did losing the object have on the owner? How do you think the object was returned? What do you think happened next?

3 ⊙ **1.17** Listen to part 3 of *Lost and found* and compare your ideas.

STRATEGY

Telling a story

When you tell a story, think about how you are going to tell it.

■ **Point of view:** decide who will tell the story: the first person or the third person?

■ **How to start:** use a 'hook', i.e. keep back a key piece of information to keep the reader interested.

■ **Show, don't tell:** let your reader learn about a character through what they say, see, hear and feel.

■ **How to end:** give your ending a twist or leave your reader guessing.

4 Read the strategy. Then answer the questions.

1 How are parts 1 and 2 of the story told: in the first person or the third person? What about part 3? What effect does this have?

2 Which part of the story uses a hook at the beginning? What is the hook?

3 Which part of the story starts in the middle of the action or situation? How does it do this?

4 In part 1, which adjectives would you use to describe the narrator? Do you think he enjoys the journey to college?

5 In part 2, what does Sarah feel, hear and see in the tutor's office? What does it say about her character and feelings?

6 Does part 3 give the reader an ending? If the story continues, what do you think happens next?

Ordering events in a story

5 Match sentences 1–4 to rules a and b, and complete the explanations. Then find two examples of rule a and two of rule b in the stories.

1 As she got off the train, she saw a poster.

2 Having searched through some photographs, she noticed a boy.

3 Looking up, he read the same advert.

4 After finishing college, he went back home.

a We use *having* + ... and .... + *-ing* to describe one action that happens before another action.

b We use .... + past simple or a .... participle to describe an action that happens at the same time as another action.

Reference and practice 3.4 | Workbook page 114

6 Rewrite the second sentence so that it has a similar meaning to the first sentence. What do you think fell out of the bag?

1 Lucas studied long and hard in the city library and then he caught the bus home.
After ....

2 An old lady sat down beside him and then started to complain about the dreadful weather.
Having ....

3 He quickly got off at the next stop and realized he'd picked up the wrong bag.
After ....

4 He hurried after the departing bus and tried to get the driver's attention.
Hurrying ....

5 He clumsily dropped the bag and something fell out.
As ....

Lost and found

Part 1: Mark

Having found it, I wasn't sure what to do with it. At first I looked around me. Perhaps the owner wasn't far away? Realizing they'd probably gone, I slipped it into my backpack and decided to hand it in at the next stop. 'All trains to Waterloo have been cancelled. London Transport apologizes for any inconvenience ... ,' announced the station loudspeaker as everyone got off the train and struggled down the narrow passageways. 'Great,' I thought as I was pulled along by the crowd. 'I'm going to miss my first lecture.'

Later that day, after finishing lunch, I remembered the folder. I pulled it out of my backpack and looked at it. It was smooth and black and had the initials S.D. on the front. Feeling a little guilty, I opened it up. Inside there were drawings – some in black and white, others in colour, all of them pretty good: a street scene in the rain, a sunny day in the park, a performer in Covent Garden.

'What's that, Mark?' asked a friend sitting next to me.

'Ah, something I found on the tube this morning,' I said, showing her.

'They're interesting. Why didn't you hand them in?'

'I forgot,' I said.

'Well, don't worry too much,' she laughed. 'You're in luck. There's an exhibition of unclaimed art from the London Transport lost property office this week, and it's at a gallery in Hoxton Square – just round the corner. Why don't you take them along?'

THE LOST COLLECTION

AN EXHIBITION OF UNCLAIMED ART FROM TRANSPORT FOR LONDON'S LOST PROPERTY OFFICE

JUNE–JULY
HOXTON SQUARE

OLD STREET

Part 2: Sarah

'Sarah Darwin?' called a cross-looking woman behind the desk as I ran through the double doors.

'Yes,' I panted. 'I'm here.' I'd just about made it, despite the delay on the Underground. It wouldn't have looked good to arrive any later. Places at Central Saint Martins College were few, the applicants were many and I was determined to make a good impression. 'They're waiting for you inside,' snapped the woman, pointing to a door at the end of the corridor.

The room was a tutor's office, with heaps of books, piles of drawings and photographs everywhere. A middle-aged woman in a black polo neck and jeans leaned against a bookcase, flicking through a portfolio, and a grey-haired man in a tweed suit was sitting in an armchair nearby. The woman looked up and smiled.

'Sarah?' she said. 'Please take a seat ...' Coughing a little, I sat in a chair opposite, then reached into my bag. That's when I noticed it was missing.

'Anything wrong?' asked the man. Outside the wind was getting stronger and it was starting to rain – to pour down, in fact.

'I think I left my portfolio on the train,' I stammered.

An hour later, having finished the interview, I was back on the street. In the end it hadn't been a total disaster; I'd borrowed a laptop and presented work from my website, although the pictures weren't as striking. Still, it was better than nothing. By now it was raining hard, but after losing my portfolio, I didn't care about getting wet. All I cared about was finding my drawings. And I wanted a place at Central Saint Martins.

WRITING GUIDE

- **Task** Write a story about an object that you have lost.

- **Ideas** Decide who is telling the story. Ask and answer *wh-* questions (*who, what, where, when, how, why*).

- **Plan** Follow the plan:

  Paragraph 1: Begin your story. Introduce the lost object, the location and the main character(s).

  Paragraph 2: Develop your story. What does the main character do next? What impact does losing the object have on their day?

  Paragraph 3: End your story. Was the object returned? Did the main characters meet?

- **Write** Write your story. Use the paragraph plan to help you.

- **Check** Check the following points:

  - Does the story start in an interesting way?
  - Have you checked grammar, vocabulary, spelling and punctuation?

Vocabulary insight 3 Phrasal verbs

The grammar of phrasal verbs

A phrasal verb is a combination of two or three words: a verb and at least one particle (a preposition or an adverb). The addition of the particle changes the meaning of the verb. Phrasal verbs can be:

1 Intransitive – these verbs do not need an object.
2 Transitive, separable – these phrasal verbs can be separated by an object (in a dictionary, there is usually sb / sth <u>between</u> the two parts of the phrasal verb).
3 Transitive, inseparable – these phrasal verbs cannot be separated by an object (in a dictionary, there is usually sb / sth <u>after</u> the phrasal verb). Three-part phrasal verbs cannot be separated.

1 Read the strategy above. Then study the dictionary entries and answer the questions.

Which verb:
1 is intransitive?
2 is transitive, separable?
3 is transitive, inseparable?
4 has one meaning as an intransitive verb and a different meaning as a transitive, separable verb?

PHR V ,opt 'in (to sth) to choose to be part of a system or an agreement ,opt 'out (of sth) **1** to choose not to take part in sth: *Employees may opt out of the company's pension plan.* **2** (of a school or hospital in Britain) to choose not to be under the control of the local authority ⊃ related noun OPT-OUT

,throw sth↔a'way **1** ☞ (also ,throw sth↔'out) to get rid of sth that you no longer want: *I don't need that— you can throw it away.* ◇ *That old chair should be thrown away.* **2** ☞ to fail to make use of sth; to waste sth: *to throw away an opportunity* ⊃ see also THROWAWAY

,turn 'out **1** to be present at an event: *A vast crowd turned out to watch the procession.* ⊃ related noun TURNOUT **2** (used with an adverb or adjective, or in questions with *how*) to happen in a particular way; to develop or end in a particular way: *Despite our worries everything turned out well.* ◇ *You never know how your children will turn out.* ◇ + adj. *If the day turns out wet, we may have to change our plans.* **3** to point away from the centre: *Her toes turn out.*

,clear sth↔'out ☞ to make sth empty and clean by removing things or throwing things away: *to clear out a drawer/ room* ◇ *We cleared out all our old clothes.* ◇ *I found the letters when I was clearing out after my father died.* ⊃ related

Understanding the meaning of particles

Knowing the meanings of the most common particles can help you to guess the meaning of any new phrasal verbs that you come across. One particle can have different meanings, depending on the verb that it is with, but almost every particle has a basic literal meaning and a metaphorical meaning. When trying to understand a new phrasal verb, think about both meanings.

2 Read the strategy above. Then read the dictionary entry and answer the questions.

OUT
The basic meaning of out is of movement from inside to outside, so it combines with many verbs of movement, for example, *storm out, rush out, go out.* Many verbs that combine with out also combine with the adverb plus preposition out of, for example, *storm out, storm out of the room.* Out and in can sometimes be used with the same verbs to express opposite meanings (for example, *go out, go in*).

1 What is the literal meaning of the particle *out*?
2 What particle has the opposite meaning?
3 What five verbs of movement do you know that can go with these two particles?

3 Read sentences 1–6. Then match the phrasal verbs in bold to the meanings of *out* a–f.

1 We decided to **check out** of the hotel.
2 The teacher **called out** all our names one by one.
3 The survey is anonymous, so **leave out** your name.
4 Can you **hand out** the test papers?
5 The factory **churns out** millions of these little toys.
6 It took me almost all day to **work out** this puzzle.

a to exclude someone or something from an activity, a list, etc.
b to search, observe, solve
c to produce (usually quickly and in large quantities)
d to share or distribute among people
e to speak or shout loudly
f to leave a place or a person, start a journey

4 Find the phrasal verbs below in a dictionary. Then add them to categories a–f in exercise 3.

▪ give out ▪ find out ▪ turn out ▪ cross out ▪ set out ▪ bark out

5 Complete the sentences with the correct forms of the phrasal verbs in exercise 4.

1 Our manager wasn't in a good mood today. She was .... orders to everyone.
2 My job for the summer was to .... leaflets to people in the underground.
3 Can you .... what time we need to be at the meeting?
4 We overslept, so we didn't .... on our journey until noon.
5 This factory .... the most cars in Europe.
6 I .... the names of the people who have already paid for the trip.

6 Guess the meanings of the phrasal verbs below. Then check your answers in a dictionary and write your own example sentence for each verb.

▪ pop out ▪ dig out ▪ spill out ▪ nap out ▪ filter out ▪ dish out

Dictionary entries from *Oxford Advanced Learner's Dictionary* 8ᵉ, Oxford University Press 2010 and *Oxford Phrasal Verbs Dictionary for learners of English* 2ᵉ, Oxford University Press.

Vocabulary

1 Match the pairs of synonyms below.

■ accumulate ■ amass ■ belongings ■ bin ■ clutter ■ get rid of ■ heaps ■ junk (n) ■ possessions ■ stacks

1 .... / ....
2 .... / ....
3 .... / ....
4 .... / ....
5 .... / ....

Marks .... / 5

2 Complete the phrasal verbs in the text with the words below.

■ reach ■ run ■ sort ■ spill ■ spread ■ throw

Dear Agony Anne,

I wonder if you can help me. My mother can't seem to ¹ .... anything out, so our house is full of junk. Whenever she starts to ² .... out of space in one room, she just moves to the next. In the kitchen, there are objects ³ .... out all over the table and things also ⁴ .... out of all the drawers. I have offered to help her ⁵ .... out the cupboards, but she refuses to let me. I don't know how to ⁶ .... out to her. What should I do?

Marks .... / 6

3 Put the adjectives in brackets in the correct position.

1 There's a rusty old statue in the square. (bronze)

2 He's a young French artist. (contemporary)

3 They drink tea in tiny china teacups. (delicate)

4 She was wearing a stunning silk outfit. (colourful)

5 There is a large wooden table in the room. (rectangular)

6 We saw a witty abstract play. (French)

Marks .... / 6

4 Complete the sentences with compound adjectives. Use the correct forms of the words in brackets.

1 There is a .... view from the tower. (take)
2 Those bags don't come out of a factory; they're .... (make)
3 We gave him our .... thanks. (feel)
4 The queue was .... (end)
5 It's a .... exhibition. (provoke)
6 He's a .... artist from Spain. (respect)
7 They had a .... break. (earn)

Marks .... / 7

Grammar

5 Choose the correct answers.

Textiles graduate Katy Bell is ¹**a(n)** / **the** / **–** entrepreneur. She runs a company called Lost Property of London, which makes ²**a(n)** / **the** / **–** quality handbags out of recycled material. ³**A(n)** / **The** / **–** bags are made using traditional techniques and ⁴**a(n)** / **the** / **–** finest accessories. They are ideal for ⁵**a(n)** / **the** / **–** people who want a product that is friendly to ⁶**a(n)** / **the** / **–** environment. Prices range from £150 to £250 ⁷**a(n)** / **the** / **–** bag.

Marks .... / 7

6 Complete the text with the words below.

■ a few ■ a little ■ almost all of ■ a lot of ■ far too many ■ few ■ little

Cornwall in the south-west of England is a popular tourist destination because it has ¹ .... beaches – over 200 to be exact. Some of them are only accessible by sea, so ² .... people go there. But most of them are easy to reach, and on days when there is ³ .... sunshine, they are occupied by ⁴ .... people, so it's hard to find a space. However, for ⁵ .... days last year the beach at Bude was not so popular because of two strange objects that were washed ashore. The first was a large white thing that ⁶ .... the residents thought was a polar bear. The second was an enormous object, which people had ⁷ .... doubt was a monster. On further investigation, however, the polar bear turned out to be a dead cow and the monster was in fact a tree!

Marks .... / 7

7 Complete sentence b so that it has a similar meaning to sentence a.

1 a You should book a guided tour of the exhibition.
  b They recommended ....
2 a Applying sunscreen regularly is fundamental.
  b Remember ....
3 a They weren't allowed to take photos.
  b The guide didn't let ....
4 a I didn't collect stamps after I was sixteen.
  b When I was sixteen, I stopped ....
5 a Buying new furniture is too expensive.
  b I can't afford ....
6 a She became a sculptor after she went to art school.
  b After art school, she went on ....
7 a After watching the travel programme, we decided to visit Greece.
  b The travel programme inspired ....

Marks .... / 7

Total .... / 45

Reading and vocabulary Perfect people

1 SPEAKING Imagine that before you were born your parents could modify your genes and change your character. Answer the questions.

1 Which two things would you have liked them:
■ to change? ■ to keep the same?

2 How would your life be different because of the changes that they made?

2 Read the article and answer the questions.

In which paragraph does the writer mention:

1 the ethical problem in relation to genetic engineering?

2 that our society is becoming similar to the one in *Gattaca*?

3 a difficult decision the parents have to make?

4 why Vincent won't realize his ambitions?

5 why genetic engineering is a logical step for society?

6 the selection process parents might go through?

7 laws which could enforce genetic engineering?

3 SPEAKING Discuss the questions.

1 How do you think Vincent feels about his brother Anton? How would you feel?

2 Do you think parents have a right to 'play God' and genetically engineer their children? Why might they be considered 'immoral' if they don't?

V **insight** Verbs and nouns with the same form

4 Study the highlighted words in the article. Complete the pairs of sentences with a highlighted word. What is the difference in meaning? Find three more examples in the article.

1 a Don't look at the computer .... for too long. You'll get a headache.

b Doctors had to .... people for bird flu, to try and stop it from spreading.

2 a Einstein had an amazing .... He thought about science in a different way from other people.

b I don't .... if you disagree with me, just listen to my point of view.

3 a Designer babies will .... a lot of problems in the future.

b This charity is a good .... to support.

4 a There needs to be a .... in attitude – we need to start accepting genetic engineering.

b Can you .... these boxes out of the way? They're blocking the corridor.

5 a The whole area of genetics will .... us with serious ethical debates.

b Old people often live in care homes because they don't want to be a .... on their children.

6 a My brother is passionate about science and mathematics. He plans to become an ....

b She tried to influence and .... the debate so she was the clear winner.

GATTACA

BY DANIEL ALLOTT

A In a scene from the science fiction film *Gattaca*, a genetic counsellor speaks with a young couple about the child they'd like to have. The couple's first child, Vincent, was diagnosed immediately after birth with several disabilities including a
5 heart defect that puts his life expectancy at just 30.2 years. So the couple decide to genetically **engineer** their second child. The geneticist explains that after screening hundreds of embryos, they are left with two healthy boy embryos and two healthy girl embryos. 'All that remains is to select the
10 most compatible candidate,' he tells them.

B They decide they want another boy, a playmate for Vincent. Reading a report, the geneticist says, 'You have specified hazel eyes, dark hair and fair skin.' He then goes on to explain that he has already got rid of genes
15 which might **cause** problems, things such as premature baldness, short-sightedness, deafness, aggression or obesity. The mother interrupts: 'We didn't want ... I mean, diseases, yes, but ...'

Her husband says, 'Right, we were just wondering if it's good
20 just to leave a few things to chance.'

The geneticist smiles and says, 'You want to give your child the best possible start. Believe me, we have enough imperfection built in already. Your child doesn't need any additional burdens. Keep in mind this child is still you, only
25 the best of you.'

Vocabulary: verbs and nouns with the same form; noun suffixes: *-ness*, *-ity*, *-ion*; phrases with body parts; word analysis; addition and contrast
Grammar: talking about habitual behaviour; future in the past

Speaking: discussing a controversial topic
Writing: a letter to a newspaper

4A

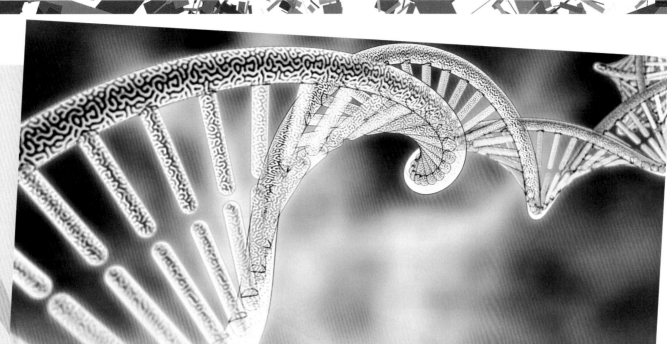

C The couple agree, and their second son, Anton, is the near genetically perfect son they had hoped for. In the past people used to leave things to chance, but in *Gattaca's* world few parents want to risk producing children who become
30 members of an underclass called 'invalids'. Anton's older brother, Vincent, wants to become an astronaut but because of his genetic profile he is labelled as an 'invalid' and can only work as a cleaner. As a result, there is a lot of pressure on parents to genetically engineer their children.

35 **D** Set in the 'not too distant future,' the film, which starred Ethan Hawke, Uma Thurman, and Jude Law, was released on October 24, 1997. Today advances in reproductive and genetic medicine might well lead to the type of society *Gattaca* warned against, a society where a drop of blood
40 decides where you can work, who you should marry and what you can achieve. In 2003 the Human Genome Project increased our understanding of the genetic roots of human traits. Currently, thanks to genetic screening, couples can learn a great deal about their children before they are born.
45 Experts predict that we will be able to screen embryos for eye and hair color within a few years. Within a decade it may also be possible to predict behavioral conditions such as depression and addiction.

E Some people believe this new technology is changing
50 parents' attitudes toward their children. 'The attitude of parents may shift from unconditional acceptance to critical scrutiny,' warned the Council on Bioethics in 2003. 'The very first act of parenting now becomes not the unreserved welcoming of an arriving child, but the judging of his or her
55 fitness, while still an embryo, to become their child.' Arthur Caplan, head of the Division of Bioethics at New York University, believes that American culture encourages this desire for genetic perfection: 'There's going to be demand in a society oriented toward doing well, toward perfection,
60 toward the value of the best you can be, even a society that says, 'I want a better life for my child than I had for myself.' So somebody's going to say 'Why won't I test my kids, to give them a better life than I had?'

F Given all these changes, how long will it be before mothers feel they have to modify the genes of their 'imperfect' 65 babies? How long until those who do not get tested will be regarded as immoral? At some point the government might come along and say 'It's so expensive to have disability, here's our policy: You can't have a baby unless you have genetic testing.' 70

G Genetic engineering raises many questions, and most of us are troubled by the idea of 'playing God'. Many people believe that children are gifts which should be appreciated as they come to us, not commodities to be manufactured. Genetic engineering fails to appreciate the value of human 75 difference, and that is an important part of what it means to be human.

5 Complete the text with the noun forms of the adjectives in brackets.

The question is …

You may suffer from ¹........................ (obese), ² .... (bald) or more serious conditions, such as autism or blindness, but it won't stop you achieving great things.

- Albert Einstein suffered from a learning ³........................ (disabled) – he could not speak until he was three and he was weak in maths. Einstein's brain processed information in a different way from his peers, but this 'defective' way of thinking enabled him to become one of the world's greatest mathematicians.

- Ludwig van Beethoven suffered from ⁴........................ (depressed) which resulted in ⁵........................ (aggressive), but also amazing creativity. Towards the end of his life, his ⁶........................ (deaf) increased, yet he carried on composing his famous Ninth Symphony.

- Claude Monet painted his *Water Lilies* paintings despite his poor vision and ⁷........................ (short-sighted). Because of his vision, these paintings are unique, and Monet didn't stop working on them until he was nearly blind.

- Michelangelo had a strange ⁸........................ (addictive) to certain routines. He would always sleep in his clothes and never take off his boots, then isolate himself for long periods of time while he worked. However, this 'mental illness' didn't stop him from painting the ceiling of the Sistine Chapel.

The question is: would these people have achieved so much without these ⁹........................ (imperfect)?

6 Put the noun forms of the adjectives in exercise 5 into the correct column. Then check your answers in the article.

-ion	-ness	-ity

7 **SPEAKING** Read the opinions below. Which do you agree / disagree with? Explain why.

1 Society encourages us to live the best life we can, and having perfect children is just part of that.

2 Children are gifts which should be appreciated as they come to us, not commodities to be manufactured.

3 Genetic engineering fails to appreciate the value of human difference, and that is an important part of what it means to be human.

Vocabulary bank Phrases with *mind* page 137

1 **SPEAKING** Look at the photos from hospital dramas and discuss the questions. Then read the text and compare your ideas.

1 Have you ever watched any hospital dramas? What sorts of characters appear in them? What types of storylines do they have?

2 Why do you think people like this type of drama? How realistic do you think they are?

Just like real life?

In 1961, the first hospital drama, *Dr Kildare*, appeared on our TV screens. It was a huge success and was quickly followed by many others. ¹Every week, these series **would show** ordinary people in extraordinary situations. People loved them because they often dealt with real-life problems, allowing viewers to reflect: 'What would I do if this happened to me?' ²They also functioned as 'entertainment education' and **would often help** viewers understand how modern hospitals operated. However, there were many medical myths in these early dramas, too – ³doctors were always portrayed as heroes and patients **rarely died** in the many years the shows were broadcast. ⁴In addition, programmes **didn't use to have** many special effects, so operations were talked about rather than filmed.

⁵Nowadays, hospital dramas **are often** more graphic than in the past, and storylines are more believable, but there are still a few myths. One popular myth is that doctors do everything. ⁶In the successful series *House*, Dr Gregory House **will usually** diagnose an illness, analyse blood samples <u>and</u> perform surgery. ⁷In real life, these jobs **are always carried out** by different people, such as lab technicians, nurses and other specialists.

Nevertheless, millions of people still enjoy *Grey's Anatomy* and *House*, although recently some fans have started to complain: ⁸'*House* **used to be** my favourite show,' commented one blogger. 'Not any more. ⁹My younger brother **will sit** there watching it for hours, but I find it predictable and boring. ¹⁰It's **always dealing with** the same issues.' She has a point. How many more illnesses can one doctor diagnose? How many more patients can he save? Maybe hospital dramas have had their day?

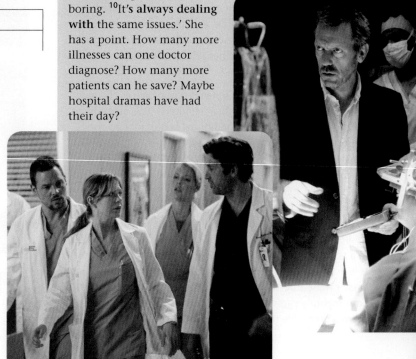

Fact or fiction

Talking about habitual behaviour

2 Read the text *Just like real life?* again and match sentences 1–10 to the uses below.

   1 Which **five** sentences describe habits in the past?

   2 Which **five** sentences describe habits in the present or future?

   3 Which **two** sentences express irritation or criticism?

3 Look at the sentences with *used to, would* and the past simple again. Then complete rules a–c below with *used to, would* or the *past simple*.

   a We use *would* and .... to talk about past states or habits in the past (that do not happen now).

   b We use .... to talk about past habits, but **not** past states.

   c We use .... to say how long a situation went on for.

Reference and practice 4.1   Workbook page 115

4 Rewrite the sentences using the words in brackets.

   1 Many medical dramas often repeat the same storylines. (will)

   2 When my mum was a nurse, she always worked very long hours. (would)

   3 My sister will insist on watching *House* when *CSI* is on! (always)

   4 A few years ago, I loved detective dramas, but I rarely watch them now. (used to / will)

   5 In early science fiction dramas, directors used simple special effects. (would)

   6 In the 1950s, westerns were one of the most successful TV genres. (used)

   7 Most evenings, we don't usually have time to watch TV. (won't)

   8 I don't like fantasy programmes, but my friend will talk about the new *True Blood* series! (constantly)

5 🔊 **1.18**   Listen to an interview with an actor from a hospital drama called *Paramedics* and answer the questions.

   1 Where did Dillon use to work? Does he work there now?

   2 Is Dillon used to seeing accidents? How often does he witness them?

   3 Are paramedics used to working long hours? Do they get exhausted?

   4 How did Dillon react when he saw someone in pain? Does he think he could get used to it?

   5 Which adjectives does Dillon use to describe the paramedics' job? What type of things do they have to get used to?

6 Study the underlined phrases in exercise 5 and match them to categories a–c below. Then decide which we can use with past, present and future tenses.

   a Events or states in the past that no longer happen now.

   b Something we are accustomed to, that is part of our life.

   c Something we are becoming accustomed to; it may have seemed strange before, but it's normal now.

7 Complete the sentences with the correct form of *used to, get used to* or *be used to*.

   1 Dillon .... (not) working long hours. He usually left the TV studio after lunch.

   2 'It may seem difficult to deal with an emergency now, but you .... it in a few weeks' time.'

   3 When we were children, we .... climb trees, until I fell and broke my arm!

   4 He gave up his job as a doctor. He found it impossible to .... the stress.

   5 I .... watch *Paramedics* every week, but I never watch it now. It's too predictable.

   6 'I can't .... my new braces. They're really uncomfortable.'
   'You need to see your dentist again.'

   7 My brother starts work at the hospital tomorrow. His biggest challenge will be getting up early – he .... lying in bed all day!

8 **SPEAKING**   Discuss the questions.

   1 Think of a TV programme you used to watch as a child, but which you do not watch now. What type of programme was it? What did you use to like about it?

   2 Think of a past change to your everyday routine that you are used to now, for example, changing schools, starting a new after-school club, doing a weekend job. What was the difference between your new and old routines? Was your new routine easy or difficult to get used to? Why?

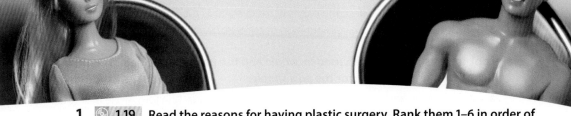

1 🔘 **1.19** Read the reasons for having plastic surgery. Rank them 1–6 in order of importance. Then listen and choose the reasons mentioned in the radio programme *Profiles*.

■ to look like a famous person ■ to correct facial deformity ■ to stop people bullying you
■ to get a better job or earn more money ■ to help with depression or other mental illness
■ to improve self-esteem and self-image

2 🔘 **1.19** Listen to the radio programme again and match people A and B to statements 1–8. There is one statement you can match both people to. There are two statements that you do not need.

A Vanilla Chamu   B Justin Jedlica

Which person:
1 was bullied when they were younger?
2 didn't receive support from their parents?
3 has decided to stop having surgery?
4 has had around thirty plastic surgery operations?
5 changed their body by working out at a gym?
6 was insulted on a television programme?
7 experienced academic success?
8 hated one part of their body in particular?

STRATEGY

Active listening (2)
When you listen to a radio programme or a lecture, or are having a discussion or debate, a good way to check understanding is to repeat or paraphrase what has been said.

3 Read the strategy. Work in pairs. Read the sentences from the radio programme, then summarize and paraphrase the ideas with your partner.

1 Their name-calling and nastiness was very upsetting … and she became increasingly depressed.
2 Like many people who suffer from a poor body image, she has put her faith in plastic surgery – it's her 'salvation', she thinks.
3 Jedlica is aware he is compromising his health, but he insists it's worth it.
4 He realizes that everyone has a different idea of perfection, and that a positive body image can allow us to thrive.
5 Jedlica claims it's impossible to stop – it would be 'like asking Picasso not to paint.'

V Phrases with body parts

4 Match the idioms in italics to their meanings a–g.
1 their cruel taunts … *broke her heart* … .
2 Has he *come to his senses* and stopped having surgery?
3 He *dug his heels in* and had the surgery without their consent.
4 He isn't concerned about his appearance any more which is *a weight off his shoulders*.
5 The comparison with Picasso … is *hard to swallow* … .
6 *There is* definitely *more to him than meets the eye*.
7 Real self-confidence comes from accepting ourselves, *warts and all*.

a difficult to believe or accept
b to refuse to change or stubbornly resist something
c not hiding faults or weaknesses
d more complicated than it seems at first
e something you no longer have to worry about
f to act sensibly after acting unwisely
g to deeply hurt someone in some way

5 Rewrite the phrases in italics using the correct form of the idioms in exercise 4.

Imagine you couldn't smile

Sometimes it's hard for us to accept other people, ¹*with all their imperfections.* Appearances matter, and life can be a misery for those who look different – cruel words and looks can be ²*tough to accept.*

It's a sunny day in Honduras and seven-year-old Zoila is playing outside a small wooden house. She's laughing and smiling like a typical child, but ³*life wasn't always so simple for this little girl.* Why? Because Zoila was born with a cleft palate. It ⁴*deeply affected her mother*, who blamed herself for her daughter's problem, and for years Ziola covered her mouth so nobody could see her smile. Then, a few months ago, her mother heard that a charity called Operation Smile was coming to Santa Rosa. The charity offered plastic surgery to people with facial deformities, and there was a chance that Zoila could be helped. At first Zoila was very frightened; she ⁵*stubbornly refused to go* and didn't want an operation. But her mother persuaded her and after a two-day bus journey, they arrived at the hospital. Today, Zoila is a different child. She's confident and happy because a simple operation ⁶*means she no longer has to worry about looking different.* She often laughs and she no longer tries to hide her smile … and it is beautiful.

6 SPEAKING Discuss the questions.

  1 How important do you think body image is? What other things can improve your self-esteem?

  2 Why do you think Chamu and Jedlica want people to notice them?

Discussing a controversial topic

7 🔘 **1.20 SPEAKING** Listen to the news story. Then discuss the questions.

  1 What was Nadia's problem? What did she do about it?

  2 Do you think school life will be easier for Nadia? Why / why not?

  3 Is Nadia's solution the best way to deal with her problem? What message might it send to other students?

8 🔘 **1.21** Listen to students discussing Nadia's choice. Are their ideas similar to or different from your own?

9 🔘 **1.21** Complete the phrases from the dialogue. Then listen again and check.

A Expressing doubts
I don't ¹................ about that (at all).
I'm not convinced by that ²................ .
I'm not sure that's true.

B Expressing your point of view forcefully
I ³................ believe it's … .
I'm totally convinced that … .

C Being diplomatic
I see ⁴................ you're coming from, but … .
I ⁵................ what you're saying, but … .

D Being undiplomatic
You must be ⁶................ !
I think you're (both) ⁷................ the point.

10 🔘 **1.22** Listen to two other people talking about plastic surgery. Tick the phrases that you hear. Then match all of them to categories A–D in exercise 9.

  ◾ I'm absolutely certain that … . ◾ I know what you're getting at, but … . ◾ Oh, come on!
  ◾ I'm completely certain that … . ◾ OK, maybe you have a point.
  ◾ There's no doubt in my mind that … . ◾ That's just not true.

11 SPEAKING Work in pairs. Read the opinions and decide whether you agree or disagree with them. Give reasons for your ideas using the phrases in exercise 9.

  1 Girls experience more pressure to look attractive than boys.

  2 Cosmetic surgery for teenagers should be banned.

  3 Teenagers who lack self-esteem should have the option of plastic surgery.

DVD extra Surgery: old and new

1 **SPEAKING** Think about the qualities that make us human. Then look at the list below and choose the three most important ones. Give reasons for your choices. Then read extracts A and B and decide which qualities Dr Frankenstein has.

- ■ morality ■ compassion ■ creativity ■ honesty
- ■ courage ■ self-discipline ■ determination ■ patience
- ■ vision ■ aspiration

2 Read extract A again. Are the statements true (T), false (F) or not given (NG)?

1 The story of *Frankenstein* warns against the misuse of knowledge.
2 People feared the changes that the Industrial Revolution would cause.
3 Mary was very well-known when she wrote the story.
4 Initially, the novel was unpopular because it was so shocking.
5 Mary had a similar character to her mother.
6 A game amongst friends inspired Mary to write the story.
7 After finishing her novel, she went on to write romantic poetry.
8 Mary wrote other books about Dr Frankenstein's creation.

V insight Word analysis

3 Answer the questions, referring closely to extract B.

1 What adjectives and adverbs does the writer use to describe the setting? What atmosphere does this create?
2 Which words does the writer use to describe Dr Frankenstein's a) physical state and b) mental state? How does the weather reflect this?
3 In line 7 of the extract, Frankenstein says 'my candle was nearly burnt out, when by the failing light, I saw the dull yellow eye of the creature open'. What do you think light represents? What might this tell us about the writer's opinion of Frankenstein's experiment?
4 Find five names that Frankenstein gives to his creation. Does he consider him human? (Clue: look at the pronouns he uses, too.)
5 What adjectives does he use to describe the creature's eyes, teeth, hair and his skin or complexion? What impression does this create?
6 Frankenstein's monster is his 'child'. Can you find evidence in the extract that the creature is behaving like a child?
7 What things might a child reasonably expect from a parent? Think about Frankenstein's treatment of his 'child'. What effect might this have on the creature?

4 **SPEAKING** Discuss the questions.

1 What issues does *Frankenstein* deal with?
2 What do you think is the book's purpose? To entertain? To warn? To inform?
3 What vision does the author have of society or people?

A

Frankenstein

On a stormy, windswept night in 1815, a young, eighteen-year-old girl had a vivid nightmare. The nightmare was dreadful and deeply distressing, but it gave her an idea for a tale – [1]<u>a tale that</u>
5 <u>would become the most recognized horror story</u>
<u>in the world</u>: the story of Frankenstein's monster.

The novel recounts the trials of an ambitious young scientist, Dr Frankenstein, who uses his knowledge to bring an inanimate body to life,
10 but then rejects the shocking 'monster' he creates. At the time of writing, the story was a powerful warning against scientific advances and [2]<u>the</u>
<u>Industrial Revolution, which was about to spread</u>
<u>across Europe</u>. Many artists and writers were
15 concerned about this industrialization and [3]<u>the</u>
<u>effect it would have on man's relationship with</u>
<u>nature</u>. They saw danger in the new scientific advances and a worrying desire to 'play God'.

The author of *Frankenstein* was called Mary
20 Shelley (1797–1851), and for many it was hard to believe that a young girl could write such a shocking story. But Mary was no ordinary eighteen-year-old. Her father, William Godwin, was a well-known philosopher and novelist, and
25 her mother, Mary Wollstonecraft, was a famous feminist. Unfortunately for Mary, her mother died shortly after she was born, but Mary inherited her rebellious spirit. At sixteen, she secretly ran away to France and then to Switzerland with the writer
30 Percy Shelley, who was later to achieve fame as a romantic poet. In Switzerland, the couple stayed with the poet Lord Byron, and in the evenings they often entertained themselves by reading ghost stories. After a while, Byron suggested they
35 write their own, and [4]<u>Mary decided she was going</u>
<u>to write about her nightmare</u>.

Mary's life with Percy was passionate and brief. When he died in a storm in Italy in 1822, Mary returned to England with her son and continued
40 writing until her death in 1851. But *Frankenstein* lived on and, almost 200 years later, it's still influencing and inspiring contemporary popular culture.

Mary Shelley
Frankenstein
1818 text

OXFORD WORLD'S CLASSICS

B

Volume 1 Chapter 4*

It was on a dreary night in November that I completed my work. With an anxiety that almost amounted to agony, I collected the instruments of life around me that I might inject a spark of
5 being into the lifeless thing that lay at my feet. It was already one in the morning; the rain fell dismally against the window panes, and my candle was nearly burnt out, when, by the failing light, I saw the dull yellow eye of the creature open; it
10 breathed hard, and a sudden movement agitated its limbs. How can I describe my emotions at this catastrophe, or how to describe the terrible wretch I had tried to form? His limbs were in proportion, and I had selected his features as beautiful.
15 Beautiful! Great God! His yellow skin scarcely covered the muscles and arteries beneath; his hair was black and flowing; his teeth of a pearly whiteness that formed a horrid contrast with his watery eyes, his shrivelled complexion and straight
20 black lips. I had worked hard for nearly two years, for the sole purpose of breathing life into an inanimate body. For this I had deprived myself of rest and health, but now that I had finished, the beauty of the dream vanished, and breathless
25 horror and disgust filled my heart. Unable to endure the appearance of the being I had created, I rushed out of the room and spent a long time pacing around my bed-chamber, unable to sleep. At length tiredness overtook me, and I threw myself on the
30 bed in my clothes, trying to find a few moments of forgetfulness. But it was in vain; I slept, indeed, but I was disturbed by the wildest dreams. [...] I started from my sleep with horror; a cold sweat covered my forehead, my teeth chattered, and
35 every limb was tense; when, by the dim and yellow light of the moon, I beheld the wretch, the miserable monster whom I had created. He held up the curtain of the bed; and his eyes were fixed on me. His jaws opened, and he muttered some
40 inarticulate sounds, while a grin wrinkled his cheeks. He might have spoken, but I did not hear; one hand was stretched out, as if to keep me there, but I escaped and rushed downstairs. I took refuge in the courtyard belonging to the house which I
45 inhabited, where I remained during the rest of the night, listening attentively, fearing each sound as if it were the approach of the monster to which I had so miserably given life.

* Adapted from Mary Shelley's *Frankenstein*

Future in the past

5 **Read the information below. Then study the underlined sentences 1–4 in extract A and answer the questions.**

We use the future in the past to talk about future events from a point of view in the past.

Which sentences are examples of:
1 a future plan or intention? (1 sentence)
2 an event that is in the very distant future or would last a long time? (2 sentences)
3 an event that is in the very near future? (1 sentence)

Reference and practice 4.2 | Workbook page 116

6 **Complete the text with the phrases below.**

- would write ■ was to emerge ■ was going to change
- were about to develop ■ would spend
- were to become ■ would find

Science fiction: the early history

At the end of the 18th century, few people had any idea of how industrial capitalism [1] .... the world. Modern scientists [2] .... the technology to build large factories, rapid large-scale transportation and new energy sources. Soon, vast numbers of people [3] .... their lives working in factories, in coal mines, on railroads and on ships. Workers [4] .... alienated from the means of production and their own products and [5] .... themselves increasingly separated from nature and from each other.

One of the first works of modern science fiction [6] .... from this period: Mary Shelley's *Frankenstein* (1818). Less than a decade after *Frankenstein*, Shelley [7] .... one of the first science fiction visions of the end of the world; in her *The Last Man* (1826), the main character wanders alone over a dead planet, sampling the useless achievements of all human society. Mary Shelley set this scene in the year 2100.

7 **SPEAKING** **Discuss the questions.**
1 Think about when you were a child. Did you dream about what you were going to be when you were grown up? Have any of these dreams changed?
2 Think about the last book you read or film you saw. How did it end? Did you guess it would end this way? Why / why not?
3 Think about yesterday. Was there anything you were about to do, but didn't? Why didn't you do it?

Vocabulary bank | Body parts page 137

1 SPEAKING Read the extract from a newspaper article. What is the main issue? What is your view on it?

The value of life

It's a sad fact, but in the near future most governments will be struggling to cover the medical costs of their ageing populations. As a result, many countries are exploring ways to save money to ease the financial burden. One way of cutting costs would be to 'punish' people with unhealthy lifestyles by making them pay for their own medical care: people who smoke, drink excessively, use sunbeds, overeat, don't wear seatbelts, etc. People who knowingly put their health at risk. The questions policy makers are asking are whether this approach will make a difference, and who is responsible for the way people behave.

STRATEGY

Taking a view and supporting your ideas

When you are asked to react to an issue:

a first decide on your point of view. What do you think is the solution to the problem? If a solution is offered, do you agree or disagree with it? What would you suggest instead?

b note down two or three main ideas that illustrate your point of view. Support your ideas with arguments or examples that will convince the reader.

2 Read the strategy. Then read letter A and answer the questions.

   1 How does the writer react to the issue?
   2 What are their two main ideas?
   3 What arguments and examples do they use to support these ideas?

3 Read ideas 1 and 2 from another letter. Match supporting arguments a–g to the ideas. Then read letter B and check your answers.

   1 People are not always entirely responsible for their actions.
   2 Poorer people with unhealthy habits are unlikely to change their lifestyles.

   a Stress and poverty can result in people making bad choices.
   b Younger people might be pressurized by friends.
   c Genetics can result in an unhealthy lifestyle.
   d When cigarette prices rose, demand stayed the same.
   e Psychological illness can lead to bad choices.
   f People will spend less on healthy food.
   g Advertising influences us to buy certain products.

V | Addition and contrast

4 Study the highlighted words and phrases in letters A and B. Which are used to add ideas and which to contrast ideas? What types of structures follow them?

5 Rewrite the sentences using the words in brackets.

   1 Advances in medicine mean we can have healthier babies, and we can live longer. (moreover)
   2 The main issue isn't about producing perfect children, it's about not appreciating difference. (less about … more about)
   3 Hospital dramas aren't very realistic, but I still enjoy watching them. (even though)
   4 Despite the risks, many teenagers still choose to have plastic surgery. (no matter what)
   5 Smoking has a bad effect on your health and makes you age more quickly. (besides, too)
   6 Some celebrities are terrible role models, but they are still very popular. (in spite of)
   7 I understand your reasons for supporting genetic engineering, although I don't agree with them. (while)
   8 Plastic surgery can improve self-image, so it's good for the mind and the body. (as well)

A

To the Editor

I was fascinated by your article *The value of life*. As a college student whose friends sometimes engage in the risky behaviour mentioned, I totally support the idea of 'punishing' people for making unhealthy lifestyle choices.

Firstly, I feel that we all have a moral responsibility to keep ourselves in good health. Furthermore, there is enough information about different lifestyles for everyone to make an informed choice. Besides the effect on our own health, most of us are conscious of the cost to the community, too. In the USA, for example, 25% of health care funding is spent on the treatment of diseases that result from smoking, overeating, alcohol abuse, etc. But even though people are aware of the consequences, they carry on doing these things.

Providing information is clearly not enough to encourage change, which brings me to my second point. Charging higher insurance payments for healthcare and increasing tax on alcohol and cigarettes would force people to come to their senses and encourage more responsible behaviour. In Canada, smoking decreased by 61% among teens when taxes on cigarettes were increased. In spite of their 'addiction', people got used to living without cigarettes fairly quickly.

In conclusion, public health care is a massive cost to the nation. Despite being informed, some people insist on making unhealthy life choices. Although more expensive health care may sound heartless to many, it could help people to lead better and happier lives. It would send a powerful warning to others, as well. Why should we pay for irresponsible behaviour? Ultimately, it's their problem, not ours.

Yours faithfully

B

To the Editor

I enjoyed reading your article on *The value of life*; however, I'm not sure I agree with your conclusions. As a youth worker, I have contact with many young people from disadvantaged backgrounds, who sometimes pursue unhealthy lifestyles. While it's true that these choices cause health problems, I think that making them pay more for treatment would be a mistake.

First of all, this idea assumes that individuals are responsible for their actions, whereas in some cases people may be uninformed, or their actions could be involuntary. For example, genetics can influence whether a person abuses alcohol or not, and psychological illness can cause compulsive overeating. What's more, there are also societal pressures: junk food adverts encourage bad food choices, and peer pressure may lead teens to smoke. In addition, once people are addicted to cigarettes, it's difficult to give up. Punishing people in these situations ignores the cause of their behaviour.

Secondly, people with unhealthy lifestyles are often poorer and increasing health care costs will make their poverty worse. Moreover, many people drink and smoke to manage the stress of being poor. If cigarettes cost more, less may be spent on healthy food, resulting in more distressing health problems. When cigarette prices rose by 40% in the USA, demand stayed the same.

To conclude, I believe that society has a moral obligation to look after the sick, no matter what their lifestyle. It's naive to think we can reduce health costs by punishing people. Ultimately, the debate is less about money, and more about the type of society we want to live in. Compassion and the desire to help make us human. To deny people health care is inhuman.

Yours faithfully

WRITING GUIDE

■ **Task** Read the extract from an article below and write a letter to a newspaper about it.

'Teen toxing' is the latest craze among Britain's image-conscious and celebrity-obsessed teenagers. A recent survey found 5% of teenage girls have considered having Botox and a staggering 48% would think about having plastic surgery. 'Excessive Botox can cause facial weakness or paralysis, and double vision,' says one doctor. 'Teenagers don't need it. It won't keep you looking young.' 'It's a question of self-esteem,' commented a parenting expert. 'Surgery isn't the answer and we can boost self-confidence without it.' It's a message all parents should be giving to their kids. But sadly, teen toxing fans would rather listen to the stars.

■ **Ideas** Make notes about:

1 your view: do you agree or disagree with the ideas in the extract?

2 your main ideas: what ideas illustrate your point of view?

3 arguments and examples you will use to support your ideas.

■ **Plan** Follow the plan:

Paragraph 1: Introduce your reason for writing. Mention your personal situation if relevant.

Paragraph 2: Present your first idea, with supporting arguments and examples.

Paragraph 3: Present your second idea, with supporting arguments and examples.

Paragraph 4: Conclusion: sum up your point of view.

■ **Write** Write your letter. Use the paragraph plan to help you.

■ **Check** Check the following points:

■ Are your point of view and the main ideas clearly stated?

■ Has each idea got supporting arguments and examples?

■ Have you checked grammar, vocabulary, spelling and punctuation?

Vocabulary insight 4 The origins of idioms

1 Work in pairs. Read the text below. Try to guess the meanings of the idioms in bold. How many other idioms can you find? Use a dictionary to help you.

> I'm studying medicine at university. I don't want to come across as big-headed, but I'm quite brainy and my lecturers say that I'm **head and shoulders above** most of the other people on my course. But my **heart's just not in it**. I'm not cut out to be a doctor. **I feel it in my bones** and the thought that I'm studying the wrong subject is always **at the back of my mind**. Maybe I should **face up to reality** and find something else to do. Perhaps I'll talk to my best friend and get her advice. After all, **two heads are better than one**.

STRATEGY

Idioms

An idiom is a commonly used group of words that has a figurative, or metaphorical meaning, so its overall meaning is different from the meanings of the individual words in it. For example, the phrase: *Ted gets my back up* does not literally mean *Ted makes my back rise*. It means *Ted annoys me*.

There are many different types of idiom, including the following:

a prepositional phrases, for example: *in vain*

b fixed phrases with two words, usually joined by *and* or *or*, for example: *body and soul*

c verb-based idioms, for example: *keep something in mind*

d noun phrases, for example: *a weight off his shoulders*

e idiomatic phrasal verbs, for example: *head out of here*

f proverbs and sayings, for example: *faint heart never won a fair lady*

2 Read the strategy above. Find one idiom in exercise 1 for each of the categories a–f in the strategy.

3 Replace the underlined phrases with the idioms in exercise 1.

1 This fitness DVD is <u>much better than</u> any other DVD I've tried. It's really fantastic!

2 Something bad is going to happen. I can <u>sense it</u>.

3 You'll definitely have to have the surgery. You need to <u>deal with this difficult fact now</u>.

4 Helen's been trying to prepare for a marathon, but <u>she doesn't feel very strongly about it</u>, so I don't think she'll succeed.

5 We should work together. <u>We'll probably be more successful if we do</u>.

6 I understand the arguments in favour of genetic testing, but the moral dilemma is always <u>something that worries me</u>.

STRATEGY

Idioms and their origins

Although idioms are figurative, or metaphorical in meaning, many of them have a literal origin. For example, the phrase *to pull the wool over someone's eyes* means to deceive them or make them believe something that isn't true. The origin of this phrase is probably because of the woollen wigs that people used to wear in the 16th and 17th centuries. If their wig slipped down from their head, it would cover their eyes and they wouldn't be able to see something. Learning about the origin of an idiom can help you to remember its meaning.

4 Read the strategy above. Then look at the explanations of idioms 1–4 and match them to meanings a–d.

1 **a feather in your cap**
   If a person did something very brave or clever, they would receive a feather which they would put in their hat or cap, so that everyone could see it – rather like wearing a medal.

2 **let the cat out of the bag**
   If a person bought a piglet at the market, they would be given the piglet in a sack or a bag. Sometimes the seller would secretly replace the piglet with a cat. If the cat escaped from the bag, the seller's dishonesty was revealed.

3 **get the sack**
   If a worker lost his job, he would have to leave his workplace and take his tools with him in a sack.

4 **on the ropes**
   In the sport of boxing, if one of the fighters is pushed up against the ropes by his opponent, then he is in a weak position and possibly about to lose the match.

a doing badly and likely to fail ....

b be dismissed from your place of employment ....

c a great achievement – something to be proud of

   ....

d uncover a secret ....

5 What do you think is the origin of these idioms? Match them to the correct categories a–c.

1 take something on the chin

2 know the ropes

3 play your cards close to your chest

4 clear the decks

5 saved by the bell

6 lay all your cards on the table

a ships and sailing ...., ...

b boxing ...., ...

c card games ...., ...

6 Use a dictionary to check the meanings of the idioms in exercise 5. Then write your own example sentences with each idiom.

Vocabulary

1 Complete the pairs of sentences with the same word.

1 a I don't want to .... you with my problems.
  b Unemployed youngsters are a .... to their parents.
2 a Our school is always supporting one .... or another.
  b The health cuts will .... many hospitals to close.
3 a They're sending an .... to fix the Wi-fi.
  b He tried to .... the interviews so that his son got the job.
4 a My little sister has a lively and enquiring ....
  b I don't .... what's for dinner.
5 a I fancy getting a mobile with a bigger ....
  b Doctors can't .... patients for every disease.
6 a Can you help me .... some furniture?
  b There was a .... in public opinion because of the scandal.

Marks .... / 6

2 Write the noun forms of the words below.

1 addicted ....
2 bald ....
3 deaf ....
4 disabled ....
5 imperfect ....
6 obese ....

Marks .... / 6

3 Complete the sentences with a phrase containing the word in brackets.

1 There's more to her .... (eye)
2 It .... to see her cry. (heart)
3 My grandparents have .... and refused to move house. (heels)
4 Ed has .... and decided against having a tattoo. (senses)
5 It was a .... when my migraines stopped. (shoulders)
6 She found the diagnosis .... (swallow)

Marks .... / 6

4 Complete the text with the words below.

■ dismally ■ flowing ■ lifeless ■ pearly ■ shrivelled ■ watery

A prince travelling through the land came across Snow White's coffin. He approached the coffin ¹........................., and with great sadness. The ²......................... body gave the impression that the girl had, indeed, passed away, but her complexion was by no means ³......................... . The Prince's eyes became ⁴......................... as he contemplated her beauty. Her ⁵......................... black hair framed a still pretty face, and her red lips were parted slightly, showing her ⁶......................... white teeth. Suddenly, the Prince realized that he was falling in love.

Marks .... / 6

Grammar

5 Choose the correct answers. Sometimes both are possible.

Today, visiting a dentist ¹**is usually / used to be** a relatively painless experience, but this has not always been the case. In the Indus Valley Civilization of 7000 BC, people ²**used to treat / would treat** tooth problems with primitive tools, like drills. Moving forward into 5000 BC, the Sumerians ³**would think / used to think** that dental issues were caused by worms. The Ancient Greeks ⁴**often extracted / would extract** teeth to keep tooth pain away and this method continued until the Middle Ages. During this period, dentists ⁵**wouldn't exist / didn't exist**, so barbers did the extractions. Modern dentistry ⁶**started / used to start** somewhere between 1650 and 1800. The French physician Philippe Fauchard was behind many of the procedures that you ⁷**will see / often see** in dental surgeries today.

Marks .... / 7

6 Complete the sentences with the correct forms of *used to*, *be used to* or *get used to* and the verbs in brackets.

1 I go to the gym every day, so I .... exercise. (do)
2 If you want to lose weight, then you'll have to .... less. (eat)
3 When we were children, we .... all day outside. (spend)
4 Max has very fair skin, so he .... in the sun. (not sit)
5 Their classes start at 8 a.m. so they .... early. (get up)
6 We .... a house on the beach when we lived in Spain. (have)
7 I .... eating vegetables, but now I love them. (not enjoy)
8 People who can't .... contact lenses usually go back to glasses. (wear)

Marks .... / 8

7 Complete the sentences with the future in the past tense. Use no more than three words, including the word in brackets.

1 Xavier was nervous because he .... have an operation. (about)
2 The scientist never imagined that his experiment .... work. (going)
3 She didn't know that she .... stay in hospital overnight. (need)
4 Alexander Fleming's discovery of penicillin .... millions of lives. (save)
5 They thought that they .... have a baby boy, but in the end it was a girl. (were)
6 We didn't realize that we .... access to medical treatment while we were away. (not have)

Marks .... / 6

Total .... / 45

Listening

1 🔘 **1.23** **Listen and match speakers 1–4 to options A–E. There is one option that you do not need.**

Which speaker wants to change a body part because of:

A an acquired disability? .... D a nasty scar? ....
B a slight imperfection? .... E a bad habit? ....
C the practical problems it causes? ....

Speaking

2 **Work in pairs. Look at the photos. What sort of illnesses might these behaviours lead to?**

3 **Work in pairs. You are preparing a poster about the dangers of an unhealthy lifestyle for teenagers. Choose one of the photos in exercise 2 for your poster. Discuss the things below.**

- the pros and cons of the behaviours in each photo
- which behaviour you think is the most unhealthy and why
- a slogan for your poster
- reasons why you chose this photo and rejected the other photos

Reading

4 **Complete the article *To clone or not to clone a mammoth?* with sentences A–H. There are two sentences that you do not need.**

A The difficulty of obtaining healthy cells from the preserved carcasses is sure to hold up the process.
B The technique requires scores of healthy mammoth cells which must have survived with their DNA intact.
C Now some scientists are talking openly about bringing them back to life.
D You stand in awe of this majestic creature, which is pacing round and round its cage.
E Researchers believe that she met her end when she fell into water or got trapped in a swamp and could not free herself.
F Elephants and mammoths each have about 4 billion DNA bases in their genes.
G The first of these concerns the welfare of the cloned animal.
H One small population was recently found to have survived to around 4,000 years ago on the Russian island of Wrangel.

To clone or not to clone a mammoth?

Imagine your next visit to the zoo. You are walking past the elephant enclosure when suddenly, you come across a new exhibit: a large, woolly mammoth.
¹.................. 'Impossible!' I hear you cry, but not all of
5 today's scientists would agree with you.

Mammoths ranged from the British Isles to eastern Asia and northern America until they disappeared around 10,000 years ago. ².................. Hunting by cavemen or climate change, or a combination of both,
10 are generally blamed for their demise.

Recently, however, the body of what has been called 'the best preserved mammoth in the history of palaeontology' was found in the Siberian permafrost. Each year, more and more frozen animals are being
15 revealed in the area because global warming is causing the ground to melt. This particular mammoth, whom scientists have named Yuka, was a female who was between six and eleven years old when she died. ³.................. Yuka's body remained in such good
20 condition because she stayed frozen for such a long, unbroken period of time – 39,000 years, to be exact. But the most exciting thing about the discovery is the fact that some of her blood has been found. Experts believe that the blood may contain cells that can be
25 used to bring the woolly mammoth back from the dead. Samples have already been sent to a laboratory in South Korea with that in mind.

However, cloning expert Sir Ian Wilmut, the stem-cell scientist whose team unveiled Dolly the sheep as the
30 first cloned mammal in 1996, regards the idea as 'wildly optimistic'. Apparently, there are formidable obstacles standing in the way of cloning the beasts.
⁴.................. In practice, the cells degenerate quickly once the snow and ice starts to melt, which is when
35 most remains are found. New cloning procedures are currently being developed but, according to Sir Ian, it could be another fifty years before these techniques are perfected.

 Literature insight 2 Workbook page 86

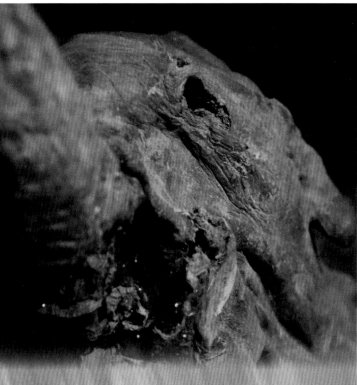

Apart from the technical difficulties surrounding the issue of resurrecting the mammoth, there are also a number of ethical questions involved. ⁵.................... Mammoths, like elephants, are highly social, intelligent animals, and at some point they would need friends and neighbours to interact with. Due to the fact that scientists will probably only be able to create one or two examples, the mammoths would be destined to a life of solitary confinement in a zoo or a research facility. The animal is hardly likely to thrive in these conditions. Another problem is the question of expense. The World Wide Fund for Nature has suggested that 10,000 species a year are becoming extinct. Many scientists believe that resources should be used for conserving existing animals rather than trying to revive just one special-interest species.

In short, despite the hopes that the discovery of Yuka ₅₅ has aroused in the field of palaeontology, it seems unlikely that a mammoth will be cloned in the near future. ⁶................... However, in the words of Sir Ian Wilmut, 'the world is full of surprises.'

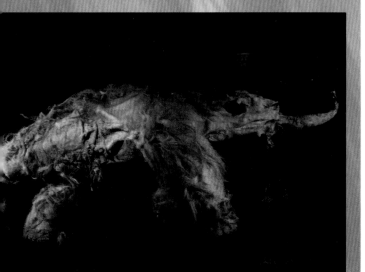

5 Read the article again and answer the questions.

  1 What is the main purpose of the article?

  2 What is the author's point of view?

Grammar and vocabulary

6 Choose the correct answers.

> In the past, it was only ¹.................... who had access to cosmetic surgery, but now it's popular with people from ².................... walks of life. Nowhere is this treatment catching on faster than in South Korea, where one in five women ³.................... under the surgeon's knife at least once in their lives. Today, cosmetic surgery is so popular that celebrities and beauty queens ⁴.................... openly discuss their treatment. Very few women ⁵.................... of the treatment if they can afford it, and it isn't uncommon for Korean high school girls to consult a surgeon. In some cases, it's the parents who encourage their children ⁶.................... surgery, because they don't want their child ⁷.................... the 'ugly one' in class. Most girls do not regret ⁸.................... their parents' advice. Of course, all plastic surgery comes with ⁹...................., including facial numbness or even paralysis. But to ¹⁰.................... women, that is the price they have to pay to look beautiful.

1   a   rich   b   the rich   c   a rich
      d   a rich people

2   a   too much   b   a lot   c   some
      d   almost all

3   a   goes   b   are going   c   has gone   d   went

4   a   are used to   b   will   c   would   d   get used to

5   a   pick out   b   spread out   c   clear out
      d   opt out

6   a   having   b   to have   c   have
      d   to having

7   a   to be   b   be   c   is   d   was

8   a   take   b   to take   c   taking   d   took

9   a   risks   b   a risks   c   the risks   d   risk

10   a   much   b   a lot   c   many   d   almost

Writing

7 Read the comment below from an article about cloning the mammoth. Then write a letter to a newspaper expressing your views.

> I think it should be done as long as we can provide excellent care for the animals. If there are reasonable prospects of them being healthy, we should do it. We could learn a lot about them.

1 SPEAKING Work in pairs. Study the words below. What do you think they mean? What is their origin? Read the article and compare your ideas.

- manga ■ embiggen ■ cyberbully ■ chillax ■ latte
- floordrobe ■ soz

STRATEGY

Skipping words that you do not understand

You can often skip unknown words and phrases when you read. This is because you do not have to know the meaning of every word or phrase in order to understand the general meaning of a text. When you come across an unknown word, follow these steps.

1. Decide if you can understand the general meaning of the sentence without understanding the meaning of the word. If the answer is 'yes', skip the word and continue reading. If the answer is 'no', go to point 2.
2. Check if you can guess the meaning from the context. If the answer is 'yes', guess and continue reading. If the answer is 'no', go to point 3.
3. Use a dictionary to help you or ask a classmate or the teacher.

2 Read the strategy. Then read sentences A–F. Follow points 1–3 in the strategy for the underlined words.

A The TV show *The Simpsons* has <u>concocted</u> several new words, and one in particular is <u>gaining</u> in popularity.

B Words that have been used for <u>aeons</u> as one part of speech often start to <u>crop up</u> as a different part of speech.

C The thirteenth-century meaning of *kill* was *hit*, but its meaning has become stronger over time through a process known as <u>hyperbole</u>.

D Abbreviations and <u>acronyms</u> also become informal words in their own right.

E Other words are adopted even when there's an existing English alternative, because the foreign word sounds superior or more <u>sophisticated</u> in some way.

F This new meaning is now so <u>ubiquitous</u> that no one today thinks of it as a metaphor.

3 Complete the article with sentences A–F in exercise 2. There is one sentence that you do not need.

DVD extra Look it up!

V insight Phrasal verbs with *on*

4 Study the highlighted phrasal verbs in the article. Match them to a–f according to the meanings of *on*.

a connecting   add on
b starting
c encouraging (×2)
d dressing
e continuing (×2)
f changing and developing

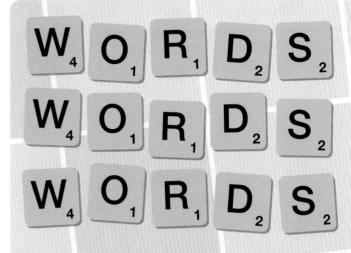

A I use hundreds, maybe even thousands of different words every day. Many of them have been part of my vocabulary since early childhood, but the words that fascinate me are the other ones, the ones that didn't even exist a few years ago. As the world changes, the vocabulary that we use moves on, too. In fact, experts tell us that at least 4,000 new English words are coined every year. Have you ever stopped to wonder where they come from and why they have the meanings that they do?

10 B It's no surprise that some of the new words come from another language, but I was amazed to find out that Modern English, which has evolved from Old English, has taken about 80% of its vocabulary from other sources: mostly from French and Latin, but also from an incredible 350 other 15 languages. Some of these loan words are used because there is no existing word in English to cover the meaning. In Britain, we now watch Japanese *manga* cartoons, eat the Greek dish *kleftiko*, and blow a South African *vuvuzela* to cheer on a football team. [1] .... People think Italian 20 coffee tastes better than the coffee traditionally drunk in Britain, so they often use the Italian word *americano* to order a black coffee in a café.

Vocabulary: phrasal verbs with *on*; verb prefixes: *en-* and *em-*; phrases with *point*; word analysis; synonyms: adjectives describing stories
Grammar: advice, obligation and prohibition; past modals; talking about ability

Speaking: choosing a book for a book club
Writing: a book review

5A

C Whenever we switch on a computer or mobile, we do things that were unheard of a few decades ago. Sometimes, the new
25 language that we need for technology evolves by giving new meanings to old words. *Hack* used to mean *chop* or *kick* and this usage carries on today. But as the internet developed, the word also started to be used with the metaphorical meaning 'access someone else's computer illegally'. **2**........................ There
30 are also new compounds of existing words, for example, *cloud computing* (computer resources delivered over the internet) and *digital footprint* (the record left on the internet of all your online activity). And then there are those useful things, prefixes. Instead of receiving an old-fashioned card bought in a shop
35 and sent in the mail, I might now receive an *e-card* bought in an *e-shop* and sent by *email*. While *e-* is an abbreviation of 'electronic', *cyber-* means 'to do with the internet': we often hear about *cybercrime* and *cyberbullies* in *cyberspace*. There's often a need to rename the old technology, too. When email
40 became popular, the mail with envelopes and stamps seemed very slow, so it got a new name: *snail mail*.

D Sometimes words are invented by comedians and scriptwriters for comic reasons. **3**........................ Take the adjective *big*, add on the prefix *en-* or *em-* and the suffix *-en*, and you
45 have the funny-sounding word *embiggen*. Just as *ensure* means 'make sure' and *widen* means 'make wider', *embiggen* means 'make bigger'. There are now more than 300,000 mentions of the word on the internet, in contexts ranging from fan fiction to physics!

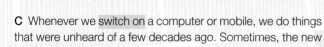

E When my friends are worrying about their exams, 50 I might tell them to *chillax* (chill out + relax). If my parents keep on complaining about the clothes on my bedroom floor, I can say that I'm using a new storage system: a *floordrobe* (floor + wardrobe). I might even slip on a *mankini* (man + 55 bikini) next time I go to the beach, but don't hold your breath! Blending two words together like this enables us to create lots of fun new words, particularly in informal English. **4**........................ *Soz* is a word that's short for 'sorry' and *yolo* stands for 'you only live once'. I 60 sometimes use it as an excuse for doing something a bit crazy, for example, 'I've just bought some £400 trainers … yolo!'

F Do you know your nouns from your verbs? Don't be too sure. **5**........................ Nouns can easily be converted 65 into verbs because in English, unlike in many other languages, verbs don't have to have a special verb ending. These days I *friend* (make friends with) people on Facebook and watch sportspeople *medalling* (winning a medal) in the Olympics. This can even 75 work with brand names. If I need to look up some information, I'll *google* it.

All these changes in English vocabulary are great fun to listen out for and you might even want to make up some new words yourself. Go on, give it a try – it's 80 *fantabulous*!

5 Complete the text with the correct form of the verbs below. Then match them to meanings a–f in exercise 4. There are two meanings you do not need.

■ throw on ■ cling on to ■ urge on ■ turn on ■ come on
■ live on

My latest skill is really improving, thanks to all the practice it's getting. I ¹................ my computer to check my Facebook account before I've even ²................ my clothes in the morning, and I update it all day on my smartphone. My texting speed is improving thanks to the use of abbreviations like *c u l8r* and *lol. dz ths mn im iliter8?* Of course not! I'm just fluent in two versions of English – standard English and textspeak. ³................ , give it a try!

Some people think that, if we want the elegance of standard English to ⁴................ , textspeak must stop, and teachers have been ⁵................ by panicky parents to ban mobile phones from schools. However, school rules are unlikely to stop a language from evolving – and why would we even want to ⁶................ an outdated language? Languages change to reflect the changing world. When they stop changing, they die.

V **insight** Verb prefixes: *en-* and *em-*

6 Read paragraph D in the article again and study the words below. Then answer the questions.

■ endanger ■ entrust ■ enlarge ■ empower ■ enable
■ enclose ■ ensure ■ encourage ■ entitle

1 When do we use the prefix *em-* instead of *en-*?
2 How does the prefix change the meaning of the root word?

7 Complete the sentences with the correct form of the words in exercise 6. There is one word that you do not need.

1 If you want to .... your vocabulary, ... that you have a good dictionary. This will .... you to look up unknown words.
2 A team of 300 people is .... with the job of updating the *Oxford English Dictionary*. They add new words, and also identify words that might disappear in the future.
3 I've .... a little book for you in the package. It's .... *Why You Say It*, and tells the stories behind lots of English words and expressions.
4 Blogs and social media .... ordinary people and allow them to influence opinion, but we must .... everyone to check their writing for spelling mistakes before they post it on the internet.

8 **SPEAKING** Discuss the questions.

1 What ways of forming new words are mentioned in the article?
2 In what ways are new words formed in your own language? Give examples.

Vocabulary bank Acronyms page 138

1 ◉ **1.24** **SPEAKING** What ways of learning and practising languages do you know? Listen to a radio programme and compare your ideas.

2 ◉ **1.24** Listen again. Which things are mentioned in the programme?

1 You **don't need to** have multilingual parents to be a brilliant language learner.
2 You **need to** be clever to match Tim's achievements.
3 You **needn't** have language lessons with a teacher.
4 You **ought not to** waste your time on smartphone language apps.
5 If you need speaking practice, you **mustn't** be shy.
6 When you're practising languages, you **ought to** do things that interest you.
7 You **had better not** practise several languages on the same day or you'll get confused.
8 The correspondent says she **must** stop making excuses for her bad language skills.

Advice, obligation and prohibition

3 Study the sentences in exercise 2. Then complete the rules with the modal verbs in bold.

a We use *should(n't)*, ... and .... to give advice.
b We use .... to express necessity or an 'internal' obligation (the speaker has decided that something is important).
c We use *have to* and .... to express necessity or an 'external' obligation (other people have decided that something is important).
d We use .... to express prohibition.
e We use *don't have to*, ... and .... to express lack of obligation or necessity.

Reference and practice 5.1 | Workbook page 117

4 Choose the correct answers.

1 In English, you **shouldn't / needn't** rely on the pronunciation of one word to work out the pronunciation of a similar word. In *cough, ought, though, through* and *enough*, you **need to / must** pronounce *-ough* in five different ways!
2 Instead of an alphabet, Japanese has more than 50,000 different characters. I **need to / must** learn more of them – I've given myself a target of 3,000. But I **don't need to / had better not** learn them all, because even Japanese people don't do that.
3 We **needn't / mustn't** learn Mandarin Chinese at school, but I've chosen to anyway. I think everyone **had better / doesn't have to** learn it because China will soon be the world's most powerful country.
4 My German teacher thinks we **ought to / must** think up funny word associations to help us memorize vocabulary, but I **mustn't / don't have to** do that because the words are quite easy to remember anyway.

5 Read about three people's experiences of trying different language learning methods. What were the advantages and / or disadvantages of each method? Have you ever tried to learn a language on your own? What method did you use?

1

When I <u>needed to</u> learn the African language Kirundi before a six-month stint in Burundi, I tried the 'spaced repetition' method. I played online vocabulary games which gradually introduced new words and then revised them at increasing intervals. It was fun, and I <u>didn't have to</u> play the games for long for them to be effective. After twenty-three hours – in short bursts of five minutes – I knew a thousand words. On the flight to Burundi, I was panicking because I didn't know any grammar, but I <u>needn't have</u> worried. I could understand quite a lot with my thousand words and I picked up the grammar easily once I was there.

Richard Webb

2

I once bought some expensive CDs that claimed to teach you a language in your sleep. According to the instructions, you <u>had to</u> go to sleep each night with one of the CDs playing, and this would enable you to speak in Italian after only a week. I <u>shouldn't have</u> wasted my time and money. At the end of the week, I knew no more Italian than I had done before!

Larissa Ingleton

3

Last year, I tried a method called 'shadowing' to improve my Arabic. You had to listen to a recording in the language and repeat it while walking around outside (the walking was meant to get more oxygen to your brain). I gave it a go for a few weeks, and it worked really well. I <u>ought to have</u> done it for longer, but people kept on staring at me and I felt like a complete idiot. I soon decided that I <u>didn't need to</u> get better at Arabic after all, and I gave up on the whole thing. I <u>should have</u> kept on learning, because I regret it now, of course … .

Felix Hope

Past modals

6 Study the underlined phrases in the texts in exercise 5 and answer the questions.

Which modal verbs do we use to:
1 express regret or to say what the right thing to do was?
2 say that something was necessary?
3 say that something wasn't necessary (and didn't happen)?
4 say that something which happened wasn't necessary?

Reference and practice 5.2 | Workbook page 117

7 Rewrite the sentences using the words in brackets.
1 In my first job, it was important for everyone to speak good Spanish. (had)
2 It was necessary for me to work hard to improve my language skills. (needed)
3 I was under no obligation to take any exams. (have)
4 I was wrong to give up Spanish at school. (ought / continue)
5 It wasn't compulsory for us to learn a modern language after the age of fourteen. (need)
6 I learned Latin to a high level, but it's never been useful to me. (needn't)
7 My parents didn't encourage me to study modern languages, but that was a mistake. (should)

8 SPEAKING Work in groups. Discuss the questions.
1 What aspects of the languages that you know make them easy or difficult to learn?
2 Do you think you started learning them at the right age and learned them in the right way? Why / why not? Discuss any regrets that you have about your language-learning experiences.
3 What advice would you give to a foreign friend who wants to learn your language?

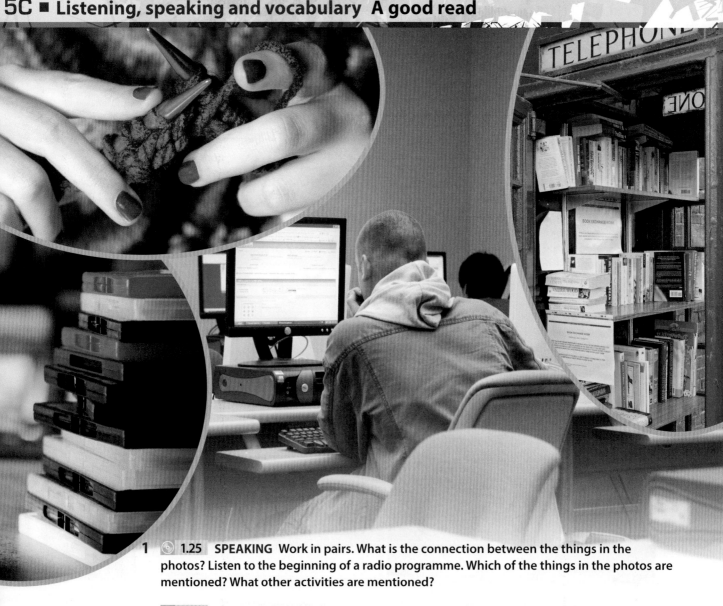

1 ◉ **1.25** **SPEAKING Work in pairs. What is the connection between the things in the photos? Listen to the beginning of a radio programme. Which of the things in the photos are mentioned? What other activities are mentioned?**

2 ◉ **1.26** **Listen to the second part of the programme. What reasons for having public libraries are mentioned? Which of them do you think are the most important?**

3 ◉ **1.26** **Listen to the second part again. Choose the correct answers.**

1 Headspace is a special area
   a that's in every library in Britain.
   b that's been designed by teenagers.
   c where people of all ages can have a chat.
   d that has manga drawings on the walls.

2 Jo says that paper books are
   a less popular with teenagers than e-books.
   b less interactive and exciting than e-books.
   c easier to use when you're studying.
   d not going to be produced in the near future.

3 She thinks that library computers are important for
   a people who don't have broadband at home.
   b people who want to borrow books online.
   c people who don't know how to use computers.
   d people who do all their banking and shopping online.

4 The radio presenter thinks that the government should
   a provide all homes with free broadband.
   b pay more to look after library buildings.
   c buy cheaper library computers.
   d help to get broadband into poorer homes.

5 According to Jo, the work of libraries is vital because
   a they support local authors and poets.
   b people don't read as much as they used to.
   c pre-school children don't have enough books at home.
   d people are losing their interest in culture.

6 In some places, telephone boxes
   a are used for storing books outside libraries.
   b have got shelves of books that belong to local libraries.
   c are full of books that people have donated.
   d are disappearing faster than libraries.

V Phrases with *point*

4 Replace the words in italics with the phrases below. In which phrase is *point* used as a verb?

■ there's no point in ■ from my point of view ■ take your point ■ the point is ■ at some point ■ up to a point ■ on the point of ■ points out

Jack Have you heard they're ¹*soon going to be* starting an Underground Library on the New York subway? ²*The important thing is*, people have time to kill on the subway, so it might encourage them to read more books.

Amy How will it work?

Jack You use your smartphone to scan a book title in the train and you get ten pages of the book for free. Later, a map on your phone screen ³*informs you* where the nearest library is, so you can go there ⁴*sometime* and borrow the whole book.

Amy It sounds good ⁵*to some extent*, but I'm on the subway for an hour every morning. For me, ⁶*it isn't worth* getting just ten pages of a book – I'd be finished half way through my journey.

Jack I ⁷*accept what you're saying*, but my subway journeys are shorter and I'm often bored. ⁸*In my opinion*, it's a great idea.

5 **SPEAKING** Work in pairs. Discuss the quotes from the radio programme. Do you agree with them? Why / why not?

1 'Public libraries these days provide a really fun and stimulating environment for teenagers.'

2 'Paper books have plenty of advantages over e-books.'

3 'I just don't think people will allow libraries to disappear.'

Choosing a book for a book club

6 **SPEAKING** Work in pairs. Look at the books. What genre do you think they are? Would you like to read them? Why / why not?

7 ◉ 1.27 Listen to the conversation. Which books do they mention? What genre are they? Do they choose a book in the end?

8 ◉ 1.27 Listen again and complete phrases 1–8. Then complete A–D in the table with the headings below.

■ Asking for a decision ■ Delaying action
■ Asking politely for information ■ Persuading

A ....
Could you tell me ¹........................ sort of books you usually read?

B ....
I was ²........................ we could ... , because ....
³........................ you think you should ... ?
⁴........................ it be better to ... ?

C ....
We don't have to ⁵........................ right now.

D ....
⁶........................ shall we decide on?
Which one shall we ⁷........................ for?

9 ◉ 1.28 Listen to another conversation and tick the phrases that you hear. Then match all of them to categories A–D in exercise 8.

■ Doesn't it make more sense to ... ? ■ Let's sleep on it and decide tomorrow.
■ Surely you have to agree that ... ? ■ Can we make a quick decision?
■ Could you let us know what the book's called? ■ We could read it another time, maybe, but ... .

10 **SPEAKING** Make a list of three books that you have enjoyed reading. Then, in groups of three, choose one book to read for a book club.

1 **SPEAKING** Work in pairs. Discuss the questions. Then read the article and check your ideas.

1 What do you know about William Shakespeare?
2 Look at the quote in the first line of the article. What does it mean? How does it relate to Shakespeare?

2 Read the article again. Are the sentences true (T), false (F) or not given (NG)?

1 Shakespeare's reputation is better now than it was during his lifetime.
2 All the stories for his plays were his own.
3 To enjoy his stories, you have to know a lot about Britain's past.
4 His heroes have more good qualities than people in real life.
5 Audiences pity Shylock in *The Merchant of Venice*.
6 Audiences today can't feel the emotion in his plays.
7 He liked to use humour after a particularly tragic scene.
8 His plays are full of words of his own invention.

V insight Word analysis

3 Answer the questions, referring closely to the article.

1 Which word is the introduction to a book or speech? How did the significance of the one mentioned change over time? (A)
2 Which word describes something strange and unusual? What type of story is it describing here? (B)
3 Which phrase means the same as *timeless stories*? What proof does the writer give that Shakespeare's stories are timeless? (B)
4 Which adjective describes behaviour aimed at getting what you want, even if you hurt other people in the process? Can this characteristic ever be a good thing? (B)
5 Which two words are types of characters in a story? What types of character are they? (C)
6 Which word means cruel treatment? Why was it experienced in this case? (C)
7 Which word describes something that makes you go cold with fear? What other emotions do Shakespeare's plays elicit from the audience? (D)
8 Which phrase says that someone is the greatest in a certain area? What metaphor is being used here? (F)

A writer for all time

A 'He was not of an age, but for all time!' stated the preface of William Shakespeare's collected plays when they were first published in 1623. At that point, seven years after the playwright's death, Shakespeare was just one of many respected writers of his era, but in the years that followed, the words of that preface proved to be prophetic. His reputation grew and grew and today Shakespeare is widely recognized as the greatest writer in the history of English literature. His plays live on, translated into at least eighty languages and performed all over the globe. Why is it that, four hundred years after his death, his work is still rated so highly?

Timeless stories

B ¹Many writers before Shakespeare could write great comedy, or tragedy, or history, but Shakespeare could tell great stories in all these genres and more: from quirky fairy tale (*A Midsummer Night's Dream*) to political thriller (*Richard III*). He rarely came up with original plots for his plays – in fact, he usually took them from traditional stories, history or other writers. In his hands, however, they became powerful tales that transcend time and culture. *Romeo and Juliet* is a story of love, hate and teenage rebellion against authoritarian parents. *Macbeth* shows the dangers of ruthless ambition. *Othello* deals with insecurity, trust and jealousy. It's no surprise that theatre and film directors return again and again to his plays for their material. As well as productions using the original language and settings, there have been imaginative reinterpretations as musicals (*Romeo and Juliet / West Side Story*), sci-fi films (*The Tempest / Forbidden Planet*), high school romantic comedies (*Twelfth Night / She's the Man*) Bollywood films (*Macbeth / Maqbool*), and even children's cartoons (*Hamlet / The Lion King*).

Complex characters

C Shakespeare portrayed the richness and variety of human life in a way that has never been equalled in English literature and many actors believe that his
40 characters are drama's most challenging and satisfying roles. Each of his protagonists has a complicated mixture of qualities and faults which feel very real to the audience. ²We can easily picture ourselves as Hamlet, a person of gentle character who
45 is led by extreme circumstances to plan violent revenge on his uncle, or as King Lear, flattered into trusting the wrong people and driving away the ones who truly love him. Every character, however bad, has a human side. ³Shakespeare even managed to make a sympathetic
50 character out of Shylock, the shockingly cruel Jewish villain in *The Merchant of Venice*, by describing his experience of anti-Jewish abuse.

Beautiful poetry

D While some parts of Shakespeare's plays are in prose,
55 his greatest speeches are in verse and their language, though old-fashioned, still resonates powerfully with modern audiences. His rude jokes ensure that the theatre is often filled with laughter, but moments later there might be an achingly beautiful passage about
60 love or chilling words about death, revenge or jealousy. As well as at least thirty-seven plays, he is known for 154 short poems called sonnets. It is thought that he started writing these in 1592 when ⁴the plague stopped Londoners from being able to go to the theatre. They
65 include some of the most famous lines about love and beauty in the English language.

Innovative language

E Shakespeare enjoyed playing with words and his language is full of interesting images and metaphors.
70 People still use many of them today, unaware that they were invented by him: *green-eyed monster* (meaning 'jealousy') and *wear your heart on your sleeve* (meaning 'show your emotions') are two examples. Even individual words were a chance for Shakespeare to show off his
75 creativity. Of the 17,000 different words that he used in his plays and poems, he made up an incredible 1,700 of them, and we are still using 800 today. They include everyday words, such as *generous, apostrophe, hurry, road* and *amazement*.

80 F ⁵Perhaps one day a writer will be able to match the achievements of William Shakespeare, but until then he stands at the pinnacle of English literature, setting the standard to which
85 all other great writers aspire.

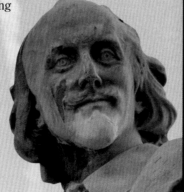

Talking about ability

4 Study underlined sentences 1–5 in the article and match them to rules a–e. Then complete the rules.

a To express ability in the present, we use .... / can't.

b To express general ability in the past, we use .... / couldn't.

c To express a particular ability in the past, we use *was / were able to*, ..., *succeeded in* (*-ing*) or *couldn't*. We only use *could* in this context with verbs of perception (*see, hear, smell, taste, feel, understand*, etc.)

d To express ability in the future, we use .... / won't be able to.

e When an infinitive or *-ing* form is needed, we use *be able to* or ....

> **Reference and practice 5.3**   Workbook page 118

5 Complete the text. Use the correct form of *can*, or if that isn't possible, the correct form of *be able to*, *manage to* or *succeed in*. Sometimes more than one answer is possible.

Shakespeare's Globe: a brief history

The Globe Theatre was part-owned by Shakespeare himself, and many of his greatest plays were first performed there. Built in 1599, it ¹........................ hold an audience of 1,500 people. Disaster struck in 1613 when a cannon, used for special effects, set fire to the theatre's thatched roof. The audience ²........................ see the flames, but at first they thought they were part of the performance. As the fire spread, they panicked. Luckily, everyone ³........................ get out safely, but they ⁴........................ (not) save the theatre. It burned to the ground.

Three and a half centuries later, American actor Sam Wanamaker dreamed of ⁵........................ see Shakespeare's drama in the theatre for which it was written. After a long fundraising campaign, he ⁶........................ building a replica of the Globe near its original site. It opened in 1997.

Come to a performance at the Globe this summer and you ⁷........................ see for yourself what the theatre was like in Shakespeare's time.

Tickets available now!

6 SPEAKING Work in pairs. Discuss the questions.

1 Have you ever seen a Shakespeare play, in a film or at the theatre? If you have, what did you think of it? If not, would you like to? Why / why not?

2 Who are the greatest playwrights in your language? Talk about their plays and other achievements.

> **Vocabulary bank**   Book structure page 138

1 **SPEAKING** Work in pairs. Make a list of things you would expect to read about in a review. Then read the book review and tick the things on your list that are mentioned.

2 Read the book review again and answer the questions.

What phrases does the writer use to:
1 describe the type of book?
2 give the setting of the book?
3 describe the plot?
4 describe the characters?
5 give reasons for liking the book?
6 recommend the book?

3 Study the phrases below. Which introduce reasons for disliking the book? Match the rest to categories 1–6 in exercise 2.

■ I could really identify with (a character). ■ I was disappointed with … . ■ I couldn't put it down.
■ There's a dramatic twist at the end. ■ I was captivated by … . ■ It was a shame that … .
■ There are some very likeable characters, including … . ■ The story opens with … .
■ The novel fails to … . ■ For me, the biggest problem was … . ■ It would appeal to anyone who … .

V insight Synonyms: adjectives describing stories

4 Study the highlighted adjectives in the book review. Then match each one to its synonym in the sentences below.

1 This **moving** / .... story about a girl's fight to survive cancer brought tears to my eyes.
2 The **complex** / .... plot is hard to follow – I found it quite confusing at some points.
3 This **insightful** / .... account of life on the streets will challenge your views on homelessness.
4 This novel is really **gripping** / .... – I wanted to carry on reading it all night.
5 The author's **meaningful** / .... use of language makes the book a pleasure to read.

STRATEGY

Avoiding repetition

When you write, it is important to vary the language that you use. Do not repeat the same words too often. You can do this by using:

1 pronouns
Use personal and possessive pronouns and *one / ones* to avoid repeating nouns.
2 *do*
Use all forms of *do* (+ *this / that / it / so*) to avoid repeating verbs and verb phrases.
3 *this / that / so*
Use *this / that / so* to avoid repeating complete clauses.
4 synonyms
Use a variety of synonyms to avoid repeating the same words.

5 Read the strategy. What do the underlined words in the book review refer to? Match them to rules 1–4 in the strategy.

6 Change the underlined parts of the sentences below to avoid repetition.

1 Tess tells Angel about her past, but <u>when she tells him about her past she</u> destroys <u>Angel's</u> love for <u>Tess</u>.
2 Mr Darcy offends Elizabeth at the ball and <u>Mr Darcy offends her</u> again when he asks her to marry him.
3 Ahab has spent his whole career killing whales, but in <u>Ahab's</u> desperation to kill the <u>whale</u> that injured his leg, he endangers the whole crew.
4 The passage in which the monster is brought to life is gripping, and the chapters that tell <u>the monster's</u> side of the story are <u>gripping</u>.
5 Most hobbits never leave the Shire, but the <u>hobbits</u> in the story <u>leave the Shire</u> to destroy the ring at Mount Doom.

THE GREAT GATSBY

The summer sizzles, the parties swing and the cocktails flow in F. Scott Fitzgerald's classic novel *The Great Gatsby*, set in the glamour and decadence of 1920s New York.

F. Scott Fitzgerald
The Great Gatsby

OXFORD WORLD'S CLASSICS

The story revolves around the self-made millionaire Jay Gatsby and his quest to win back his lost love, Daisy Buchanan. The narrator is Daisy's cousin, Nick Carraway, who starts renting a house across the bay from the <u>one</u> where Daisy lives with her rich, but unfaithful husband Tom. Nick's mysterious next door neighbour, Gatsby, throws spectacular parties every weekend, and Nick discovers that he <u>does this</u> with one purpose: to tempt Daisy back into his life. Gatsby asks <u>him</u> to reunite <u>them</u>. Nick succeeds in <u>doing so</u>, and <u>that</u> sets in motion a tragic chain of events which expose some ugly truths about love, wealth and the American Dream.

The novel has a fast-moving and riveting plot, but what appealed to me most was the way that the protagonists' complex personalities are revealed over the course of the story. Daisy has a touching vulnerability and charm, but is self-centred and shallow, whereas Gatsby, a fake and a liar, has a moral integrity unmatched by the characters who grew up with money. Fitzgerald's <u>insightful</u> comments on the materialistic values of the 1920s still feel relevant today, and his concise but expressive prose is a delight.

The Great Gatsby is a perceptive portrayal of a fascinating time in US history and the gripping and moving story is told in expressive and intricate detail. It's a must-read.

WRITING GUIDE

- **Task** Choose a fiction book set during an interesting period of history and write a review.

- **Ideas** Make notes about:
  - the title, author and genre.
  - the setting, main themes and characters.
  - the plot.
  - what you liked and didn't like about it.
  - why it feels / doesn't feel relevant to the modern day.
  - who you would recommend it to.

- **Plan** Follow the plan:

  Paragraph 1: Introduction to the book. Give its title, author and setting in an interesting way.

  Paragraph 2: Concise summary of the plot. Use the present simple and include information about the main characters and themes. Give readers enough information to understand your comments in paragraph 3.

  Paragraph 3: Your opinion. Say what you liked and / or disliked most about the book. Use the present simple or past simple.

  Paragraph 4: Conclusion. Summarize your opinion and / or give a recommendation.

- **Write** Write your review. Use the paragraph plan to help you.

- **Check** Check the following points:
  - Have you used a clear paragraph structure?
  - Have you managed to avoid repetition?
  - Will readers who do not know the book be able to understand all your comments?
  - Have you checked grammar, vocabulary, spelling and punctuation?

Vocabulary insight 5 Verbs and nouns

1 Work in pairs. Study the dictionary entry for *google*. What part of speech is it? Where does the word come from?

> **google** /ˈguːgl/ *verb* [T, I] ~ (**sb/sth**) (*computing*) to type words into the SEARCH ENGINE Google® in order to find information about sb/sth: *You can google someone you've recently met to see what information is available about them on the Internet.* ◇ *I tried googling but couldn't find anything relevant.*

Verbification

Verbification or *verbing* is the process of making a noun or an adjective into a verb without changing it. There are thousands of verbs in the English language which were originally nouns or adjectives. Categories of verbified nouns include:

a brand names, e.g. *Google* and *Facebook*: *I Facebooked you last night.*

b words associated with tools, for example: *hammer the nail*

c words associated with business, for example: *chair a meeting*

d words associated with communication and technology, for example: *email a company*

e words associated with parts of the body, for example: *foot the bill, eye a competitor*

2 Read the strategy above. Rewrite sentences 1–10 using verbified nouns. Then match them to the categories of verbified nouns in the strategy.

1 I want to put this shelf onto the wall using <u>screws</u>.

2 Ben is going to be the <u>chair</u> of our next debate.

3 She pushed me in the chest with her <u>elbow</u>!

4 Can you send me a <u>text</u> with your email address?

5 Whenever I find an interesting website, I add it to my <u>bookmarks</u>.

6 Peter can write the <u>minutes</u> of the meeting.

7 I'm out of the country, but I can talk to you on <u>Skype</u> tomorrow.

8 I wanted to find out more about the place, so I just searched for it on <u>Google</u>.

9 He hit the ball with his <u>head</u> and scored a goal.

10 You'll need to use a <u>drill</u> to make a hole for the hook.

Nominalization

Sometimes, when we want to make our writing more formal or academic, we can use *nominalization*. This means using a noun instead of a verb or an adjective. Note that the rest of the sentence also changes.

For example, we can change the verb *illustrates* in this sentence:

Shakespeare's Sonnet 73 brilliantly <u>illustrates</u> his use of metaphor in poetry.

to the noun *illustration* in this sentence:

Shakespeare's Sonnet 73 is a brilliant <u>illustration</u> of his use of metaphor in poetry.

Nominalizations are often followed by prepositions (*illustration of, arrival at, investment in*, etc.), so it is important to know which prepositions follow which nouns.

3 Read the strategy above. Rewrite sentence b so that it has a similar meaning to sentence a. Nominalize the underlined words. Use a dictionary to check which prepositions you need to use with the nouns.

1 **a** The supermarket often <u>delivers</u> my orders late.
  b The delivery of my orders from the supermarket is often late.

2 **a** The company <u>invested</u> several million pounds in these products.
  b The company's .... was several million pounds.

3 **a** We <u>failed</u> to complete the course and therefore we didn't get the qualification.
  b Our .... meant that we didn't get the qualification.

4 **a** The report <u>concluded</u> that more research was needed.
  b The .... the report was that more research was needed.

5 **a** The teachers <u>rejected</u> the head teacher's proposals. This shocked the students.
  b The teachers' .... shocked the students.

6 **a** The photos were <u>perfect</u>. He was very pleased with them.
  b The .... pleased him.

7 **a** When the star <u>arrived</u> at the hotel, she was greeted by many fans.
  b The star's .... was greeted by many fans.

8 **a** Her cooking is <u>excellent</u>, which makes me always want to eat here.
  b The .... always makes me want to eat here.

4 Make nouns using the words below. Then write one example sentence for each verb or adjective form and one example sentence using the nominalized form.

■ beautiful ■ believe ■ refuse ■ hate ■ grow ■ shocking

    Dictionary entry from *Oxford Advanced Learner's Dictionary* 8ᵉ, Oxford University Press 2010.

Vocabulary

1 **Replace the words in italics with the correct forms of the phrasal verbs below.**

■ carry on ■ cheer on ■ move on ■ throw on ■ switch on

1 My parents don't understand that the world .... (*has developed*) since they were kids and everyone now owns a smartphone.

2 The sound engineer .... (*started*) the equipment to record the interview.

3 We didn't win the quiz because nobody .... us .... (*was encouraging us*).

4 I .... (*will continue*) studying until I fall asleep.

5 Dan .... (*got dressed in*) a pair of jeans, but then decided to change into a suit.

Marks .... / 5

2 **Add *en-* or *em-* to make verbs.**

1	...........danger	5	...........large
2	...........trust	6	...........courage
3	...........title	7	...........close
4	...........power	8	...........able

Marks .... / 8

3 **Complete the sentences with the phrases below.**

■ from my point of view ■ on the point ■ up to a point ■ take your point ■ there's no point

1 ...., that website is a load of rubbish.

2 .... in shouting. They don't speak the same language as you.

3 I agree with you ...., but not completely.

4 I ...., but I still think you're making a terrible mistake.

5 She was .... of giving up when a publisher finally accepted her manuscript.

Marks .... / 5

4 **Match the words below to meanings 1–6. There is one word that you do not need.**

■ abuse ■ chilling ■ pinnacle ■ protagonist ■ quirky ■ ruthless ■ transcend

1 cruel (behaviour) ....

2 frightening ....

3 cruel treatment ....

4 strange and unusual ....

5 the best or most successful part of something ....

6 the main character in a play, movie or book ....

Marks .... / 6

Grammar

5 **Complete sentence b so that it has a similar meaning to sentence a. Use the words in brackets.**

1 a It's compulsory to study a foreign language. (must)
  b Students ....

2 a We recommend watching films in English. (ought to)
  b You ....

3 a It isn't necessary for students to bring their own dictionary to class. (needn't)
  b Students ....

4 a It's a good idea to study vocabulary every day. (had better)
  b You ....

5 a Cheating in exams is prohibited. (mustn't)
  b Students ....

6 a It's important to speak in English in class. (need to)
  b You ....

7 a We don't recommend using online translation services. (ought not to)
  b Students ....

Marks .... / 7

6 **Complete the text with the past forms of the modals and verbs in brackets.**

As soon as Jan turned up for his interview, he realized that he **1**................................ (should / research) the company more carefully. He **2**................................ (ought to / know) it was an American multinational and that all the employees were expected to speak English. The receptionist asked him something when he arrived and he **3**................................ (have to / ask) her to repeat the question several times. When he eventually understood what she had said, he **4**................................ (need / think) for a long time how to respond. He **5**................................ (not have to / wait) for long for the interviewer to call him into the room. As he sat struggling to answer the questions, he became aware that he **6**................................ (should not / take) his English classes so lightly. When Jan left the room five minutes later, he already knew that he **7**................................ (not need / bother) to apply for the job.

Marks .... / 7

7 **Choose the correct answers. Sometimes both are possible.**

1 Amy **can / is able to** speak Chinese because she was born in Beijing.

2 If you download the app, you'll **can / be able to** study the vocabulary more easily.

3 We **were able to / succeeded in** making ourselves understood, despite our poor language skills.

4 To pass the writing paper, you must **can / be able to** write a formal letter.

5 Sorry I haven't **could / been able to** call you.

6 They **could / managed to** find the way, although they couldn't read the road signs.

7 I was frustrated because I **couldn't / wasn't able to** remember the right word.

Marks .... / 7

Total .... / 45

6 The media and the message

Reading and vocabulary Who controls the news?

1 SPEAKING Work in pairs. Discuss the questions. Then read the article and compare your ideas.

1 Think about the biggest news story in your country at the moment. How did you first hear about it?

2 How has technology influenced the way we hear about news stories?

3 What do you understand by 'citizen journalist'?

2 Match headings 1–6 to sections A–F in the article.

1 Human interest
2 Whistle-blowing
3 Breaking news
4 A lot to learn
5 Responsible reporting
6 A new kind of reporter

3 Read the article again and answer the questions.

1 What can give an early indication of an important global news story?

2 Why are citizen journalists able to post news stories more quickly than professional journalists?

3 How are citizen journalists' reports different from professional reports? What reasons does the writer give for this?

4 How can citizen journalists help investigative journalists?

5 Why does Mimiboard post anonymous contributions? What does it achieve?

6 What is the problem with anonymous reporting?

7 What effect did the Reddit story have on the student and his family?

8 Can you answer professor Clay Shirky's question? Think about the benefits and drawbacks of citizen journalism.

V insight Collocations: journalism

4 Study the highlighted phrases in the article and explain their meaning. Then complete the text below with the correct form of the highlighted phrases.

How to stop a Facebook hoax

In 2012, Nolan Daniels posted a picture of himself on Facebook with a 'winning' lottery ticket and offered $1 million to one lucky person who shared his photo. He'd never posted a public status on Facebook before, but he wanted to see who would ¹.................... and share it. Two days later, his photo ².................... as more than 2 million Facebook users shared his picture. It even ³.................... in respected online newspapers. Then an anti-hoax website exposed the story as a scam.

Unfortunately, misinformation, scams and hoaxes are everywhere on the web. News stories can sometimes do good and ⁴.................... or wrongdoing, but at other times they can be inaccurate or false. So how can we deal with this misinformation?

- Don't ⁵.................... about people or post stories that aren't verified.
- If a story ⁶...................., check one of the many websites that ⁷.................... and make sure the facts are true.

As Facebook users, we ⁸.................... for the type of information that is spread. When we post or share a story on our timeline, we have a responsibility to make sure that these stories are accurate and true.

Armed with a smartphone

A Friday 11 March 2011 started like any other day on Twitter. A celebrity story was trending that morning, along with business news about Google, when suddenly, at 12.46 a.m., thousands of tweets started coming out of Tokyo. Something big had happened in the area, and Twitter was first to report it: a massive earthquake had hit Japan, followed by a huge tsunami. Eyewitness testimonies from cities rocked by the quake flooded the web, and then as the tsunami swept the coastline, people scrambled up bridges and buildings and posted footage on YouTube and Facebook. The camera work was shaky, but the content was compelling – their world was falling apart, yet they continued to film.

B Over the last few years, the big news stories, such as the Japanese earthquake in 2011 and Hurricane Sandy in 2012, have been reported mainly by ordinary individuals. It was citizen journalists armed with smartphones who brought these stories to the world. Mobile technology has enabled people at the scene of the event to post videos, photos and commentary more quickly than paid journalists. The landscape of reporting and of deciding what is newsworthy has changed: news organizations and their reporters no longer set the agenda.

C The content of the news has changed, too, as stories told by citizen journalists are often more personal and have more emotional appeal. Unlike investigative journalism, these blog posts and tweets seldom include background information or give a broad overview. People haven't got time to collect and scrutinize facts or explore the bigger picture. A YouTube video may cover battles between police and protestors at a G20 demonstration, but it probably won't delve into why there was a protest, what may have caused the situation and what the possible outcomes could be.

Vocabulary: collocations: journalism; word analysis; idioms with *in* and *out*; documentaries; discourse markers
Grammar: speculation about the past, present and future; emphasis and inversion

Speaking: choosing front page news
Writing: an article

6A

D But in other ways, citizen journalism supports investigative journalism. It is now easier for ordinary people to expose corruption and cover-ups in government and private companies. In Africa, a virtual noticeboard called Mimiboard helps people to report rigged elections and human rights abuses. These noticeboards create pressure for change and reform, and sometimes they work – corrupt government officials have been sacked and international companies have changed their working conditions. But because of the risks involved, Mimiboard relies on anonymous posts, and anonymous publishing comes with its own set of challenges: it makes it very difficult to verify information.

E The freedom to publish whatever we want is exciting and empowering, but there are serious ethical implications. Unlike traditional journalism, citizen journalism is largely unregulated, with little or no accountability – there is no one to check the facts or trace sources. People can spread rumours or anonymously post a defamatory article and get away with it. An example of this happened after the Boston Marathon bombing in 2013, when a student who was watching the event was named as a suspect on Reddit*. The story lacked credibility and had very few facts to support it, but it still went viral and made headlines in the national papers. The student turned out to be seventeen-year-old Salah Eddin Barhoum, a high school sports star who had moved to the USA from Morocco four years before the incident. Eventually his name was cleared, but Salah and his family were devastated. 'I was terrified,' he said later. 'I have never been in trouble, and I feared for my security.'

Because posts are rarely checked and verified, citizen journalism is more vulnerable to scams and can help to spread false information. In 2012, a sixteen-year-old girl from New Jersey tweeted that someone was in her house. When she mysteriously disappeared shortly afterwards, many Twitter users thought she had been kidnapped and tweeted #HelpFindKara. The call for help trended worldwide, with 34,000 people retweeting the message. Everyone believed Kara's story and fell for the scam, until the police found her walking alongside a highway. She had faked her own kidnapping and had run away from home. Luckily for Kara, she didn't get prosecuted.

F Incidents like this show that citizen journalism is still finding its way. Yet, despite the challenges, this new way of reporting the news has had a largely positive and democratizing effect. Armed with our smartphones, we are now telling our own stories, controlling our own destinies and creating impact and change around the world. 'The choice we face,' says Clay Shirky, professor in new media at New York University, 'isn't whether or not this is the media environment we want to operate in. This is the environment we've got. The question we all face now is, "How can we make the best use of this media?"'

Glossary
*Reddit: a social news website

V insight Word analysis

5 Answer the questions, referring closely to the article.

1 Which verbs of movement does the writer use to describe the disaster? What effect does this have? (A)

2 Citizen journalists are 'armed with smartphones'. What context is the verb *to arm* usually used in? What does using this verb imply? (B)

3 Which three verbs are used to mean *examine*? (C)

4 Which noun is used for something that is hidden, usually illegally? (D)

5 Which adjective describes something that has been changed or altered dishonestly? (D)

6 Which noun is used to mean *public responsibility for something*? (E)

7 Which two adjectives describe Salah and his family's reaction to the accusations? (E)

8 Which adjective is used to mean *exposed to danger and risk*? (E)

6 Complete the sentences with the words below.

■ armed ■ scrambled ■ delved into ■ rigged ■ a cover-up
■ accountability ■ vulnerable ■ devastated

1 The new laws protected .... workers from exploitation by big companies.

2 The journalist .... the reasons why the factory fire had happened.

3 When a news story revealed that the football manager had .... the match, he was sacked.

4 During the flood, people .... to the top of buildings for safety.

5 The soldiers were .... with guns and hand grenades.

6 There needs to be more .... in today's government. Politicians should answer to the people.

7 The director was .... when he read the terrible review of his film.

8 The government was accused of .... ; politicians had been accepting 'gifts' from companies.

7 SPEAKING Work in pairs. You are going to post your own news story. Agree on what you are going to write about. Think about:

■ a local issue you would like to cover.
■ sources you could use.
■ the main point of your story and its purpose.
■ where you are going to post it.

| **Vocabulary bank** | Headlines page 139 |

| **DVD extra** | Good news travels fast |

1 SPEAKING Work in pairs. Look at the stills from a TV advert and answer the questions.

1 Describe what is happening in the photos, then agree on the correct order.

2 Describe the appearance of the younger man. What do you think he wants to do?

3 Describe the older man. What is he carrying? Where might he be going?

4 How does the camera angle affect what we see? How does it affect what we think?

2 ◉ 2.01 Listen to a journalist talking about the TV advert and compare your ideas in exercise 1. What is the advert advertising?

Speculation about the past, present and future

3 Study sentences a–h from the recording. Then answer questions 1–3.

a (The younger man) **has to** be running away from a bad situation.

b He **must have** done something wrong.

c He **might have** stolen someone's wallet or someone **could have** been hurt in a fight.

d He **can't** be doing anything good.

e (The older man) **may** be a businessman on his way to work.

f The bricks **might** fall and they **could** both be badly hurt.

g That **can't have** happened because he's a troublemaker, right?

h He **can't have** been trying to help him.

1 Which sentences express:
a) certainty b) possibility?

2 Which sentences refer to:
a) the past b) the present c) the future?

3 Which modal verbs can be used to refer to both the present and the future?

4 Study these words and phrases from the recording. Which ones express certainty and which express possibility?

■ most probably ■ looks like ■ it's (not) possible that ■ He's bound to be ■ It seems likely that ■ It's safe to say that ■ He looks as if ■ I'm almost sure

Reference and practice 6.1 | Workbook page 119

5 Rewrite the second sentence so that it has a similar meaning to the first sentence. Use the modal verbs in brackets.

1 The photo must be from a citizen journalist. (has to)
A citizen journalist ....

2 I'm sure they were at work when the news story broke. (must)
They ....

3 It seems likely that the police have already caught the escaped criminal. (may)
The police ....

4 I'm almost sure he was watching TV when the disaster happened. (must)
He ....

5 It's not possible that he heard about it on the radio. He never listens to the news. (can't)
He ....

6 They're surely at the scene of the incident by now. They left two hours ago. (bound to)
They ....

7 It's safe to say that the report isn't accurate. It lacks credibility. (can't)
The report ....

8 It's possible that he'll read the news headlines today. (seems)
It ....

6 SPEAKING Look at the still from another advert and discuss the questions. Use modal verbs to speculate.

1 Where is it? What can you see?
2 Why do you think it is there? Who could have put it there?
3 What might happen when someone pushes the button?
4 How might people react?
5 What might be its purpose? What product could it be advertising?

7 ◎ 2.02 Listen and compare your ideas.

1 **SPEAKING** Can you think of any news stories about people who have done something in order to be famous? Think of publicity stunts, breaking a world record or doing something for the first time.

STRATEGY

Adapting to authentic listening situations

When we listen to broadcasts on the radio or TV, we sometimes start listening in the middle or halfway through. In order to quickly identify the topic and context, answer these questions:

1 How many speakers are there?
2 What is the topic?
3 What type of recording is it?
4 Why might people listen?

Once you have finished listening, think about:
■ what you heard.
■ what you think happened before.
■ what you think happened after.

2 🔊 **2.03** Listen to the middle of a news item. Then answer questions 1–4 in the strategy and discuss what might have happened before and after.

3 🔊 **2.04** Listen to the complete news item. Were your predictions correct? Did anything surprise you?

4 🔊 **2.05** **SPEAKING** Why do you think people want to be famous? Choose the three most common explanations in the list below. Then listen to a radio programme about life in the public eye. Are you three choices still the same?

■ financial rewards ■ parental neglect ■ the adrenaline rush ■ survival instinct
■ desire to influence people ■ unpopularity at school ■ possibility of a longer life
■ possibility of a happier life ■ need for approval

5 🔊 **2.05** **SPEAKING** Listen again and match the speakers, David (interviewee 1), Tom (interviewee 2) and Ginny (interviewee 3), to statements 1–8. Then discuss the opinions.

1 Children who don't get a lot of attention may crave fame.
2 The need for approval can be traced back to primitive civilizations.
3 You have to please your audience if you want to remain famous.
4 The body's physical reaction to fame can be addictive.
5 Most people want to be famous because of the financial rewards.
6 Fame does not guarantee a long and happy life.
7 Despite the attention, celebrities can feel lonely.
8 People want to be famous because they want to feel immortal.

V insight Idioms with *in* and *out*

6 Which of the phrases below go with *in* and which with *out*? Explain their meaning. Use a dictionary to help you.

■ of one's depth ■ the limelight ■ on a limb ■ step with ■ of character ■ of favour ■ one's element
■ the offing

7 SPEAKING Complete the questions with the correct form of the phrases in exercise 6. Then discuss the questions. Give reasons for your answers.

1 Do you agree that fame is very much in .... for everybody, and that anyone can become a celebrity?
2 Are you a risk-taker? Would you feel in .... on stage or as the focus of attention?
3 Why do you think people get out .... and fail to cope with fame?
4 Why might famous people act out ....? Why is their public image so important?
5 How might someone famous feel if they fell out .... with their fans and lost popularity?
6 What do you think is the main reason for people wanting to stay in ....?

Choosing front page news

8 SPEAKING What makes a good news story? Rank these qualities in order of importance.

■ human interest ■ local relevance ■ educational ■ global perspective ■ controversial ■ entertaining ■ celebrity content ■ inspirational ■ humorous

9 ⦿ **2.06** Listen to three students discussing which story to include on a student news website. Which one do they choose? Which of the qualities in exercise 8 does it have?

> ### Park festival rained off
>
> ## World Cup wonder
>
> ### Reality TV star: caught on camera
>
> ## Supergran tackles mugger
>
> ### Local boy wins US scholarship

10 ⦿ **2.06** Listen again and tick the phrases that the students use. Then match the phrases to categories A–C.

1 We might as well … .
2 Let's go with it.
3 So, do we all agree that … ?
4 You can say that again!
5 I wouldn't do that.

6 I'm just trying to point out … .
7 It ticks lots of boxes.
8 Hang on a minute, are you saying that … ?
9 I didn't mean that exactly.
10 In other words, … .

A Using modals to comment and suggest
B Agreeing on a choice
C Restating a point of view

11 ⦿ **2.07** Listen to a similar discussion. Put the phrases below in the order they are used. Then match them to categories A–C in exercise 10. Which story did the students choose and why?

.... a Which one is it going to be, then?
.... b We could include … .
.... c I couldn't believe it!

.... d Let's put it this way: … .
.... e Which one should we choose?
.... f I'm just saying that … .

12 SPEAKING Work in groups. You are working on a student news website. Which two stories below would you cover and why? Which two would you not cover? Give reasons for your choices using the phrases in exercises 10 and 11.

> ## Fast food chain funds new sports centre
>
> ## Graffiti – art or eyesore?
>
> ## Local youth hostels to close down
>
> ## Rise in knife crime worries teens
>
> ## Radio station sponsors drama school hopefuls
>
> ## Protest over education cuts

1 SPEAKING What makes a good documentary? What are the similarities and differences between a documentary and a fiction film?

2 Read the article and match missing paragraphs A–F to gaps 1–5. There is one paragraph that you do not need. Then compare your answers in exercise 1.

3 SPEAKING Discuss the questions.

1 What was the main purpose of Flaherty's films? Do documentaries have the same purpose today?

2 In what ways were early newsreels an 'adapted reality'? Are news reports today more truthful? How might they adapt reality?

3 Do you agree that documentaries are 'the most trusted form of the news'? Justify your opinions.

V Documentaries

4 Match the words in A to the words in B. Then check your answers in the article.

A ■ staged ■ archival ■ musical ■ voice- ■ crowd ■ fly-on-the-wall ■ shot on ■ docu-

B ■ footage ■ funding ■ ganda ■ scenes ■ location ■ over ■ score ■ style

5 Complete the text with the correct form of the phrases in exercise 4.

Want to make your own documentary?

First, choose a hard-hitting story; then, write your script. Get your friends to tell the story and ¹................ (it's cheaper than in a studio). If you need some money to get going, try ²................ on the internet.

Always use a hand-held camera – your mobile phone camera is ideal – and follow your subject. Make your film look more realistic by using a ³................ of filming. Sure, you will probably need to have a few ⁴................ with some scripted dialogue, but try to make them sound as spontaneous as possible.

When you've finished filming, it's time to edit. You can add a ⁵................ , although I prefer to show, rather than tell people what to think. If there's a political message, it's better for your audience to draw their own conclusions, rather than producing ⁶................ .
If you can, use ⁷................ from time to time as a bit of history will give your film more credibility. You could also add a ⁸................ , but be careful the song doesn't distract the audience from your message.

SEEING IS BELIEVING

A steam train slowly pulls into a station, a boat docks at a port, and workers swarm out of factory gates after a hard day's work. These are the subjects of the first moving images, produced by the Lumière Brothers and first
5 shown in a café in Paris over a hundred years ago. Known as 'actualities', these short black and white films were shot on location at a single place and had no storyline or political agenda. ªWhat they did was show simple scenes from everyday life. These scenes had a dramatic impact
10 on people who had never witnessed a moving image before. In one famous incident the audience ran out of the theatre as an on-screen train speeded towards them. ᵇNever before had people seen such realistic images; for these first audiences, 'seeing was believing'.

1 ....

15 Flaherty's documentary starred locals and looked natural and spontaneous, but the film was very much a romantic interpretation of the Inuit way of life, and included many staged scenes. In one such scene, a walrus is killed with a harpoon rather than a shotgun, although in the 1920s
20 Inuit people no longer hunted with harpoons. These early documentaries were very much an interpretation of reality – ᶜwhat happened was that they presented the film-makers' idea of life, rather than showing life as it actually was.

2 ....

25 Interestingly, this type of 'adapted reality' was used in newsreels, too. Much archival war footage from the early twentieth century was staged, with cameramen arriving after a battle, then filming re-enacted scenes.

3 ....

Gradually, this direct cinema style started to influence
30 other genres, and some mainstream films became more 'realistic'. In the 1970s, British film-maker Ken Loach used a 'fly-on-the-wall' style to make his 'drama-documentary' films appear as unscripted and as natural as possible. These hard-hitting stories often dealt with
35 real-life issues, such as homelessness (*Cathy Come Home*) and unemployment (*Riff-Raff*), and they had clear social and political messages.

4 ....

As well as instructing audiences, these new documentaries use musical scores, emotional
40 storytelling and dramatic re-enactments. In fact, in many ways, contemporary documentaries are becoming indistinguishable from mainstream Hollywood films. *Super Size Me*, *March of the Penguins* and *An Inconvenient Truth* all rely on techniques from fiction
45 films to manipulate the audience's emotions and interest.

5 ....

Nowadays, the influence of documentary film-makers can be found in many places: in reality TV shows, such as *Big Brother*, and in mainstream 'mockumentary' films, such as *The Blair Witch Project*. Cheap digital
50 technology, computer-based editing and the internet are making it much easier for anyone to produce a documentary film. As well as watching these films online, ordinary people can now try their hand at creating them. But as documentaries become more like Hollywood
55 movies, and Hollywood movies become more like documentaries, can any of these films truly document reality? Can we still claim that 'seeing is believing'?

A This tradition of shaping 'reality' continued when, ten years later, a British director John Grierson started to produce documentaries with a similar stylized approach. *The Nightmail* began as an information film about the mail train from London to Edinburgh, but as it progressed, the film became more poetic and less realistic, concentrating on movement, light, rhythm and sound. 60 65

B It wasn't until 1922 that documentaries as we know them today started to emerge. An American director called Robert Flaherty produced a feature-length documentary called *Nanook of the North*. The film introduced audiences to Inuit life in Northwest Alaska, helping to broaden their knowledge of the world. ᵈIt was this desire to educate and present people with the 'truth' that motivated early film-makers, but just how truthful were their documentaries? 70

C Despite this manipulation, documentary film-making is becoming more and more popular, and in many ways is one of the most trusted forms of news reporting: 'I think there is a thirst for a meaningful relationship with reality,' explains Martijn te Pas at Amsterdam's International Documentary Film Festival. 'And documentaries can offer that … People today want more than escapism.' 75 80

D In the 1950s and 1960s there was a backlash against staged reality and re-enacted scenes in a movement called direct cinema. Direct cinema started in the USA, and gave the impression that the events on the screen had been recorded spontaneously and were presented exactly as they happened in real life. Thanks to technological developments, directors had more freedom to follow people during a crisis and capture their personal reactions. ᵉAll they did was use a hand-held camera with synchronized sound. 85 90

E ᶠNot only do these new documentaries deal with local problems, but they also focus on global issues, like the environment, poverty and hunger. Cheapness is what is helping to push the trend of home-made documentaries, but when directors need money to create more ambitious projects, they turn to crowdfunding – raising money via internet donations. 95

F More recently, directors such as the American film-maker Michael Moore have also focused on hard-hitting stories. They've taken documentaries to a new level of popularity, although Moore's films have also been criticized for being 'docu-ganda' – films that spread propaganda using a documentary style. Some people think his voice-overs tell audiences how to react to a topic. However, this approach is nothing new in documentaries, and audiences have come to expect it. 100 105

Emphasis and inversion

6 Study sentences a–f in the article. Then match them to rules 1 and 2 below and answer the questions.

To create emphasis we can:
1 add an extra clause beginning with *It* … , *All* … or *What* … .
  - What do we use after *What / All they did was* … ?
  - What do we use after *What happened was (that)* … ?
  - What do we use after *It was … that* … ?
2 start with a negative expression, for example: *Seldom, Not only, Hardly, Never, Rarely*.
  - How does the word order change in sentences that start with negative expressions?

Reference and practice 6.2 | Workbook page 120

7 Rewrite the second sentence so that it has a similar meaning to the first sentence.

1 The director used documentary techniques to make the film seem realistic.
  What the director ....
2 Michael Moore's documentary *Fahrenheit 9/11* won awards at several major film festivals.
  It ....
3 Film-makers only spent eight days on *The Blair Witch Project*.
  All they did ....
4 He drank a milkshake and ate a big bag of popcorn during the film.
  Not only ....
5 The controversial political documentary was banned from some cinemas.
  What happened ....
6 I have never seen such a fascinating documentary.
  Never ....

8 **SPEAKING** Read the opinions. Do you agree with them? Why / why not?

1 'Not only is it difficult to separate documentaries from Hollywood films, but it's also often impossible to separate fact from fiction.'
2 'Documentaries are just movies. Seldom are they about real life.'

Vocabulary bank | Film-making page 139

1 **SPEAKING** Study the headings on page 77 from articles about the news. What issues would you expect to appear in them?

2 Read articles A and B and match them to two of the headings in exercise 1. Which arguments do you agree with and why?

STRATEGY

Creating emphasis

When you write an article, you can use different ways to emphasize your points.
The most common ways are:

a beginning with a negative expression, for example, *Never*.
b using a fixed emphatic phrase, for example, *whatsoever, by far*.
c adding an emphatic verb, for example, *do*.
d adding an extra clause, for example, *All they did was ... .*

3 Read the strategy. Then match sentences 1–7 in the articles to a–d in the strategy.

4 Rewrite the second sentence so that it has a similar meaning to the first sentence.

1 Citizen journalists were first to break the story.
It was ....
2 The paper didn't check the facts before they published the article.
What ....
3 When news stories are entertaining, teenagers read them.
Teenagers do ....
4 Young people often don't care about international events.
Rarely ....
5 In my opinion, the best news stories are about celebrities.
By far the ....
6 He had just finished writing his Facebook update when his friends arrived.
Hardly ....

V Discourse markers

5 **Match highlighted phrases a–g in the articles to definitions 1–7. Then match the words below to the same definitions.**

■ undeniably ■ probably ■ in all honesty ■ undoubtedly ■ hypothetically ■ in reality ■ distressingly

1 it's likely that   presumably
2 I acknowledge this point, although I'd rather not   admittedly
3 to be honest with you
4 there is no doubt about this
5 in fact, really
6 in theory
7 I'm concerned about this

6 **Choose one word you <u>cannot</u> use to complete the sentences.**

1 Teenagers aren't interested in the world around them. **Theoretically / Frankly / As a matter of fact**, all they care about is what other teenagers are doing.
2 Young people often talk about 'the news'. **Admittedly / Probably / In reality**, 'the news' is usually about the party last weekend!
3 Eighteen-to-thirty-four-year-olds are less knowledgeable than their elders. **Presumably / Obviously / Hypothetically**, it's because they don't have time to read the news.
4 Newspapers should make news more relevant to young people. **In reality / Worryingly / Probably**, they don't seem to be doing this.
5 Many top journalists are middle-aged. **Hypothetically / Undoubtedly / Obviously**, they reflect a middle-aged view of the world.
6 Newspapers need to engage younger readers. **Undeniably / Frankly / Distressingly**, they need to write about issues that matter to them.

7 **SPEAKING** Do you agree or disagree with the opinions in exercise 6? Give reasons for your answers.

'No news is good news'

News sites bore Generation Zzzz

Teens today: the dumbest generation?

No news? That's not an option!

A

Newspapers are part of our daily life; without them we'd be cut off from reality. We read the news to know what is going on in the world, and this knowledge shapes our attitudes and actions. Newspapers educate us, exposing us to new ideas and words, which are good for the mind, too.

[1]It's a sad fact, but much of the younger generation have no interest whatsoever in the news. [a]Worryingly, in a recent survey, young people scored an average of 5.9 out of twelve questions in a general knowledge test about world events. [b]Frankly, ignorance is dangerous and it's reckless to ignore reality; by following the news, we become stronger, more valuable citizens, able to form our own opinions about national and international events. And as we find out about other people's problems, we can try to work out how to help them.

So, [c]theoretically, reading the news makes us better citizens. In addition, it's good for the mind. Fresh perspectives and new concepts broaden our outlook, and learning new words and ideas helps our minds to stay sharp. [2]What reading does is encourage comprehension and our ability to focus, as well as improving our vocabulary.

In short, make the most of the news and try to read it every day, even for just a few minutes. Visit different news sites and challenge your ideas by looking at different points of view. [3]Not only is the news about accessing information, but it's also about inspiration. People who change the world always read the news, forming opinions on the biggest challenges facing our planet today.

B

Whoever said 'No news is good news' had a point. If we don't read the news, we can pretend nothing bad has happened. But look at the headlines and there it is: [4]rarely do we find good news in the papers. [d]As a matter of fact, journalists seem to like bad news. So why do we read it? And wouldn't we be better off without it?

[e]Presumably we read the news because we think that it deals with issues that we might be able to influence in some way. But think about news stories you have read recently. Could you change any of the situations? Events in the news are usually about things we cannot influence. [5]Hardly have we finished reading one depressing story, when another appears that we can't do anything about.

So are we better off without it? Probably, as studies have shown that bad news stories can have a negative effect on our minds and on our bodies. [6]It is this negative news that is one of the causes of stress, which can lead to serious illness. And the huge amount of news available is [f]obviously difficult for our minds to process. As a result, we often skim-read articles, rather than reading them deeply for understanding. This overworks our short-term memory, which in turn weakens our long-term memory.

[g]Admittedly, in this information-rich age, it's impossible to switch ourselves off from the news completely – but we can change our habits. [7]Try having 'no news' days to give your brain a break, and when you do read, try to read more deeply and focus on issues that are relevant to you. No news can sometimes be good news.

WRITING GUIDE

- **Task** Choose one of the headlines in exercise 1 and write an opinion article.

- **Ideas** Brainstorm ideas and then select the main points you want to make. Try to include unusual angles on the topic, or facts and opinions that the reader may not have considered.

- **Plan** Follow the plan:

  Paragraph 1: State the topic and main purpose of your article. Outline your main ideas.
  Paragraph 2: Present your first point.
  Paragraph 3: Present your second point.
  Paragraph 4: Restate the main points you have covered.

- **Write** Write your article. Use the paragraph plan to help you.

- **Check** Check the following points:
  - Is the topic clearly stated?
  - Have you used emphasis to underline your main ideas?
  - Have you checked grammar, vocabulary, spelling and punctuation?

hope verb

ADV. **certainly, desperately, fervently, really, sincerely, very much** ◇ *They ~d desperately that their missing son would come home.* ◇ *I sincerely ~ that you will be successful.* | **only** ◇ *I only ~ you're right.* | **secretly** ◇ *He secretly ~d that she wouldn't be home.*
VERB + HOPE **(not) dare (to)** | **hardly dare, scarcely dare** (esp. BrE) ◇ *I hardly dared to ~ the plan would succeed.* | **begin to** | **continue to**
PREP. **for** ◇ *We are hoping for good weather.*
PHRASES **~ against ~** (= to continue to hope for sth even though it is very unlikely) | **~ for the best** (= to hope that sth will happen successfully, esp. where it seems likely that it will not)

regret verb

ADV. **bitterly, deeply, greatly, really, seriously, sincerely, truly, very much** ◇ *The president said that his country deeply regretted the incident.* | **rather** | **immediately, instantly** ◇ *I immediately regretted not asking for his name and address.* | **quickly, soon** ◇ *It was a decision she would soon ~.* | **later** ◇ *Pierre told them some things he later regretted telling.* | **never**
VERB + REGRET **begin to** | **come to, grow to, live to** ◇ *She knew that she would live to ~ this decision.* | **seem to**

STRATEGY

Adverb intensifiers

We can use adverb intensifiers to modify verbs or adjectives. There are three types of adverb intensifiers.

a emphasizers: these words make the verb or adjective stronger.

That new programme is really boring.

b amplifiers: these words enlarge the meaning of the verb or adjective. We can only use amplifiers with non-gradable adjectives.

The standard of journalism today is absolutely appalling.

c downtoners: these words reduce the meaning of the verb or adjective.

They're somewhat concerned about recent developments.

1 Read the strategy above. Identify the adverb intensifiers in the sentences below.

1 It was an extremely challenging time for the whole family.
2 I was fairly surprised to hear the news.
3 Do you really think that's a good idea?
4 I'm utterly exhausted from trying to understand his politics.
5 The politician exposed in the documentary was absolutely furious.
6 We're slightly concerned about the lack of information in this report.
7 Her story is undoubtedly true. You must believe her.
8 They were pretty annoyed about the article in the newspaper.
9 It's a very interesting documentary.

2 Put the adverb intensifiers in exercise 1 under the correct heading in the table.

emphasizer	amplifier	downtoner

STRATEGY

Adverb intensifiers: collocations

Some adverb intensifiers collocate with specific verbs to make emphatic expressions. You can find which adverbs to use with which verbs in a collocations dictionary.

3 Read the strategy above. Then study the dictionary entries for *hope* and *regret* and answer the questions.

1 Which adverbs are commonly used to intensify both verbs?
2 Which adverbs are used only with *hope*?
3 Which adverbs are used only with *regret*?

4 Replace the words in italics with the correct adverbs. Use the dictionary entries in exercise 3 to help you.

1 The residents of the burning building (*in a way that shows despair*) .... hoped that there wasn't anyone left inside.
2 You will (*not long from now*) .... regret what you wrote about the incident.
3 They (*in an instant*) .... regretted posting the photos online.
4 I (*in a genuine way*) .... hope that you accept my apology.
5 She (*after some time*) .... regretted spreading all the rumours.
6 Jack (*without wanting anyone else to know*) .... hoped to win the Young Journalist of the Year award.

5 Choose the correct intensifier for the sentences below. Use a collocations dictionary to help you.

1 I **honestly / readily** believe that there should be no censorship of the media.
2 The documentary-makers **freely / sincerely** regretted the distress caused to some of the people featured in their programme.
3 My teachers **positively / utterly** encouraged me to take the journalism course at college.
4 We **utterly / fully** refuse to read anything published by this newspaper.
5 Mr Gruber **categorically / deeply** rejects all accusations that he broke the law.
6 I **strongly / freely** recommend that you watch this documentary.
7 She **sincerely / readily** hopes that her photographs will help to inform more people about the war.
8 They **fully / honestly** appreciate the seriousness of the crime.

Vocabulary

1 Match the words in A to the words in B to make collocations.

A ■ expose ■ fall for ■ go ■ make ■ set ■ spread

B ■ the agenda ■ corruption ■ headlines ■ rumours ■ a scam ■ viral

1 .... 4 ....
2 .... 5 ....
3 .... 6 ....

Marks .... / 6

2 Complete the text with the words below. There is one word that you do not need.

■ accountability ■ armed ■ cover-up ■ delve into ■ devastated ■ rigged ■ vulnerable

Investigative journalism is a style used by reporters to ¹.................. one topic in order to get to the bottom of it. The journalists start their research ².................. only with an idea, but by the end of it, they may be able to reveal information about a ³.................. election or a police ⁴.................. . Investigative journalists are not very popular, because the subjects of their reports don't want to take ⁵.................. for their actions. This makes these journalists very ⁶.................. , and they have to take special care to ensure their own safety.

Marks .... / 6

3 Choose the correct answers.

You would think that the publishers of magazines would find themselves out ¹**of character / on a limb / of their depth** since the arrival of the internet. Today, news about famous people in ²**the limelight / their element / the offing** can be found on numerous different websites. Although it is true that some of the celebrity titles have fallen out ³**of character / of favour / of their depth**, other specialist titles are doing well. This is because they have found a way to keep in ⁴**the limelight / their element / step with** digital technology. Far from being out ⁵**of character / favour / of their depth**, they have learned to embrace new platforms, such as tablets and smartphones. Due to their popularity, there are sure to be some new titles in ⁶**their element / the limelight / the offing**.

Marks .... / 6

4 Complete the definitions with the words below. There is one word that you do not need.

■ crowdfunding ■ docu-ganda ■ fly-on-the-wall ■ footage ■ score ■ staged ■ voice-over

1 .... scenes are carefully planned parts of a film or documentary.
2 .... style makes the action look natural.
3 Films that spread propaganda using a documentary style are known as ....
4 A .... is the information in a film given by a person who is not seen on the screen.
5 The .... is the music written for a film.
6 .... is the act of raising small amounts of money from a large number of people.

Marks .... / 6

Grammar

5 Complete sentence b so that it has a similar meaning to sentence a. Use *must*, *might (not)* or *can't*.

1 a That story is in all the papers, so it's probably true.
   b That story .... because it's in all the papers.
2 a It isn't possible that that singer is dying – she's so young!
   b That singer is so young – she ....
3 a It's possible that the reporters were trying to help the injured man.
   b The reporters .... to help the injured man.
4 a Perhaps the police didn't arrest the right person.
   b The police .... the right person.
5 a I'm sure that the newsreader made a mistake.
   b The newsreader .... a mistake.
6 a It's possible that it will rain in the morning.
   b It .... in the morning.
7 a It's impossible that they started the fire.
   b They .... the fire.

Marks .... / 7

6 Complete the news item with the phrases below.

■ sure ■ is bound ■ looks as if ■ most probably ■ possible that ■ safe to ■ seems likely

Police are appealing for information about an attempted robbery at a cash machine in Worcester Park last night. The thief is ¹.................. a local man, although it is ².................. he lives some distance away, because he was riding a bike. It ³.................. that this was not his first attempt as he did not hesitate to approach the two girls who were at the cash machine. CCTV footage shows that he ⁴.................. he is going to ride straight past the machine at first, but at the last minute he leans over to try and grab the cash. Police are ⁵.................. that he went home after the incident because the girls pulled him off his bike. He ⁶.................. to be hurt because they hit him quite hard. It's ⁷.................. say that he will think twice about robbing girls in pairs in the future.

Marks .... / 7

7 Rewrite the sentences.

1 The film had only just begun when there was a newsflash.
   Hardly ....
2 I was surprised about the style of the report.
   What ....
3 It's the first time I've been so shocked by a news item.
   Never ....
4 The driver and the passengers got injured in the crash.
   Not only ....
5 Citizen journalists helped the victims of the crash.
   It ....
6 They took lots of photos and immediately uploaded them online.
   What ....
7 The fans have rarely witnessed such a defeat of their team.
   Seldom ....

Marks .... / 7 **Total** .... / 45

Listening

1 🔘 **2.08** **Choose the correct answers.**

Recording 1 How should the piece of news be headlined?

a Woman makes online plea for fire victims
b Fame for resident of block hit by fire
c Animated film of fire hits the internet

Recording 2 What do the speakers think about the new libraries?

a They are convenient.
b They are unusual.
c They are useless.

Recording 3 The extract comes from

a an advert.
b a documentary.
c a debate.

Recording 4 Which of the following does the caller state as a fact and not an opinion?

a Features of textspeak, such as *LOL*, are corrupting the English language.
b The function of the word *LOL* has changed since it was first used.
c Abbreviations like *LOL* are only ever used in textspeak.

Recording 5 The speaker is

a a careers advisor.
b a university professor.
c a journalist.

Speaking

2 **Work in pairs. Make a list of sources where you can get all the latest news from. Then discuss which sources you use and why.**

3 **Work in pairs. Choose one photo each and describe it to each other. Then answer the questions.**

1 Which source of news is the fastest and which the slowest? Why?
2 Which source is the most reliable and which the least reliable? Why?
3 How do you think the ways we get our news will change in the future?
4 Is it important for teenagers to follow the news? Why / why not?

Wildlife documentaries
Sixty years of change

A Natural history fans will probably be familiar with the nine seasons of the *Life* series made by British broadcaster and naturalist David Attenborough. Famous for his hushed, yet enthusiastic delivery
5 and his ability to find any sort of plant or animal interesting, he is one of the most enduring presences on UK television. In a career spanning more than sixty years, Attenborough has been a key witness to the development of the wildlife documentary.

10 **B** When Attenborough's career began in 1952, people's attitude towards nature was very different. Everybody thought that animals were to be tracked, captured, tied up and brought back home to be gawped at. As a typical naturalist of the age, Attenborough admits to
15 being no different from the rest. He would go along, chase a giant anteater and pull it by the tail so that it could be filmed. He is also known to have done a sequence with an under-sized crocodile, filming it up close so that it appeared to be bigger, and jumping on it
20 to give the false impression of a fight. But in those days, things were different, and Attenborough is by no means proud of his actions.

C In addition to this change of attitude towards nature, Attenborough has also seen a leap in the
25 technology used to film wildlife documentaries. He started his career in broadcasting when those people lucky enough to own a television possessed a very basic black and white set. The images were captured with a lightweight, wind-up camera, which was positively
30 primitive compared to the technology used to film his latest series. New cutting-edge 3D technology has been used to capture mesmerising images, such as plants flowering. The pictures more than compensate for the difficulty of transporting the equipment – it takes two
35 or three men to carry each 3D camera.

Literature insight 3 Workbook page 88

D However, improvements in technology have not been the most important development in the last six decades. During this period, a number of scientific revolutions have changed our perspective on the natural world. One of the new concepts is continental drift, an idea which helps explain the variation in the plants and animals on the different continents. Attenborough says, 'At university I once asked one of my lecturers why he was not talking to us about continental drift and I was told, sneeringly, that if I could prove there was a force that could move continents, then he might think about it. The idea was moonshine, I was informed.' Another is the discovery of the structure of DNA, which has completely changed the way we see the world. David Attenborough has responded to these new theories by travelling to every conceivable part of the planet to find evidence to support them. He has also interviewed many of the scientists behind them in his documentaries.

E Unfortunately, there is also a negative side to the changes that Attenborough has witnessed over the years. Today, wildlife documentaries are more about the importance of conserving nature rather than purely showing the wonders of the living world. This is because these marvels are being destroyed at an alarming rate. In their films, naturalists like Attenborough want to inform people about the state of the world in the hope that a worldwide protest will slowly grow, with younger people wanting something to be done to protect the planet. 'The truth is: the natural world is changing. And we are totally dependent on that world. It provides our food, water and air. It is the most precious thing we have and we need to defend it.'

Reading

4 Read the article and answer the questions. There are two questions that have no answer.

In which paragraph does the writer:
1 acknowledge a negative change the naturalist has witnessed? ....
2 comment on the naturalist's plans for the future? ....
3 illustrate behaviour that the naturalist regrets? ....
4 refer to the new techniques in filming? ....
5 mention the style of one particular naturalist? ....
6 remark on a conflict the naturalist has been involved in? ....
7 comment on the naturalist's approach to interviewing scientists? ....

Grammar

5 Complete the second sentence so that it has a similar meaning to the first sentence. Write between three and five words, including the word in brackets. Do not change the word in brackets.

1 I'm sure that the reporter broke the rules to get this information.
The reporter .... to get this information. (must)
2 I haven't heard such an outrageous accusation before.
Never .... such an outrageous accusation before. (heard)
3 It was a bad idea to write your essay late at night.
You .... your essay late at night. (ought)
4 Were you able to get any tickets for the play?
Did .... any tickets for the play? (succeed)
5 My brother has never walked with crutches before.
My brother .... with crutches. (isn't)
6 The surgeon was on the point of making an incision when the patient opened her eyes.
The surgeon .... an incision when the patient opened her eyes. (about)
7 We weren't allowed to touch the sculptures in the exhibition.
They .... the sculptures in the exhibition. (let)
8 She started painting landscapes when she was six.
She .... she was six. (has)

Writing

6 Read the statement below. Write an article for your school magazine stating your opinion and giving a review of a documentary that has been popular among people your age.

> Teens would rather be entertained by reality shows than informed about real events.

Reading and vocabulary Before I die …

1 SPEAKING List five things that you would like to achieve before you die. Now imagine you will never die. Would your objectives be the same or different? Why / why not?

2 Read the article. Are the sentences true (T), false (F) or not given (NG)?

1 Dmitry Itskov claims that only powerful people will benefit from his project.

2 At the end of his long life, Jiroemon Kimura was tired of living.

3 The writer says immortality would result in more crime.

4 He believes that longer lives would mean more opportunities to explore different careers.

5 He thinks that older generations usually prevent progress and societal evolution.

6 The writer predicts that in an immortal world, there would be fewer differences between people.

7 He claims that immortality would offer us infinite, exciting possibilities.

8 He believes that it's a mistake to try and control our own destinies.

STRATEGY

Critical thinking: evaluating pros and cons

When you read an article discussing the pros and cons of an idea or situation, make a list of the pros and cons the writer identifies. This will help you to understand the argument and judge how 'balanced' it is. It will also help you to evaluate the writer's ideas and decide whether you agree or disagree with their conclusion.

3 Read the strategy. Make a list of the pros and cons of living forever presented in the article. Then answer the questions.

1 Does the writer present a balanced argument?

2 Can you think of any other pros?

3 Do you agree with the writer's conclusion? Why / why not?

V insight Phrasal verbs with *off*

4 Study phrasal verbs 1–6 in the article. Then match them to the meanings of *off* below.

a become less
b depart
c reject or dismiss
d postpone
e resist
f remove

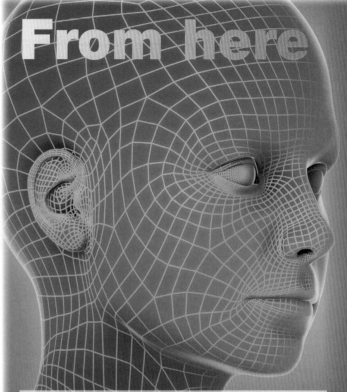

From here

Tyler Jamieson has a strict daily routine. He goes jogging every morning at 6 a.m., reads the newspapers, then ¹<u>sets off</u> to work an eighteen-hour day. Tyler is the CEO of a huge corporation and works in a pressured and stressful environment. But despite this – and the fact that he is nearly 100 years old – he has no serious health problems. In fact, Tyler expects to live for many centuries more. His original body 'died' several years ago, but his brain lives on in an avatar robot.

This may sound like an idea from a science fiction film script, but it actually comes from a serious business proposal. In 2013, a thirty-one-year-old media entrepreneur called Dmitry Itskov sent a letter to billionaires offering them a new lease of life. Itskov had thirty scientists working on an immortality project whose aim was to transplant a human mind into a robot body by 2023. 'Our research has the potential to free you, as well as the majority of all people on our planet, from disease, old age and even death,' claimed Itskov in his letter. 'A person with a perfect avatar will be able to remain part of society. People don't want to die.'

Fundamentally, he's right. Most people's shelf life is a mere eighty-five to eighty-nine years, so it's hardly surprising that we want to ²<u>put off</u> the inevitable. Even the world's oldest man, 116-year-old Jiroemon Kimura, insisted that although he was tired, he didn't want to die. But is eternal life as attractive as it sounds? What would be the consequences of immortality?

From a purely practical point of view, immortality poses quite a few problems. The most obvious is the increase in overpopulation, putting more pressure on our planet's already strained resources. Other problems would stem from the effects on society. Crime rates

Vocabulary: phrasal verbs with *off*; phrases with *life*; the old and the young; analysing meaning
Grammar: conditionals, mixed conditionals; unreal situations

Speaking: discussing old age
Writing: an opinion essay

7A

to eternity

'Immortality is the next logical step'

would rise because a few years in prison would no longer deter criminals, and how could the state afford 'life sentences'? Another big change would be in the length of our working life. People could spend thousands of years in the same job, resulting in severe depression. There would be fewer career opportunities for younger, less experienced generations, too.

Immortality would also influence how society develops and progresses. As demographics changed and the population grew older, there would be more resistance to progress. Imagine if everyone from the eighteenth century were still alive today. Chances are that racial segregation would still exist and women wouldn't have the right to vote. Older generations need to die in order to let the younger generation breathe life into new concepts and allow society to progress; in a brave new 'immortal' world, older people could continue to [3]fend off innovation in favour of the status quo. 'A new scientific truth does not triumph by convincing its opponents and making them see the light,' said Nobel physicist Max Planck, 'but rather because its opponents eventually die and a new generation grows up that is familiar with the idea from the beginning.'

Itskov claims that people from every walk of life will benefit from immortality, but in reality, only the very rich and powerful will be able to afford it. It could lead to a new world order with billionaire immortals living charmed lives and running the world in much the same way as the gods ruled the ancient world in Greek mythology. The divide between the rich and the poor could widen to the extent that they may even become two different species.

Yet those in favour of immortality projects argue that it's unethical to condemn everyone to death when the possibility of indefinite life exists. Modern medicine cures diseases and keeps people in the prime of life for as long as possible; surely, they argue, immortality is the next logical step? People could explore endless possibilities, witness how the human race evolves and dedicate themselves to doing good. Supporters don't believe that the novelty of life might one day [4]wear off. They don't consider that once we have passed all the milestones in life and [5]crossed everything off our bucket lists, we could be condemned to an eternity of boredom.

Today, it is not only Dmitry Itskov who is promising the gift of immortality; scientific research is also uncovering nature's secrets of longevity. Living forever really is a matter of life and death and the problems it creates cannot be easily [6]shrugged off. Ultimately, by accepting that life is finite, we're able to give more value to the time we have, and to think carefully about how we are using it and what we hope to achieve, because we might not get another chance. As a wise man once said, 'The bad news is, time flies. The good news is, you're the pilot.'

5 **Match the sentence halves. Then match the phrasal verbs in italics to meanings a–f in exercise 4.**

1 We may *laugh off* the idea of eternal life,
2 Scientists *called off* the news conference
3 We can *fight off* disease and infections,
4 As we get older, physical activity *eases off*
5 The shoplifter *made off* with an anti-ageing cream
6 Very old people often feel *cut off* from society
7 Most people *brush off* the idea of immortality
8 He *rubbed* the dirt *off*

a because the results of their study were inconclusive.
b and we become more sedentary.
c but we ultimately have to accept our own mortality.
d as it's unlikely to happen in their lifetime.
e and find it difficult to keep up with new changes.
f that was worth a lot of money.
g his face.
h but scientists predict that some babies born today will live for hundreds of years.

V **Phrases with *life***

6 **Study the highlighted phrases in the article. Then match them to their meanings below.**

1 an important event or point in someone's life
2 an urgent or very important issue
3 length of time for which an item remains usable
4 the best and healthiest time in someone's life
5 bring ideas and energy to something
6 all occupations and statuses
7 a new opportunity to live longer and have a better quality of life
8 to always be lucky and safe from danger

7 **SPEAKING Discuss the questions.**

1 What are the main milestones in life? Which have you already completed?
2 What age do you consider to be the prime of life? Why?
3 What types of situations might be a matter of life and death?
4 Would you say you live a charmed life? What types of people might be considered to have such a life?

Vocabulary bank Phrases with *time* page 140

The luckiest man alive?

1 **SPEAKING Look at the life events below. Which would you consider to be lucky escapes and which lucky breaks? Have you read about any lucky escapes or lucky breaks in the news recently? Describe what happened.**

■ winning the lottery ■ surviving a plane crash
■ getting out of a burning car ■ surviving a train accident
■ meeting the love of your life ■ getting your dream job
■ recovering from a serious illness

2 **2.09 Listen to a report about Frank Selak. Which events in exercise 1 did he experience?**

Conditionals

3 **Read the sentences from the recording and answer questions a–e.**

1 If you were Frank, you'd be happy to be alive.
2 Unless he lost everything, he wouldn't buy another ticket.
3 If it hadn't been for the people in the village, Frank could have drowned.
4 If he hadn't landed in the hay, he mightn't have survived.

a Which sentences talk about an imaginary or unlikely situation in the past? Which conditional are they?
b Which sentences talk about an imaginary or unlikely situation in the present or future? Which conditional are they?
c Which tenses do we use to form conditionals in sentences 1 and 2? Which tenses do we use in sentences 3 and 4?
d Which verbs can we use instead of *would*?
e Can you rephrase sentence 2 using *if*?

Reference and practice 7.1 Workbook page 121

4 Rewrite the second sentence so that it has a similar meaning to the first sentence.

1 Frank ended up in the crash because he missed an earlier train.
If he hadn't ....

2 He managed to break the train window; that's why he survived.
Frank might not ....

3 Frank should believe in good luck – I would in his situation.
I'd believe ....

4 The pilot flew too low; that's why the plane crashed.
If the pilot ....

5 The children had already got off the bus, so they weren't hurt.
The children could have been ....

6 It'd be amazing to live a charmed life like Frank.
If I ....

Mixed conditionals

5 Read the sentences from the recording and answer questions a–c.

1 If Frank's luck had run out, this would be the end of his story.
2 If Frank was a greedy man, he would have kept the money for himself.

a Which sentence talks about a past condition with a present result?
b Which sentence talks about a present condition with a past result?
c Which conditionals are used in each clause?

Reference and practice 7.2 | Workbook page 121

6 Complete the sentences with the correct form of the verbs in brackets. Are the sentences second, third or mixed conditionals? In the mixed conditionals, which part of the sentence refers to the present and which to the past?

1 My life might be better if I .... (make) different choices in the past.
2 If I .... (be) you, I wouldn't put off applying for college.
3 If they hadn't spoken English every day, they .... (not be) so fluent now.
4 If he .... (not learn) from his mistakes, he wouldn't have made any progress.
5 If I were in the prime of life, I .... (hitchhike) round the world.
6 We'd be better off today if we .... (buy) that winning lottery ticket last week!
7 She'd be a teacher by now if she .... (not drop out) of university.
8 She .... (not be) happy unless she did all the things on her list.

7 Complete the text with the correct form of the words in brackets.

THE L②TTERY ②F LIFE

Most people's definition of luck is winning a lot of money. But if you suddenly won the lottery, [1] .... (it / really / make) your life better? Everyone would know who you were. If you [2] .... (go) to your local supermarket, people would stop and stare. They'd probably ask you for money and they'd want a piece of your good luck. This is what happened to Jacqueline King, who won £14 million in the lottery. 'It was overwhelming,' she says. If she [3] .... (know) this before, would she have bought the ticket? Probably, she admits.

Today, King lives in a much nicer house, but she is divorced from her husband. Winning the lottery helped her to end an unhappy relationship. If it [4] .... (not be) for the money she received, she would still be married today. But apart from that, if she hadn't chosen the winning numbers, her life [5] .... (not be) so different. She still lives in the same area and sees the same people, but she's happier than before. However, some winners claim that their lives [6] .... (be) much better today if they hadn't won the lottery. These winners are usually people who [7] .... (make) the same mistakes if they hadn't won the jackpot. When you ask most winners about their good luck, they simply smile and say that if they [8] .... (not have) such good fortune, their lives would be nowhere near as happy.

8 SPEAKING Discuss the questions.

1 What do you define as 'good fortune' in life?
2 If you had won the lottery two years ago, how would your life be different today?
3 If you could choose one thing to change in your life, what would it be?

1 SPEAKING Look at the photo and discuss the questions.

1 How old are the women in the photo? What does the picture suggest we forget when we look at older people?
2 Think about old people you know. What do you talk to them about? How do you relate to them?
3 If you pass an old person in the street, do you smile and say 'Good morning' or avoid eye contact?
4 If you see an old person get on a full bus, do you give up your seat or let them stand?
5 How does your society treat older people? What might be the reasons for this?

2 ⊚ **2.10** Listen to a radio programme about growing old in different societies. Tick the ideas that are mentioned.

■ physical fitness ■ mental deterioration ■ dependence vs independence ■ depression
■ loneliness ■ poor diet ■ job opportunities ■ community projects

3 ⊚ **2.10** Listen again and choose the correct answers.

1 According to the presenter, what is happening to society today?
   a It's becoming more tolerant.
   b It's becoming much older.
   c It's becoming less caring.
2 What is the attitude to young people in countries like America?
   a They don't have much to say about important issues.
   b They come up with new ideas.
   c They gain experience quickly.
3 According to the speakers, why do old people lose respect?
   a Because they retire too early.
   b Because they don't value young people.
   c Because they lose their independence.
4 In the East, young people
   a send the elderly to nursing homes.
   b take care of the elderly.
   c are looked after by the elderly.
5 How is the way that old people are treated in Japanese culture explained?
   a It forms part of their upbringing and customs.
   b They don't value young people as much.
   c Children rely on their parents to support them.
6 Tribal societies are helped by
   a the resilience of old people during famine and hardship.
   b old people's knowledge of tribal history.
   c old people's ability to fight in battles.

V The old and the young

4 Study the words and phrases from the radio programme. Which do you think describe the old and which the young? Which can describe both? Use a dictionary to help you.

■ over the hill ■ adolescent ■ (in)dependent ■ wise ■ juvenile ■ long in the tooth ■ youthful
■ elderly ■ infantile ■ dynamic ■ supportive ■ (in)experienced ■ self-reliant ■ vulnerable ■ childish
■ set in their ways ■ foolish ■ mature

5 **SPEAKING** Work in pairs. Discuss how you would describe the people in 1–3. Use the words in exercise 4 and justify your answers.

1 Seventy-five-year-old Olive lives alone in a bedsit with her cat. She doesn't like going out and prefers to watch game shows most of the day. Her only son moved abroad two years ago.

2 Ed is sixty-five years old and a volunteer at the local community centre. He served in the army for many years and used to be a boxer. He gives youngsters self-defence lessons.

3 Seventy-year-old Irene lives with her daughter and son-in-law. She helps look after the grandchildren and does most of the household chores while her daughter works. She often gives her grandchildren advice when their parents aren't around.

6 **SPEAKING** Discuss the questions.

1 Do you agree that older people are 'invisible'? Give reasons for your answer.

2 What value can older people bring to your local community? How can they contribute?

| **Vocabulary bank** | Generation gap page 140 |

Discussing old age

7 Read the statement below. Do you agree? Why / why not?

'Societies should value youth over age and experience.'

8 🔊 **2.11** Listen to students having a class discussion about the statement in exercise 7 and compare your ideas.

9 🔊 **2.11** Complete the phrases from the discussion. Then listen again and check.

A Supporting a statement	**C Discussing hypothetical situations**
One of the ¹................... reasons for … is … .	If society didn't value its youth, we
I ²................... support that idea.	⁶................... make no progress.
The most obvious reason for this is … .	Society ⁷................... become … .
	Perhaps fewer mistakes ⁸................... be
B Opposing a statement	made … .
One of the biggest ³................... of … .	
What ⁴................... me is … .	
I can't ⁵................... support that point of view … .	

10 🔊 **2.12** Listen to some other students discussing the same statement. Tick the phrases that you hear. Then match all of them to categories A–C in exercise 9.

■ The main benefit that … . ■ One positive aspect of … is … . ■ A significant problem is … .
■ My main worry would be … . ■ That might result in … . ■ What if … ? ■ Even if … .
■ The best thing about it is … .

11 **SPEAKING** Work in small groups. Discuss one of the statements below.

1 'Young people aren't valued enough by society.'

2 'There is too much pressure on young people today.'

3 'Old people should be cared for by their families.'

1 SPEAKING Think about an important decision you have made in your life, such as deciding which school to go to, applying for a part-time job or taking up a new sport. Discuss the questions.

1 Who or what influenced you when you made the decision?

2 Was it an easy decision to make? Did you make it quickly or did you consider all the options first?

3 Do you think you made the right decision? Why / why not?

2 🔘 **2.13** Read and listen to the poem. What decision did the writer have to make?

3 Match summaries A–D to verses 1–4 in the poem.

A One road seemed less used than the other road, but when I took a closer look they were really no different.

B I was walking through a wood one day, when I came across two roads. I didn't want to choose which one to take, but I had to.

C In the future I'll probably tell people that I took the road that looked less used (even though it wasn't) and that choosing that road made a big difference to my life.

D Even though there was no difference, I decided to take the second road. I hoped I might go back and explore the other road another time, although I knew this was unlikely.

V insight Analysing meaning

4 🔘 **2.13** Read and listen to the poem again and discuss the questions.

1 Can the poet see where the two roads lead? Which phrase tells us this?

2 The wood is yellow and the road covered in leaves. What time of year is it? What does this suggest about the poet's age? Why might this make his choice more difficult?

3 What type of decision-maker is the poet? Does he feel comfortable making a choice or is he hesitant?

4 When he tells the story in the future, what sort of 'sigh' does the poet give? Is it a sigh of regret or relief? Give reasons for your answer.

5 How will he change his story in the future? Why? What type of person might take 'the road less traveled'?

6 What do you think the road is a metaphor for?

5 Read Robert Frost's biography and put his life events in the correct order.

▪ dropped out of university ▪ met the love of his life
▪ worked for a newspaper ▪ had his first child
▪ became famous ▪ lived on a farm
▪ travelled to England ▪ his father died

DVD extra Making decisions

The Road Not Taken
by Robert Frost

1
Two roads diverged in a yellow wood,
And sorry I could not travel both
And be one traveler, long I stood
And looked down one as far as I could
To where it bent in the undergrowth;

2
Then took the other, as just as fair,
And having perhaps the better claim,
Because it was grassy and wanted wear;
Though as for that the passing there
Had worn them really about the same,

3
And both that morning equally lay
In leaves no step had trodden black.
Oh, I kept the first for another day!
Yet knowing how way leads on to way
I doubted if I should ever come back.

4
I shall be telling this with a sigh
Somewhere ages and ages hence:
Two roads diverged in a wood, and I –
I took the one less traveled by,
And that has made all the difference.

Robert Frost (1874–1963)

Robert Frost is one of America's most popular poets. By the end of his life he was a living legend, but in the beginning, it was a very different story. Born in 1874, Frost spent his first eleven years in San Francisco. Sadly for Robert, several years later his father died, so the family moved to Massachusetts and lived with relatives. It was there that Frost met the love of his life, Elinor White. **5**

Later, Robert and Elinor got engaged and Robert went off to study at Dartmouth College. But one term into his course, he dropped out and went home to work as a reporter for a local newspaper and teach at a high school. Soon after, Robert and Elinor got married and had a baby boy called Elliot. The same year, he managed to get a place at Harvard University. Unfortunately, he dropped out after two years of study. [1]It was as if he hadn't wanted to carry on, although quite the opposite was true. The fact was that Robert had to support his wife and family. As a result, they moved to a farm in New Hampshire and made money raising chickens. [2]Perhaps he'd rather have had more time to write poetry, but life on the farm was hard. However, he did manage to write a little, early in the morning, before work. During this period, he completed some of the poems that would eventually make him famous. **10** **15** **20** **25**

Robert wasn't good at farming, so after nine years he returned to education and taught English at an academy. Five years later, frustrated by his lack of success, Robert moved his family to England. There, he found a publisher for his work and soon became popular in poetry circles in England as well as in America. **30**

In 1915, he went back to America, where he wrote *The Road Not Taken*. He was forty-two at the time and the poem's theme of indecision probably reflected Robert's own regrets. [3]Suppose he'd moved to England sooner, perhaps he'd have found fame earlier? [4]Imagine he'd finished his degree, maybe success would have been easier? In 1960, he was asked to read his poem *The Gift Outright* at President Kennedy's inauguration. Today, Robert Frost's poetry is read and enjoyed by poetry lovers all over the world. **35** **40**

Unreal situations

6 Study sentences 1–4 in the biography and answer the questions.

1 Do they talk about real situations?
2 Do they refer to the past, present or future?
3 Which tenses are used in each sentence?

7 Study the underlined sentences below and answer the questions in exercise 6.

1 John hasn't been to class for a while. It's as though he didn't want to carry on.
2 My brother is a journalist and he's always chasing deadlines. Perhaps he'd rather there was more time to write.
3 Ruth says she can't move away from New York until she's finished her studies. But suppose she moved to England next month, couldn't she study the same subjects there?
4 My cousin wants to quit college, but he can't find a good job. Imagine he finished his degree, maybe success would be easier?
5 I'd sooner we didn't have a test today.
6 Hannah can't afford a new moped, but supposing she was offered that new job, maybe she'd buy one then.

> We can use the present simple instead of the past simple after *suppose / supposing* and *as if / as though* with little difference in meaning.
>
> John hasn't been to class for a while. It's as though he doesn't want to carry on.

Reference and practice 7.3 | Workbook page 122

8 Choose the correct answers.

1 Imagine you **lived / had lived** in America today. How would your everyday life be different?
2 Imagine you **didn't study / hadn't studied** English last year. What would you be doing now?
3 Supposing she **told / had told** him the truth. What would he have done?
4 Suppose I **dropped out / had dropped out** of school, would I find a job?
5 My best friend wouldn't talk to me. It was as if I **did / had done** something wrong.
6 I'd sooner we **hadn't studied / didn't study** poetry today. Can we listen to a song instead?
7 I'd rather he **was / had been** honest with me. He lied about having his poem published.

9 SPEAKING Discuss the questions.

1 Imagine you'd left school last year, how would your life be different?
2 Supposing you passed your exams, what would your plans for the future be?
3 Do you agree that one road leads to another in life? Why / why not?
4 Have you ever changed your mind after making an important decision?

1 SPEAKING Who do you think has a better quality of life: older or younger people? Justify your answers. Then read the opinion essay and compare your ideas.

STRATEGY

Persuasive writing

When you want to persuade your reader to do something, support something or change the way they think, use the language of persuasion to get your message across. Think about:

1 **Repetition:** repeating key words and ideas for emphasis.
2 **Word order:** put information you want to emphasize at the beginning or end of the sentence.
3 **Sentence length:** shorter sentences are more emphatic. Use them for points you want to emphasize.
4 **Examples from real life:** giving real examples can make your argument more compelling.

2 Read the strategy. Then read the essay again. What persuasive language does the writer use? Find examples in the essay of points 1–4 in the strategy.

3 Rewrite the sentences below so that they are more persuasive. Use the clues in brackets to help you.

1 Today, old people are treated well in Mediterranean countries and in Japan. (Repeat *are treated well* and add *too*.)

2 My grandmother is the most interesting person I've met. (Begin with *I've never met such* … .)

3 Older people aren't good with technology and they can't multitask or concentrate for long periods of time. (Use three sentences instead of one.)

4 Young people aren't considerate and they lack compassion towards older people and can be quite rude. (Use three sentences instead of one.)

5 In the past, society respected older people far more than it does today. (Begin with *Older people were* … .)

6 My grandparents have more friends, money and security than I'll ever have. (Repeat *more*.)

Making comparisons

4 Study the highlighted words and phrases in the opinion essay and answer the questions.

Which phrases are used to describe:
1 differences? ....
2 similarities? ....
3 one thing changing over time? ....
4 two or more things changing? ....

5 **Rewrite the second sentence so that it has a similar meaning to the first sentence.**

1   In the past, people used to respect old people more.
    Old people aren't ....

2   Today, old people are treated well in Mediterranean countries and in Japan.
    Today, old people are treated just ....

3   My grandmother is the most interesting person I've met.
    You're unlikely to meet ....

4   Older people aren't as good with technology as younger people.
    Younger people are ....

5   My grandparents have a better social life than I do.
    I don't have such ....

6   If you exercise regularly, you'll live a lot longer.
    The more ....

'Older people have a better quality of life than younger people.' Do you agree?

Growing old is something we all have to face. For young people, old age may seem a long way off. It may also seem depressing with many disadvantages, but in my opinion getting older has a lot to offer. Older people can have a better quality of life than younger people.

Firstly, I believe that the older people become, the happier they get. They are older and wiser, and have more self-knowledge and life experience than younger people. They know where they've come from, they know where they're going and they've got nothing to prove.

Secondly, as people get older, they have more and more time to do what they want. Old people can learn new things just as easily as young people, and they can broaden their horizons just as much as the younger generation.

On the other hand, it's also true that older people are less active and more likely to fall ill. They are not always as mentally alert, and not so good at multi-tasking as younger people. However, medical advances mean that the older generation have far more active lifestyles than before. Seventy-six-year-old Ernestine Shepherd is a good example – you're unlikely to meet such an energetic pensioner as this body builder. Ernestine gets up at 2 a.m. every day and runs ten miles!

All things considered, in my opinion, older people definitely have a better quality of life than younger people. They have more life experience, they are healthier than previous generations, and they have the time to follow their dreams.

WRITING GUIDE

■ **Task** Write an opinion essay on one of the topics below.

1   'Old people were better taken care of in the past than they are today.' Do you agree?

2   'Young people today have no time or respect for the old.' Do you agree?

■ **Ideas** Match the ideas below to the essay topics. Do you agree or disagree with them? Brainstorm more ideas to support your opinion.

a   Society places more value on youth and forgets what older people have to offer.

b   In the past, society had more respect for older people as they passed on their knowledge to the younger generation. Today, that knowledge is on the internet.

c   Older people are no longer cared for by their families. Most are put into care homes and forgotten.

d   Older generations used to live at home. Children don't want that responsibility any more.

e   Care homes have qualified individuals to look after older people. They are better off there.

f   Young people have nothing in common with old people. Why should they make time for them?

■ **Plan** Follow the plan:

Paragraph 1: State the topic of the essay and give your point of view.

Paragraph 2: Introduce the first argument which supports your opinion.

Paragraph 3: Introduce a second argument to support your opinion.

Paragraph 4: Sum up any arguments against your opinion.

Paragraph 5: Summarize and restate your opinion.

■ **Write** Write your essay. Use the paragraph plan to help you.

■ **Check** Check the following points:

■ Have you stated your opinion in the introduction and the conclusion?

■ Have you used persuasive language?

■ Have you made comparisons to illustrate your point of view?

■ Have you checked grammar, vocabulary, spelling and punctuation?

Vocabulary insight 7 Using a dictionary: *would* and *could*

1 Work in pairs. Read sentences 1–7 from the unit. What does *would* mean in each sentence?

1 Crime rates <u>would</u> rise because a few years in prison <u>would</u> no longer deter criminals.

2 There <u>would</u> be fewer career opportunities for younger, less experienced generations.

3 The writer says immortality <u>would</u> result in more crime.

4 If Frank's luck had run out – this <u>would</u> be the end of his story.

5 If I were you, I <u>would</u>n't put off applying to college.

6 People <u>would</u> stop and stare.

7 If she had known this before, <u>would</u> she have bought the ticket?

STRATEGY

would

would has multiple meanings and functions depending on how, where and in what way it is used. Identifying these meanings and functions will help you to understand more complex texts and use more sophisticated language in a correct way. Always use the context (the information before and after the word) to infer the word's meaning. A good dictionary will provide all the different meanings of a word, as well as examples of its use.

2 Read the strategy above. Then study the dictionary entry for *would* and answer the questions.

> **would** 0-ᴡ / *strong form* wʊd; *weak form* wəd; əd/ *modal verb* (*short form* ʼd /d/, *negative* would not, *short form* wouldn't /ˈwʊdnt/)
> **1** 0-ᴡ used as the past form of *will* when reporting what sb has said or thought: *He said he would be here at eight o'clock* (= His words were: 'I will be there at eight o'clock.'). ◇ *She asked if I would help.* ◇ *They told me that they probably wouldn't come.* **2** 0-ᴡ used for talking about the result of an event that you imagine: *She'd look better with shorter hair.* ◇ *If you went to see him, he would be delighted.* ◇ *Hurry up! It would be a shame to miss the beginning of the play.* ◇ *She'd be a fool to accept it* (= if she accepted). **3** 0-ᴡ used for describing a possible action or event that did not in fact happen, because sth else did not happen first: *If I had seen the advertisement in time I would have applied for the job.* ◇ *They would never have met if she hadn't gone to Emma's party.* **4** 0-ᴡ **so that/in order that sb/sth ~** used for saying why sb does sth: *She burned the letters so that her husband would never read them.* **5** 0-ᴡ **wish** (**that**) **sb/sth ~** used for saying what you want to happen: *I wish you'd be quiet for a minute.* **6** 0-ᴡ used to show that sb/sth was not willing or refused to do sth: *She wouldn't change it, even though she knew it was wrong.* ◇ *My car wouldn't start this morning.* **7** 0-ᴡ used to ask sb politely to do sth: *Would you mind leaving us alone for a few minutes?* ◇ *Would you open the door for me, please?* **8** 0-ᴡ used in polite offers or invitations: *Would you like a sandwich?* ◇ *Would you have dinner with me on Friday?* **9** 0-ᴡ **~ like, love, hate, prefer, etc. sth/(sb) to do sth | ~ rather do sth/sb did sth** used to say what you like, hate, etc.: *I'd love a coffee.* ◇ *I'd be only too glad to help.* ◇ *I'd hate you to think I was criticizing you.* ◇ *I'd rather come with you.* ◇ *I'd rather you came with us.* **10** 0-ᴡ **~ imagine, say, think, etc. (that)...** used to give opinions that you are not certain about: *I would imagine the job will take about two days.* ◇ *I'd say he was about fifty.* **11** 0-ᴡ **I would...** used to give advice: *I wouldn't have any more to drink, if I were you.* **12** 0-ᴡ used for talking about things that often happened in the past **ꜱʏɴ used to**: *When my parents were away, my grandmother would take care of me.* ◇ *He'd always be the first to offer to help.* **13** (usually *disapproving*) used for talking about behaviour that you think is typical: *'She said it was your fault.' 'Well, she would say that, wouldn't she? She's never liked me.'* **14** **~ that...** (*literary*) used to express a strong wish: *Would that he had lived to see it.* ⊃ note at MODAL, SHOULD

---

1 What verb is *would* the past form of?

2 What is a synonym of *would* when it is used to talk about past events?

3 When *would* is used with requests, invitations and offers, is it polite or impolite?

4 Which phrases is *would* used with to say why somebody does something?

5 How can you express opinions that you are not certain of?

3 Match sentences 1–7 in exercise 1 to meanings of *would* in the dictionary entry in exercise 2.

4 Complete sentence b so that it has a similar meaning to sentence a. Use the correct form of *would* or *wouldn't*.

1 a We used to spend hours dreaming about the future.
  b We .... dreaming about the future.

2 a Doing more exercise will probably make him feel better.
  b If he did more exercise, he ....

3 a My brother refused to apply for a place at university.
  b My brother .... for a place at university.

4 a 'I won't retire,' he told me.
  b He told me that ....

5 a She slipped off the roof and broke her leg.
  b If she hadn't .... her leg.

6 a I want you to stop worrying about the future.
  b I wish that ....

5 Use a dictionary to find the entry for *could*. Then read about situations 1–5. Write a sentence with *could* and the words in brackets.

1 You want to look at someone's magazine. (borrow)

2 You're annoyed because your friend was rude to you. (be more polite)

3 You feel very upset about something. (so / cry)

4 You think that your friend's bedroom is too hot. (do with / some fresh air)

5 You think your teacher didn't remember to set any homework. (forget)

6 Study the dictionary entries for *would* and *could* again. Write three sentences with different meanings of *would* and three sentences with different meanings of *could*.

Dictionary entry from *Oxford Advanced Learner's Dictionary* 8ᵉ, Oxford University Press 2010.

Vocabulary

1 Replace the words in italics with the correct forms of phrasal verbs with *off* formed from the words below.

■ brush ■ call ■ cut ■ ease ■ fight ■ laugh ■ make ■ warn

1 My grandfather always .... (*makes a joke about*) any suggestions that he is going to retire.

2 An old farmer .... (*told us to leave*) his land when we were going for a walk.

3 My birthday party .... (*has been cancelled*).

4 Thieves .... (*have left*) with the old lady's jewels.

5 The pain .... (*became less*) after he had had his treatment.

6 My grandmother .... (*resists*) any attempts to put her in a home.

7 She .... (*is separated*) from her children because they have all emigrated to Canada.

8 Our elderly neighbour .... (*ignored*) our offers of help.

Marks .... / 8

2 Complete the sentences with phrases with *life* and the words in brackets.

1 Teenage girls sometimes consider their clothes as .... (matter)

2 A hip replacement gives some old people .... (lease)

3 He died when he was barely 30 and .... (of)

4 Marriage is an important .... (in)

5 Some young people .... and never do anything to help at home. (live)

6 During the tour, we met people from .... (walk)

7 Cookery programmes can teach the elderly how to .... into their cooking. (breathe)

8 Some medicines have a limited .... and should not be taken if they have expired. (shelf)

Marks .... / 8

3 Choose the correct answers.

Some would say that 101-year-old Fauja Singh from Ilford, East London is a little **[1]dependent / long in the tooth / self-reliant** to be running marathons. However, for the last twelve years, this **[2]elderly / over the hill / supportive** gentleman has been doing just that. Far from regarding Mr Singh as a **[3]dynamic / foolish / wise** old man, his family has always been **[4]independent / set in their ways / supportive** of his running. Not only does Mr Singh have children and grandchildren, but he also has great-grandchildren who are now **[5]adolescent / childish / juvenile**. Mr Singh was not an **[6]elderly / experienced / infantile** runner in his youth, but a farmer in Punjab, India. He moved to Britain in the 1960s and started running at the **[7]mature / wise / youthful** age of 89, when he lost his wife. People as old as that are usually firmly **[8]dynamic / long in the tooth / set in their ways**, but this is not true of Mr Singh, who has been known to take part in races to raise awareness about social issues, such as women's rights.

Marks .... / 8

Grammar

4 Complete the text with the correct conditional forms of the verbs in brackets.

People who see Margaret Dunning in her classic car often wonder which of the two is older: the 1930 Packard 740 Roadster or its driver. Margaret **[1]**................................ (not draw) as much attention if she wasn't so old – she was 102 on her last birthday. But she insists that she wouldn't be on the road if she **[2]**................................ (not have) a driving licence. Margaret officially received her licence at the age of twelve, when her father died. She wouldn't have got it at that age if the same thing **[3]**................................ (happen) today. Margaret **[4]**................................ (not learn) so much about cars if it hadn't been for her father. If she **[5]**................................ (not help) him mend the machinery on the farm, she **[6]**................................ (never / find out) how an engine worked. Margaret has several cars, and she **[7]**................................ (buy) more if she had the money. She still changes her own oil, and she would do her own repairs if she **[8]**................................ (be able) to get under the car.

Marks .... / 8

5 Complete the sentences.

1 a My grandmother doesn't live with us because she found a place in a retirement home.
  b If my grandmother ....

2 a I didn't visit them because they don't like me.
  b If they ....

3 a I speak French because I was born in Paris.
  b If I ....

4 a My parents didn't shout because they weren't angry.
  b If my parents ....

5 a My aunt is alive because she had an operation.
  b If my aunt ....

6 a Your dad bought you a car because he is rich.
  b If your dad ....

7 a She looks old because she didn't have an easy life.
  b If that woman ....

Marks .... / 7

6 Complete the sentences with the correct forms of the verbs in brackets.

1 Imagine you .... (win) the lottery. What would you spend the money on?

2 Suppose you .... (make) a different choice. What would have happened?

3 My grandmother never used to make a sound. It was as if she .... (not be) there.

4 She'd sooner he .... (not write) that poem for her. She doesn't really like him.

5 Supposing you .... (be) a poet. What kind of poems would you write?

6 I'd rather you .... (not tell) me what to do. I'm capable of deciding myself.

Marks .... / 6

Total .... / 45

1 SPEAKING Work in pairs. Discuss the questions.

1 Look at the photos. What is happening? Why is it happening? How does it make you feel?

2 Study the list of animals. Which ones would you eat? Are there any animals you would not eat? Why?

■ horse ■ cow ■ snake ■ cat ■ dog ■ shark ■ grasshopper ■ crocodile ■ chicken ■ scorpion ■ dolphin

2 Read the article about a popular Asian food. Why do some people eat this food? Why do others want it banned?

3 Read the article again and choose the correct answers.

1 What is difficult for Aamir to do?
a make enough money to live on
b find and kill sharks
c throw sharks off the boat
d carry dead sharks in the hull of his boat

2 What will happen if sharks disappear?
a Smaller predators will die out.
b The food chain will be more or less the same.
c Marine ecosystems could be devastated.
d Marine biologists can't predict the result.

3 Why are sharks being hunted?
a Because they are not endangered.
b Because they are like dolphins.
c Because they bring in a lot of money.
d Because they are used to make cheap food.

4 How does the article describe shark fin soup?
a It has a very strong taste.
b It has some health benefits.
c It has been enjoyed by ordinary people for centuries.
d It has been eaten for a long time.

5 What does Yuli Tan say about shark fin soup?
a It should be served at important events.
b She ate it when she was younger.
c It's a significant part of Asian culture.
d It's a tradition that should be preserved.

4 SPEAKING What are your food choices based on? Rank the things below in order of importance. Explain your ideas.

■ taste ■ price ■ health issues ■ culture ■ ethical issues ■ environmental issues

V insight Synonyms: intensity

5 Find the synonyms of words 1–10 in the article.

1 painful (line 13)
2 impressive (line 15)
3 upsetting (line 19)
4 destroyed (line 23)
5 important (line 25)
6 numerous (line 39)
7 banned (line 60)
8 kill (line 70)
9 huge (line 73)
10 cruel (line 77)

Would you eat it?

It's five in the morning and the sea off Oman is bright red. Aamir Mohammed has just thrown a bloodied carcass over the side of his small fishing boat. It's a shark and it's Aamir's first catch of the day. It's still
5 alive, but it's badly injured because its fin has been cut off. As Aamir tosses the fin into the empty hull of his boat, he worries about how he will support his family – shark numbers are down and the fish that he finds now are smaller than before. Meanwhile,
10 under the boat, the shark is still struggling and unable to swim. As it slowly floats down to the bottom of the sea, smaller fish start to eat it alive. Its death will be long and agonizing.

In seas and oceans across the world, these
15 awe-inspiring animals are being hunted to extinction. On average, three sharks are killed every second, or over 70 million a year. It's hardly surprising that in the last few years there has been a 90% decline in most shark populations. These are distressing statistics, but
20 sharks don't have the same appeal as dolphins, so we don't feel much empathy for them. After all, these man-eating 'monsters' kill around ten people every year, so why should we care if they are being wiped out? Aren't we better off without them?

25 For 400 million years sharks have played a critical role in maintaining balanced, healthy marine ecosystems. Sharks are apex predators and the caretakers of our oceans. Based on current evidence, marine biologists predict that losing this caretaker
30 could bring about a significant rise in the number of smaller predators like stingrays. This would result

Vocabulary: synonyms: intensity; prepositions; phrases with *face*; adjective + noun
collocations: food
Grammar: the passive; the passive: verbs with two objects; the passive with reporting verbs

Speaking: talking about photos
Writing: a for and against essay

8A

in fewer fish, and also fewer shellfish, which keep the seas and oceans clean. An imbalance in the food chain could ultimately lead to the collapse 35 of the underwater ecosystem, with a reduced fish population and more pollution. Everything and everyone who depends on the ocean for a living, or simply for recreation, would suffer. It'd be an environmental disaster with countless consequences 40 for us all.

So why are people like Aamir Mohammed killing sharks? The reason is simple: shark fins are big business. The fins are the main ingredient in China's most prized dish – shark fin soup. This soup plays a 45 significant part in Chinese culture and is often served at New Year and other important celebrations, where one bowl can cost as much as $100. The price is surprising because shark fin is tasteless and mercury levels in the meat mean the soup is 50 relatively unhealthy. Nevertheless, shark fin has a long culinary history, first appearing on the tables of the wealthy in 960 AD. This association with wealth and exclusivity continued through the centuries until the 1980s, when, thanks to a rise in prosperity in 55 Asia, ordinary people started to buy it. The increased demand has put 181 different shark species on the 'threatened with extinction' list.

But there is a glimmer of hope – a ban on finning could still save the shark population and, encouragingly, it has already been outlawed in some 60 countries. However, not everyone supports this approach. Some people feel that banning shark fin soup is an attack on Chinese culture, and that we all have the right to eat our traditional foods.

Seventeen-year-old Yuli Tan disagrees. 'I ate shark 65 fin soup as a child,' she says. 'If it wasn't offered at important events, the host would lose face in front of his guests. But traditions can change, especially when they do more harm than good. Is it really necessary to slaughter 200,000 sharks a day just for 70 a bowl of soup?'

In Oman, Aamir takes the fish he has caught to the market. Next to his tiny boat are monstrous fishing ships with hundreds of shark carcasses on board. More than a thousand can be sold here in a single day, 75 but the sharks at these markets are only a fraction of the animals actually killed. It's a cold-blooded trade, but most fishermen aren't concerned about ethics because they need to make a living. Aamir looks at the long rows of shark fins, lined up on huge slabs in the 80 market. Behind them the Arabian Sea, which used to be alive with fish, looks dead and still. Is this the future of our seas and oceans?

6 Study the synonyms in exercise 5. Which synonym in each pair is stronger? Why has the writer chosen to use these words? What effect might they have on the reader? What do they tell us about the writer's point of view?

7 Complete the text about a stunt eater. Then look at the highlighted words in *Would you eat it?* and check your answers.

It's hard not to feel empathy ¹............... the live scorpion, as Louis Cole chews it enthusiastically. Like the ragworm before it, it swiftly ends up in his stomach. Twenty-eight-year-old Louis has been eating unusual food for over a year now, including eyeballs, a live frog, and, most controversially of all, 'my pet goldfish' (which resulted ²............... hundreds of critical comments). Everything is recorded on his YouTube channel *Food for Louis* and this week, thanks ³............... the scorpion, there's been a rise ⁴............... the number of visitors.

As a stunt eater, the main ingredient ⁵............... Louis's diet is shock. Most viewers find his videos disgusting, but a small fraction ⁶............... the people who watch them think they're fine. Louis argues that people's reactions depend ⁷............... the type of food they're used to. Eating a tarantula may be unusual in England, but it's a delicacy in Cambodia. Insects are also nutritious – are we really better off ⁸............... them on the menu?

However, others see his videos as an attack ⁹............... animal rights and some are concerned ¹⁰............... animal welfare. Louis claims that most of his meals die within five seconds, and that none of them are species that are threatened ¹¹............... extinction. His view is that they are no different from the animals we eat every day. Perhaps Louis's stunts are a reminder that many of our food choices are based ¹²............... culture and prejudice.

8 SPEAKING Work in pairs. Discuss the questions.

1 Should people who have few food choices worry about ethical food? Are ethical food choices only for the wealthy?
2 Would you still eat traditional food if you knew it was unethical in some way? Would you support a ban?

Vocabulary bank	Environmental threats and protection page 141

1 SPEAKING Look at the photos. What do you think is the connection between them? Think about how the objects are made and what they are made of.

2 🔘 2.14 Listen to a radio programme about 'wet wealth' and compare your ideas.

3 🔘 2.14 Listen again. Are the sentences true (T) or false (F)? Correct the false ones.

1 Nine million computers were sold in the UK last year.
2 Rare minerals are being used up very quickly.
3 The deep sea has been mined for minerals before.
4 The seabed was being explored by companies thirty years ago.
5 Some mining projects had been agreed, but didn't happen.
6 In the future, new machines will be used to do the work.
7 The consequences of mining in the sea are known.
8 The food chain can't be damaged by mining.

The passive

4 Match the passive sentences in exercise 3 to a–h below. Then rewrite the sentences that can be changed in the active. If the subject is not clear, use *people*.

a present simple
b present continuous
c past simple
d past continuous
e past perfect
f present perfect
g future simple (*will*)
h modals

5 Study the sentences in exercise 3. Answer the questions.

1 How do we form the passive in all the tenses in exercise 4?
2 Why do we use the passive? Match the sentences in exercise 3 to explanations a–c.
   a The person / thing who does the action is obvious, unknown or unimportant.
   b The person / thing is important and added to the end of the sentence, after *by*.
   c We are more interested in the action rather than the person / thing who does it.

Reference and practice 8.1	Workbook page 123

More passive structures

6 Study sentences 1–4 from the radio programme. Then complete rules a–c.

1 Companies expect billions to be made from this 'wet wealth'.
2 But why should we care about the seabed being destroyed?
3 Our seas and their ecosystems need to be protected.
4 Can we prevent electronic equipment being sold?

a After verbs such as *prevent*, *enjoy*, etc., we use *being* + ...
b After verbs such as *expect*, *want*, etc., we use ....
c After prepositions, such as *of*, *about*, etc., we use ....

Reference and practice 8.2   Workbook page 123

7 Choose the correct answers.

1 'Wet wealth' began **to be / being** explored decades ago.
2 How can we object to the sea **to be / being** mined?
3 Can we stop flat-screen TVs **to be / being** sold?
4 Would companies care about **to be / being** fined?
5 Some companies don't want **being / to be** told what to do.
6 Many companies still hope **being / to be** given mining rights.

8 Complete the text with the correct passive form of the words in brackets.

You get home from school, kick off your trainers, grab a piece of pizza from the fridge and watch some TV. The trainers and pizza are things we take for granted, but the beef on your pizza and leather on your trainers may come from cattle that can ¹ .... (trace back) to a tropical rainforest.

Today, half of the world's rainforests ² .... (destroy), and at the moment, in countries like Brazil, trees ³ .... (cut down) illegally. In recent years, three-quarters of this destruction ⁴ .... (cause) by cattle ranching, because for every cow raised, an area of rainforest the size of two football fields ⁵ .... (destroy). In the past, ranchers could avoid ⁶ .... (catch), but things are starting to change. At the moment, satellite images ⁷ .... (use) by environmental organizations to track deforestation, especially in Brazil.

Brazil is one of the world's biggest exporters of leather. Last year, pictures of Brazilian cattle ranches ⁸ .... (compare) with maps which marked their legal boundaries. The pictures showed that a lot of the protected forest ⁹ .... (clear away), and some ranches ¹⁰ .... (prosecute) as a result. In the future, thanks to satellites, we can expect forests ¹¹ .... (protect) more effectively. We still may not know the origins of the beef on our pizzas, but soon some leather products ¹² .... (certify) deforestation-free – just remember to check the label!

9 **SPEAKING** Work in pairs. Look at the photos of everyday items. Discuss the points below.

- where they might have come from
- how they are made and what they are made of
- whether they should be avoided or not and why

A

B

C

D

1 SPEAKING Work in pairs. Discuss the questions.

1 Which of these things do we always use to grow food? Which of these resources are limited?
■ land ■ water ■ light ■ heat ■ fertilizer ■ animal feed

2 What problems do you think we might face with food in the future? Can you think of any solutions?

STRATEGY

Taking notes

When you take notes while listening to a talk, pay attention to:

■ the opening paragraph. This will outline the structure and the content of the talk. For example: *The subject of today's talk is … , I'm going to examine … , It's important to consider …* .

■ explanations, definitions or examples. These will help you to understand the content. For example: *In other words, … , To put it another way, … , … or what we would call … , Let me explain what I mean.*

■ key content words and phrases. These nouns, verbs and adjectives will show you how ideas develop.

2 ⊚ **2.15** Read the strategy. Then listen to the opening of a talk. What is the talk going to be about? Which phrases from the strategy does the speaker use to introduce the topic?

3 Look at the key content words and phrases below. Which of the photos on the left do you think they describe?

■ bland taste ■ pink slime ■ people squeamish ■ needs land to grow
■ tastes good ■ high cost ■ easy to farm ■ affect natural ecosystem

4 ⊚ **2.16** Listen to the rest of the talk and complete the lecture notes.

Feeding the world

Solution 1: micro-livestock
Explanation: [1] _____
Advantages: rich in protein, less space needed
Disadvantages: [2] _____

Solution 2: cultured meat
Explanation: meat grown in a lab
Advantages: [3] _____
Disadvantages: [4] _____

Solution 3: green super rice
Explanation: [5] _____
Advantages: can grow in hostile environments, feeds more people
Disadvantages: [6] _____

Solution 4: greening deserts
Explanation: [7] _____
Advantages: frees up land to grow food on
Disadvantages: [8] _____

V Phrases with *face*

5 Replace the words in italics with the phrases below.

■ let's face it ■ in the face of (e.g. difficulties or danger) ■ put on a brave face ■ on the face of it
■ talk until we're blue in the face ■ face the music ■ face up to the fact

1 *When you first look at the problem*, GM crops appear to be the answer. Organic food is for the rich and selfish as it uses up more resources. However, GM is not problem free.

2 What about a new national dish made of insects? If some celebrities could *pretend they are happy* and eat it, perhaps other people might try it.

3 We can *have many pointless discussions* about future foods, but it doesn't matter what we eat, we just have to eat less.

4 *As we are confronted by* the problem of global food shortages, we should all become vegetarian.

5 We need to *accept* that food miles equal global warming. Buy local and grow your own food!

6 Don't waste food: supermarkets and restaurants should *accept the punishment for what they have done* and be fined for throwing it out.

7 *We have to admit it to ourselves*: food habits are not going to change any time soon. People are too busy and too worried about other things to care.

6 SPEAKING Work in pairs. Decide on the two best solutions for food shortages and give reasons.

Talking about photos

7 SPEAKING Look at the photos above from a book and discuss the questions.

1 Who are the people in the photos? Where are they? What do you think their everyday life is like?
2 The photos are all from the same book. Why were the photos taken? What do you think the book is about?

8 2.17 Listen to two students discussing two of the photos. Answer the questions.

1 Which photos are they talking about?
2 Match the opinions to the speakers: girl (G) or boy (B). Who:
   a thinks the man in photo A is from Germany?
   b notices typical American food?
   c thinks the man eats 8,000 calories a day?
   d says the boy in photo B sells food?
   e thinks the boy's diet is unhealthy?

9 2.18 Listen to the first part of the dialogue again and complete the phrases. Then complete A–C with the headings below.

■ Speculating and reflecting ■ Clarifying an opinion ■ Conceding a point

A ....
It doesn't ¹.. a healthy diet.
It looks as though he ... .
².. by the food ... , I reckon ... .
It's ³.. from the photo.
... He's obviously a ... he might be ... .

B ....
Fair ⁴.., I didn't notice that.
Well-⁵..!

C ....
What I ⁶.. is ... .
That's all I'm saying.

10 2.19 Listen to the second part of the dialogue again and tick the phrases that you hear. Then match all of the phrases to categories A–C in exercise 9.

■ That's an interesting point. ■ In other words, ... ■ Supposing that ... . ■ It's hard to say.
■ That depends. ■ It's safe to say that ... . ■ I see what you mean. ■ That would explain ... .
■ It can't be. ■ I wonder if he (sells) ... .

11 SPEAKING Choose a different photo in exercise 7 and discuss the points below.

1 Identify the food in the photo.
2 Estimate the number of calories.
3 Identify the country.
4 Guess what activities / jobs the person does every day.
5 Decide if it is a healthy / environmentally-friendly diet.
6 Compare it with a diet from a different photo.
7 Compare the diet with your own diet.

1 SPEAKING Work in pairs. Talk about food which:

1 reminds you of a traditional festival in your country.
2 people eat on a certain day of the week or at a certain time of year.
3 acts as 'comfort food' when things are not going well.
4 represents your country in some way.

2 Read the article about a typical British food. Where did fish and chips originate?

3 Read the article again. Then complete the article with sentences A–G. There is one sentence that you do not need.

A As a result, by the early 1900s there were more than 30,000 'chippies' – traditional fish and chip shops – in England, satisfying the needs of the growing industrial workforce.

B Fish and chips was also heavily relied on throughout the two World Wars.

C And it's food worth queuing for: the chips are hot and fluffy, the fish moist and flaky and the batter crisp and golden.

D Many workers frequented eating houses where you could buy a meal including chipped potatoes for tuppence (or 2p).

E In the north-east it's known as a 'fish lot', in Leeds 'fish and nerks', in Manchester 'a chippy tea' and so on.

F People have been doing the same thing for almost 160 years, in all weathers, through good times and through bad.

G Consequently, migrant workers were able to travel from town to town, looking for jobs.

4 SPEAKING Think of a traditional dish in your country. Where does it come from? What are its origins? Who brought it to your country?

V insight Adjective + noun collocations: food

5 Study the highlighted nouns in the article and complete the table.

types of meal	
food in general	
requests for food	
quantities of food	

6 Look back at the article and at the adjectives that go with each highlighted noun. Then match the nouns to the adjectives below. Use a dictionary to help you. Some adjectives may go with more than one noun.

■ classic ■ six-course ■ light ■ emergency ■ Chinese
■ individual ■ side

DVD extra Farmers' markets

Exploring Britain's fish and chips

Journalist Jack Newberry explores the origins of one of the nation's favourite dishes.

It's a cold, wet afternoon in Manchester, but there's still a long queue outside Hammond's fish and chip shop. 'Fridays are always busy,' says forty-two-year-old fryer Terri Thomas. 'Most of our customers
5 come after work and have fish and chips with curry sauce – it's our most popular order.' [1] _____ As Terri liberally sprinkles on salt and vinegar from supersized bottles, it's hard to resist the mouth-watering smell. She offers me a double portion,
10 neatly wrapped in newspaper, and I grab a plastic fork and tuck in. Delicious!

In a recent UK survey, people were asked to name things they considered typically British. At the top of the list (in front of the Queen) was fish and chips, a
15 traditional dish that has been enjoyed by the British for generations, and can be described in at least twenty-six different ways. [2] _____ Battered fish and fried chips are a classic double act, yet they started life as solo performers, and their roots are
20 not as British as you might think.

Fish fried in batter was introduced to England in the fifteenth century, arriving in London with Jewish immigrants who had fled their homes in Portugal to escape persecution. As these new immigrants settled
25 down in the East End, their *pescado frito* became standard fare – so much so that on a visit to London in the late 1700s, Thomas Jefferson wrote that he had eaten 'fish fried in the Jewish fashion.' By the Victorian era, fish fried in batter had become a regular part of
30 the British diet, often sold by street sellers who carried it on large trays hung around their necks.

The origins of the chip are less clear. Depending on who you believe, we were given the chipped potato by either France or Belgium in the seventeenth century.
35 According to popular folklore, one winter when the rivers froze over and there were no fish to fry, an adventurous housewife cut up some potatoes in the shape of fish and fried them instead. However, the first recorded appearance of chips in England was in
40 Charles Dickens' novel *A Tale of Two Cities* (1859), which mentions 'husky chips of potatoes, fried with

some reluctant drops of oil.' Fried chipped potatoes were popular with the working classes during this time, especially migrant labourers. ³ ....

Then, in 1860, a Jewish Londoner called Joseph Malin, noticing the success of fried fish and chipped potatoes, decided to combine the two. He started a fish and chip shop on Cleveland Street in the East End of London and business was so good that many other shops opened soon after. Luckily, fresh fish was in plentiful supply thanks to the rapid development of steam trawling in the North Sea, and new railways were connecting ports to major industrial cities. ⁴ .... This rise in the number of fish and chip shops shows that the Industrial Revolution was fuelled by fish and chips!

⁵ .... According to one historian, 'the government knew it was vital to keep families on the home front in good heart' – and giving them fish and chips helped! During World War II, the government acknowledged the power of this traditional dish again, and made sure fish and chips weren't included in the wartime ration* book.

Today fish and chips is still one of the most popular fast-food takeaways in the UK, with about 10,500 'chippies' selling nearly 276 million meals a year. Some people eat them as a lunchtime snack, others as an evening meal, and a few people actually serve them at wedding banquets! They're also a popular 'comfort food' in tough times, which might explain the rise in sales during the economic crisis.

At Hammond's chip shop, the queue is getting smaller now. I watch the locals trudging back home through wind and rain, clutching their wrapped-up portions, and feel a sense of continuity, belonging and pride. ⁶ .... Fish and chips are a great British tradition with a fascinating history; a tradition which, like many others, has its origins elsewhere.

Glossary
* ration: a fixed amount of food

45
50
55
60
65
70
75

7 Complete the text with the nouns in exercise 5.

THE BEST OF BRITISH?

The British have an unfortunate reputation for bland food. The question is, why?

The 1940s have a lot to answer for in terms of Britain's culinary reputation. When food rationing started in 1939, every family got a wartime ¹ .... of meat, cheese, eggs, butter and sugar – even bread and potatoes were in short supply. With such limited ingredients, people cooked small, unimaginative meals in their homes – there were no double ² .... or supersized treats! Meat and two vegetables were standard ³ ...., usually followed by sponge pudding and custard. Lunchtime ⁴ .... were often warmed-up leftovers from the previous day's dinner.

Eating out was less adventurous, too. During the same period, 'British Restaurants' selling cheap basic meals were set up by the government, and their most popular ⁵ .... was soup, mashed potato and minced meat. There were no Chinese or Indian fast-food ⁶ .... – just plain fish and chips. There were few grand meals to celebrate special events. At one 1940s wedding ⁷ ...., boiled tongue and beetroot were served to the lucky guests.

But on the positive side, the health of the nation improved, as everyone ate a lot more vegetables than we do today!

The passive: verbs with two objects

8 Study the pairs of passive sentences in 1 and 2. Is there any difference in meaning between the sentences? Why are there two passive forms for these sentences? Write the active sentence for each pair.

1 a Fish fried in batter was introduced to England by Jewish immigrants.
 b England was introduced to fish fried in batter by Jewish immigrants.
2 a We were given the chipped potato by either France or Belgium.
 b The chipped potato was given to us by either France or Belgium.

Reference and practice 8.3 | Workbook page 124

9 Rewrite the passive questions in another way. Use the words in brackets.

1 Which foreign foods have been introduced to your country? (has your country)
2 Have you ever had food from other cultures cooked for you? (has food from)
3 When was the last time you were taught a new recipe? (a new recipe was)
4 Are you given free food samples in your supermarket? (are free food samples)
5 How often are 'classic' dishes made for you at home? (how often are you)

10 SPEAKING Ask and answer the questions in exercise 9. Find out more information by asking *who, what, why, where* and *when* questions.

Vocabulary bank | Ways of cooking page 141

1 **SPEAKING** **Think about the places you can buy food where you live and answer the questions.**

  1 Is there much food from different cultures and traditions? Give examples.
  2 Does trying new food show that we accept other cultures? Why / why not?

2 **Read the for and against essay. Which question does it answer?**

  1 In the future, more and more people will become vegetarian. What would be the pros and cons of giving up meat?
  2 We should put food ethics before affordability, health or anything else. Discuss.
  3 The impact of globalization on our diet is more positive than negative. Discuss.

STRATEGY

Talking about cause and effect

When you write a for and against essay, you need to look at the pros and cons, or costs and benefits, of different ideas. In order to write about them, you need to use the language of cause and effect.

3 **Study the highlighted phrases in the for and against essay. Which introduce a cause and which introduce an effect?**

4 **Which of the phrases below introduce a cause and which introduce an effect?**

  ■ owing to ■ as ■ therefore ■ hence ■ the effect of ■ for this reason

5 **Make as many sentences as you can with the phrases below.**

It's difficult to decide where to eat	since	his vegetarian diet.
We grabbed a burger at a fast-food restaurant	due to	too much choice!
The food was grown locally	result in	she lived to a ripe old age.
Eating too much fast food can	hence	we didn't have much time.
They couldn't make spaghetti bolognese	owing to	obesity and heart disease.
She had a Mediterranean diet	consequently	they'd run out of pasta.
He lost a lot of weight	as	it had a smaller carbon footprint.

The passive with reporting verbs

6 We can also make passive sentences with reporting verbs, such as *know, believe, think, claim, consider, understand* and *report*. Study sentences 1–5 in the for and against essay and match them to the rules.

  a *It* + passive (past or present) + *that* ...., ...
  b Subject + passive (past or present) + *to do something* ....
  c Subject + passive (past or present) + *to have done something* ....
  d Subject + passive (past or present) + *to be doing something* ....

Reference and practice 8.4 | Workbook page 124

7 **Rewrite the sentences to make them more impersonal. Use the passive and the verbs in brackets.**

  1 The first Indian curry appeared in a British cookbook in the eighteenth century. (believe)
  It ....
  2 At the time, people said spicy food was good for your health. (consider)
  At the time, spicy food ....
  3 Today, Indian curries have changed to accommodate British tastes. (know)
  Today, Indian curries ....
  4 A restaurant in Glasgow invented chicken tikka masala. (think)
  It ....
  5 Last year, chicken tikka masala was Britain's most popular dish. (report)
  Last year, it ....
  6 Today, supermarkets are selling more ready-made curries than ever before. (said)
  Today, supermarkets ....

[1]It is often said that globalization has had a positive impact on our food, giving us more adventurous diets and promoting international understanding. However, globalization has also resulted in problems, especially in relation to the environment and health. In this essay I intend to examine both the positive and negative aspects of globalization.

One advantage of globalization is variety in our supermarkets, which means more exciting meals. In the 1950s, [2]the average British supermarket is thought to have stocked fewer than 700 different items, whereas nowadays supermarkets have around 35,000. At the moment, [3]one supermarket is believed to be selling more than seventy different varieties of coffee! But this huge amount of choice has an environmental cost. Due to advances in technology and transportation, most foods are available all year round and are often shipped hundreds of miles. Consequently, there has been an increase in the carbon footprint of our food thanks to these out-of-season products.

A second advantage of globalization is the variety of restaurants on our high streets. Eating food from different cultures can help to promote tolerance and understanding. [4]London, for example, is known to have restaurants from more than 200 different countries. Many Londoners are more open and broad-minded on account of this diversity. However, since America has the biggest global influence, there are cheap American-style fast-food restaurants on the high streets, too. [5]It is claimed that one American fast-food restaurant chain welcomes 1% of the world's population in 188 different countries every day. This has led to a rise in poor eating habits and obesity.

To sum up, globalization has had some positive influences on our diet, especially in terms of cultural exchange. However, because of environmental costs and the dominance of fast-food restaurants, it is clear that the negatives outweigh the positives. It is time to return to home-grown food and local cuisine.

WRITING GUIDE

- **Task** Choose a different topic in exercise 2 and write a for and against essay about it.

- **Ideas** Make notes about:

Essay 1
- the health benefits of eating less meat.
- the environmental advantages.
- the challenges of a vegetarian diet.
- the health benefits of eating more vegetables.

Essay 2
- food ethics (give examples of ethical and unethical food).
- why people might choose unethical food.
- the consequences of eating unethical food.
- how people can make more ethical / better choices.

- **Plan** Follow the plan:

Paragraph 1: Introduction: state the subject of the essay, summarize the main areas you want to cover, and state your purpose.

Paragraph 2: Present your first argument for or against and any counter-arguments.

Paragraph 3: Present your second argument for or against and any counter-arguments.

Paragraph 4: Conclusion: sum up the main arguments and restate your opinion.

- **Write** Write your essay. Use the paragraph plan to help you.

- **Check** Check the following points:

- Is the development of your argument clear? Have you used cause and effect language?
- Have you presented a balanced argument? Have you included all the points you want to cover?
- Have you used neutral language?
- Have you checked grammar, vocabulary, spelling and punctuation?

Vocabulary insight 8 Dependent prepositions

1 Read the extract. Identify the parts of speech in the highlighted words.

> ¹Based on current evidence, marine biologists predict that losing this caretaker could bring about a significant ²rise in the number of smaller predators like stingrays. This would ³result in fewer fish, and also fewer shellfish, which keep the seas and oceans clean. An ⁴imbalance in the food chain could ultimately ⁵lead to the ⁶collapse of the underwater ecosystem, with a reduced fish population and more pollution. Everything and everyone who ⁷depends on the ocean for a living, or simply for recreation, would suffer. It'd be an environmental disaster with countless consequences for us all.

STRATEGY

Dependent prepositions

Many English nouns, verbs and adjectives are followed by specific prepositions. These prepositions are called dependent prepositions because the kind of preposition that is used depends on the word and its meaning. When you come across a new word, always check which prepositions it goes with and how they change the meaning of the word.

2 Read the strategy above. Then study the dictionary entry for *rise* and answer the questions.

> **rise** 0ᴍ /raɪz/ noun, verb
> ■ *noun*
> ▸ INCREASE **1** 0ᴍ [C] an increase in an amount, a number or a level: *The industry is feeling the effects of recent price rises.* ◇ **~ in sth** *There has been a sharp rise in the number of people out of work.* ⊃ LANGUAGE BANK at INCREASE **2** 0ᴍ [C] (*BrE*)
> ▸ IN POWER/IMPORTANCE **3** 0ᴍ [sing.] **~ (of sb/sth)** the act of becoming more important, successful, powerful, etc: *the rise of fascism in Europe* ◇ *the **rise and fall** of the British Empire* ◇ *her meteoric **rise to power***

1 What part of speech is *rise* in this entry?
2 Which prepositions does it go with?
3 How do the prepositions change the meaning of *rise*?

STRATEGY

Dependent prepositions: patterns

Dependent prepositions can follow many patterns. The most common are:
a verb + preposition + object
b verb + preposition + object + preposition
c verb + direct object + preposition + indirect object
d noun + preposition + noun / -*ing* form
e noun + preposition + noun + preposition
f adjective + preposition

3 Read the strategy. Then match the highlighted words in the extract in exercise 1 to patterns a–f in the strategy. There is no example for one of the patterns.

4 Use a dictionary to check the dependent prepositions for the words below. Pay attention to the patterns in the strategy. Then check the meaning of the words.

1 (be) better / worse ....
2 pay (sb) .... (sth)
   pay .... cash
   pay .... credit card
   pay sth .... (sb)
   pay .... (a loan, a mortgage, etc.)
3 imbalance .... / .... sth
   imbalance .... A and B
4 fork ....
   fork .... sth .... / ....
   sth
5 save sth .... (................... sth)

5 Complete the sentences with the correct prepositions.

1 I recently noticed an imbalance .... my account. More seems to be going out than coming in.
2 The imbalance .... the economies of the developed and developing countries is staggering. Something needs to be done about it.
3 We forked .... a fortune .... our new house; now we need to ask for a loan to do it up.
4 The bank manager told me I wouldn't get a new credit card until I paid .... all my loans.
5 Our family will be better .... once I go back to work.
6 I'm saving all my money ....
   .... a trip around the world.
7 We don't take credit cards, so you'll need to pay .... cash.

6 Use a dictionary to check if the highlighted words in exercise 1 go with any other prepositions. Then write your own example sentences with each word and preposition that you find.

   Dictionary entry from *Oxford Advanced Learner's Dictionary* 8ᵉ, Oxford University Press 2010.

Vocabulary

1 Match the synonyms below. Then complete the text with the pairs of synonyms.

■ awe-inspiring ■ banned ■ countless ■ distressing
■ huge ■ impressive ■ kill ■ monstrous ■ numerous
■ outlawed ■ slaughter ■ upsetting

Whales are some of the most ¹........................ /
.... animals that live in the sea.
Although whale hunting has been ² .... /
.... in most places, some countries still
³ .... / .... them for their meat.
The mammals don't stand a chance against the
⁴ .... / .... fishing boats that go
after them. As a result, ⁵ .... /
.... species are already in danger of extinction. It's
⁶ .... / .... to think that one day
these magnificent creatures might disappear.

Marks .... / 6

2 Complete the text with the correct prepositions.

Most doctors recommend a diet based ¹ ....
the five main food groups. However, recently there
has been a rise ² .... the number of vegetarians
in the UK. The reasons for their choice depend
³ .... a number of factors. 'Classic' vegetarians
feel empathy ⁴ .... the animals that are killed.
'Green eaters' are concerned ⁵ .... the impact
of eating meat on the environment. And, there are
people who feel that they are better ⁶ ....
without meat for health reasons.

Marks .... / 6

3 Complete the sentences with phrases with *face* and the words in brackets.

1 Most animals try to protect themselves ....
.... (danger)
2 Although the hiker had hurt his foot, he ....
.... and went on walking. (brave)
3 We can .... , but we'll never agree. (blue)
4 It's time for you to ....
and admit what you have done. (music)
5 .... , you didn't want
to give up meat in the first place. (it)
6 Why don't you .... ? You're
overweight because you eat too much fast food. (fact)

Marks .... / 6

4 Match the words in A to the words in B to make collocations.

A ■ fast-food ■ lunchtime ■ popular ■ standard
■ traditional ■ wedding
B ■ banquet ■ dish ■ fare ■ order ■ snack ■ takeaway

1 ....   4 ....
2 ....   5 ....
3 ....   6 ....

Marks .... / 6

Grammar

5 Complete the text with the correct passive form of the verbs in brackets.

During the 1970s, scientists discovered that the ozone layer
¹ .... (destroy). One of the main factors
contributing to the problem was the use of CFC gases. Up
until then, these gases ² .... (use) in
refrigerators, air conditioning and aerosol sprays. In 1988,
CFCs ³ .... (ban) at an international
convention in Montreal. Since then, alternatives to CFCs
⁴ .... (develop), which do not damage
the ozone layer. Currently, measures to control the use
of CFCs ⁵ .... (implement) under the
Montreal Protocol and the Kyoto Protocol. According to
these agreements, CFCs ⁶ .... (phase
out) completely by 2030. Unfortunately, the regulations
⁷ .... (not follow) by all of the countries
in the world.

Marks .... / 7

6 Complete sentence b so that it has a similar meaning to sentence a. Use *to be* or *being* + past participle.

1 a She hopes that they'll offer her a place on the course.
  b She hopes ....
2 a My dog enjoys it when I take it for a walk.
  b My dog enjoys ....
3 a Some people want the government to ban hunting.
  b Some people want ....
4 a How can farmers prevent people stealing their animals?
  b How can farmers prevent .... ?
5 a They expect someone will beat them at the next election.
  b They expect ....
6 a He only cares about the money his company makes.
  b He only cares about ....

Marks .... / 6

7 Write two passive sentences for each active one.

1 Someone introduced them to me at a party.
  a ....
  b ....
2 They give all visitors a bag for their rubbish.
  a ....
  b ....
3 They might send you the tickets by courier.
  a ....
  b ....
4 The teacher is showing us a new documentary.
  a ....
  b ....

Marks .... / 8

Total .... / 45

1 ⊙ **2.20** You are going to listen to a radio programme about the first stem cell burger. Look at the notes below and try to predict the missing information. Then listen to the recording and complete the notes.

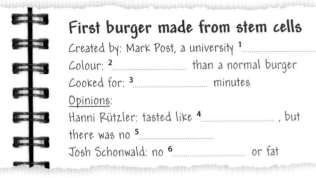

First burger made from stem cells

Created by: Mark Post, a university [1] ....
Colour: [2] .... than a normal burger
Cooked for: [3] .... minutes
Opinions:
Hanni Rützler: tasted like [4] .... , but there was no [5] ....
Josh Schonwald: no [6] .... or fat

2 ⊙ **2.20** Listen again. Are the sentences true (T) or false (F)?

1 Meat production is said to be one of the contributing factors of climate change.
2 Research for the lab burger was carried out in the USA.
3 The lab burger looked exactly like a normal burger.
4 The chef didn't notice any difference in the smell of a lab burger and a normal burger when cooking.
5 Stem cells for meat can be obtained from any part of a cow.
6 Producing meat in a lab is a costly and time-consuming process.

Speaking

3 Work in pairs. Look at the photos and discuss how the fruit is sourced in each case.

4 Work in pairs. Decide what is the most a) practical, b) economical and c) environmentally-friendly way for a family to eat fruit. Give reasons for your answers.

Reading

5 Make a list of the pros and cons of eating insects. Then read the article and compare your ideas. What other pros and cons does it list?

Anyone for a grasshopper sandwich?

A Two billion people already eat bugs as part of their regular diet, according to the United Nation's Food and Agriculture Organization (FAO). Most people in Europe, however, reject the idea of entomophagy, the technical term for the human consumption of insects. The activity is usually associated with the grim tasks set for celebrities in the jungle on reality shows. If citizens of Europe are going to have to start eating insects to combat world hunger, as the FAO has suggested, somebody will have to persuade them that it is a good idea.

B The main barrier to the proposal is consumer disgust. A plate of locusts in a salad, where they look as if they are about to jump up at you, is more likely to put European diners off their food than encourage them to try it. One approach to dealing with this obstacle is to disguise the insects contained in the food by grinding them into a powder to make 'protein flour'. This process is already underway at an insect farm in Malaga, Spain, which makes fishmeal for fish farms on the Andalusian coast. But 'protein flour' can potentially be used in food meant for human consumption as well.

C However, there are those who would rather see insects served in their original shape and form. René Redzepi, chef and co-founder of the world's most fashionable restaurant, Noma in Copenhagen, regularly includes insects on the menu. Redzepi's research unit, Nordic Food Lab, does experiments into insect 'deliciousness'. Researchers at the

Literature insight 4 Workbook page 90

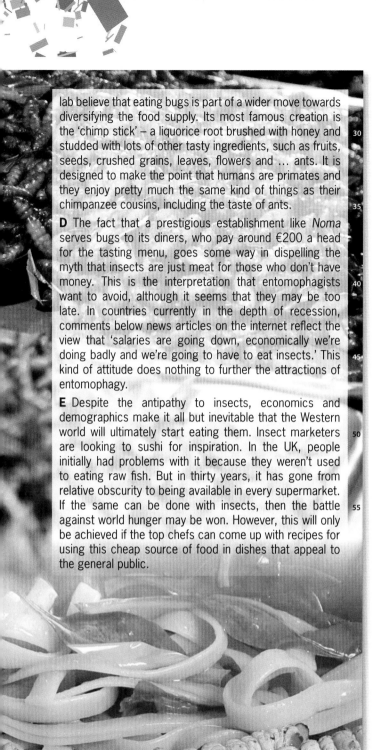

lab believe that eating bugs is part of a wider move towards diversifying the food supply. Its most famous creation is the 'chimp stick' – a liquorice root brushed with honey and studded with lots of other tasty ingredients, such as fruits, seeds, crushed grains, leaves, flowers and … ants. It is designed to make the point that humans are primates and they enjoy pretty much the same kind of things as their chimpanzee cousins, including the taste of ants.

D The fact that a prestigious establishment like *Noma* serves bugs to its diners, who pay around €200 a head for the tasting menu, goes some way in dispelling the myth that insects are just meat for those who don't have money. This is the interpretation that entomophagists want to avoid, although it seems that they may be too late. In countries currently in the depth of recession, comments below news articles on the internet reflect the view that 'salaries are going down, economically we're doing badly and we're going to have to eat insects.' This kind of attitude does nothing to further the attractions of entomophagy.

E Despite the antipathy to insects, economics and demographics make it all but inevitable that the Western world will ultimately start eating them. Insect marketers are looking to sushi for inspiration. In the UK, people initially had problems with it because they weren't used to eating raw fish. But in thirty years, it has gone from relative obscurity to being available in every supermarket. If the same can be done with insects, then the battle against world hunger may be won. However, this will only be achieved if the top chefs can come up with recipes for using this cheap source of food in dishes that appeal to the general public.

6 Read the article again and choose the correct answers.

1 Where can ground insects currently be found?
a in processed food
b in salad dressings
c in bread-making products
d in animal feed

2 What is the logic behind Nordic Food Lab's 'chimp stick'?
a Eating insects is chic.
b Eating insects is natural.
c Eating insects is delicious.
d Eating insects is unnatural.

3 Which of the following is stated in the article as a fact, not an opinion?
a Westerners aren't used to eating insects because chefs don't know how to cook them.
b Eating insects is confined to those who cannot afford anything else.
c People in the West have a different attitude to eating insects from the rest of the world.
d Only professional chefs know how to make insects look appetizing.

4 What do insects and sushi have in common?
a Neither is traditionally part of the western diet.
b Both are prepared in the same way.
c Both are relatively inexpensive.
d Neither is currently popular with consumers.

Grammar

7 Complete the sentences with the correct form of the words in brackets and any additional words if necessary.

1 Drift net fishing catches other sea creatures as well as fish. Environmentalists think .... (nets / should / ban).

2 Pizza originated in Naples, Italy. It .... (bring / America / immigrants).

3 If my brother had gone to university, he .... (might / become / engineer).

4 Julia wouldn't be so miserable if she .... (not / lose / job).

5 The thief (must / have / key) .... because the front door is open.

6 If you're going to work in Moscow, then you (better / learn / speak) .... some Russian before you go.

7 I used to hate wearing glasses when I was little, but now I (get / used / it) ....

8 The author decided to take a break because (she / write / dawn) ....

9 You're late. (who / stop / talk) .... on the way home?

10 This time tomorrow (I / arrive / Paris) .... I'm really looking forward to my trip.

Writing

8 Write a for and against essay on the topic below.

People in my country should start eating insects. Discuss.

9 Technology

Reading and vocabulary What's new?

1 SPEAKING Make a list of technologies that you use now, but did not use five years ago. How have these changes in technology affected your life? Then read the article. What technologies from your list does the writer mention?

STRATEGY

Making inferences

Writers sometimes leave out ideas that do not need to be explained. This is to keep the focus of the text on the most important information.

In order to understand the missing information, you will need to make guesses called *inferences*. Inferences are made based on information in the text and the reader's own knowledge about the world.

---

2 Read the strategy. Are the sentences true (T) or false (F)? Is the information stated or implied?

1 The writer first found out about mobile social networking from her mother.
2 The webcams in the writer's house were usually used to keep in touch with her international friends.
3 It was difficult for video conferencing companies to become successful in the mid-1990s.
4 The writer's mother had a business selling pens.
5 The writer is one year older than her sister.
6 Successful technology doesn't appeal to the writer's mother as much as technology that might be successful in the future.
7 The writer enjoyed her first taste of augmented reality glasses.
8 The writer is now a technology addict because of her upbringing.

V insight Word analysis

3 Answer the questions, referring closely to the article.

1 Which phrase says that something could be successful? What is it referring to? (B)
2 Which phrase means *speak quietly to calm someone down*? (C)
3 Which phrase says that something started with a lot of noise to grab people's attention? (D)
4 Which word does the writer use to say that the businesses failed? Why did they fail? (D)
5 Which phrase means that people have caught up with the world described in the mother's slogan? Why did the mother laugh? (E)
6 Which word says that something was made for a particular purpose? (F)
7 Which phrase expresses the writer's negative feelings about the new phone? (H)
8 Which phrase means *distinguishing features of someone interested in technology*? (I)

The next big thing

A In 2007, my mom's new favorite phrase was 'mobile social networking'. It was a big thing in Asia and Africa, she told me.

'What is it supposed to be?' I asked.

She said you joined a social network on your phone, and then you could express opinions about things. You could send something to your friends, and they would say if they liked it or they didn't like it – on their phones.

'That sounds really stupid,' I said.

B But, as I don't think I need to stress, the idea turned out to have legs. In my defence, the first iPhone was still six months away. And though I was one of the first few million users of Facebook, the 'Like' button wouldn't come along for years.

C The future arrived much earlier in our house than anywhere else because my mother is an emerging technologies consultant. She has lived by her unusual ability to see beyond the glitchy demos of new tech to the faint outlines of another reality, just over the horizon. She takes these new-born ideas in her arms, murmurs reassurances, and runs as fast as she can into the unknown.

D In the mid-1990s, video conferencing was my mom's thing. I grew up in a house full of webcams displaying pictures of strangers in Hong Kong, New York and the Netherlands, to whom I'd have to wave when I got home from school. My mother worked with companies who wanted to develop software and hardware for video conferencing, and she wrote reports about the state of the market, which, at that point, was a slender stream of early adopters. Internet connections were so slight, and the hardware so bulky and expensive, that it was slow going. Tech start-ups launched with fanfare and sank within months.

E But my mom is a futurist, that peculiar subclass of optimists who believe they can see the day after tomorrow coming. In the 1990s, she ordered pens customized with her consultancy name and the slogan: 'Remember when we could only hear each other?' Years later, when an unopened box of them surfaced in her office, she laughed and laughed. It would be another several years before Skype with video brought the rest of the world up to speed with her pens.

F In 2004, the year I went to college, I took a video phone with me. It was a silvery chunk of plastic with a handset on a cord, a keypad, and

Vocabulary: word analysis; technology; phrases with *under*; adverbs
with two forms; evidence verbs
Grammar: reported speech; verb patterns in reported speech

Speaking: giving a presentation
Writing: a report

9A

a four-inch screen on a hinge on which I could see
my family every week or so. The next year, when
my sister went away to college, she did not take
one. That fateful Skype release had occurred in the
intervening twelve months, and the days of dedicated
hardware were through.

G Strangely enough, after the video revolution came,
it no longer seemed to interest my mom. I had not
fully grasped it until that point, but her interest was in
premature things – full of potential, unready to take
their place in the world, in need of her talents. Unlike
almost every consumer of technology, for her, and
for a few others like her, the sleek final product held
much less interest, except as a sign that their instincts
had been correct.

H These days, the devices strewn around my
parents' apartment are augmented-reality glasses
and headsets. Mom's latest projects include turning
a city's publicly available data into an app that
lets people see the transit system or sewer pipes
projected over the reality before them. She's been
talking to hang-gliders and hot-air-balloonists about
whether they would like to see the wind unfurling
across the sky ahead. And years before Google Glass
was even on the horizon, my mom had me try out
a pair of glasses that were to provide an immersive
movie theater experience. (The earbuds mounted on
the frames, I regret to say, had not been designed
with young women in mind.) But while there have
been some industry successes – mainly in the form
of games – augmented reality is going through an
awkward adolescent phase. It's good for PR stunts,
like the billboard that went up in Stockholm a couple
of years ago and let passers-by win McDonald's
food by playing ping-pong with their smartphones.
But will there ever be, as my mom thinks, a secret
digital world underlying the real one, visible through
your phone, and soon, she hopes, through glasses?
Several months ago I went to a release party for a
phone loaded with augmented reality features, and
the demo was a groan-inducing animation. We're not
there yet.

I Sometimes I think I could sell my services to these
people with the tagline: 'I come from the future.'
I don't have all the hallmarks of a standard techie:
my cell phone lives peacefully unconnected to
the internet, and I belong to relatively few social
networks, but I am from a bubble in time, a place
where these things have always existed. I can tell you
what users are going to want, because I have seen,
over the course of my short life, so many things fail,
and so many unlikely things succeed.

4 Complete the sentences with the correct form of the words and phrases in exercise 3.

1 The report will bring you .... on this year's emerging technology.

2 She .... about the new product's potential and he soon felt much more confident that it ....

3 We need a .... phone for emergencies so that people can contact us at all times.

4 The company .... because people were annoyed by its .... adverts and didn't buy its products.

5 One of the .... of a good marketing executive is being able to .... a new product ....

V Technology nouns

5 Study the highlighted words in the article. Then complete the text with the correct singular or plural form of the words.

Technology giants like Apple and Google and thousands of small ¹............... around the world are trying to come up with the next big thing. Here's a quick round-up of the ²............... that we think will be big in the next few years.

Augmented reality glasses
Some ³............... are already wearing these incredible glasses, which can make phone calls, use the internet, respond to voice commands and take photos. Instead of using ⁴............... for audio, the glasses vibrate the bones in your ear. Will they one day replace our mobile phone ⁵............... ? Only time will tell.

Brain-controlled games
Once you needed a long ⁶............... to connect your controller to your games console. Now most controllers are wireless, and soon even they may be a thing of the past. Instead, you'll wear a ⁷............... with brain sensors positioned over different parts of your head, which will pick up your thoughts and use them to control video games.

Airwriting gloves
Pressing buttons on the ⁸............... of your mobile can be a frustrating way to write messages, so these gloves may be just what you've been waiting for. Write in the air, and your message will appear on screen.

6 SPEAKING Work in pairs. Discuss the questions.

1 Compare the writer's attitude to technology with her mother's. What different attitudes to technology do people in your family have?

2 What technologies do you know of that were popular for a short time and then abandoned?

3 Which of the technologies that you currently use would be hardest to live without? Why?

4 Which of the things described in exercise 5, or other emerging technologies that you know about, will be most popular in the future? Why?

| **Vocabulary bank** | Describing gadgets page 142 |
| **DVD extra** | Robot cars |

1 🔘 **2.21** SPEAKING Work in pairs. What do you need to become a good scientist or inventor? Put these things in order of importance and add your own ideas. Then listen to the radio programme. Which of the things in the list apply to Kelvin Doe?

- original ideas ▪ a university degree
- access to a laboratory ▪ enthusiasm ▪ hard work
- encouraging parent / teacher ▪ money for research

Reported speech

2 🔘 **2.21** Rewrite the statements and questions in reported speech using the words in brackets. Then listen again and check.

1 'My interest <u>started</u> five years ago.' (Kelvin told me that)

2 'By the age of thirteen I <u>had invented</u> a new type of battery.' (He said that)

3 'Why <u>did you want</u> a home-made battery?' (I asked him)

4 'I <u>have</u> a whole team of kids working for me.' (He told me)

5 'I <u>am visiting</u> an American university for three weeks so <u>I'll be able to learn</u> from the professors there.' (He said)

6 'I <u>must do</u> three more years of high school before I <u>can think</u> about a degree.' (He said that)

7 '<u>Have you decided</u> on your next invention?' (I asked him)

8 'I <u>would like to build</u> solar panels.' (He told me that)

9 'Sierra Leone <u>should have</u> a lot more solar power.' (He said)

3 Study the examples in exercise 2 and answer the questions.

1 Look at the underlined verbs. Which tenses and modal verbs usually change in reported speech? To what? Which tenses and modals do not change?

2 What other types of words often change?

3 How is the word order in direct questions and reported questions different?

4 Which word, apart from *if*, can introduce a *yes* / *no* reported question?

| **Reference and practice 9.1** | Workbook page 125 |

4 Rewrite the sentences in reported speech.

1 'Have you had fun at our university?' they asked Kelvin.
2 'I'll never forget my fantastic experience here,' he replied.
3 'I'd never seen technology equipment like this before I came to the USA,' he told them.
4 'I must thank the professors for their help,' he said.
5 'I'd like to learn more from them in the future,' he said.
6 'I can't wait to see my family again,' he admitted.
7 'When are you going home?' they asked.
8 'I should be there tomorrow, if there aren't any problems with my flight,' he told them.

5 Study these examples of reported speech from the recording. Change them into direct speech. Then answer questions 1 and 2.

a Experts say that we don't have enough science and technology students in our universities.
b Maybe in a few years he'll tell us that his solar inventions are powering the whole of Sierra Leone!

1 Do tenses change in reported speech when the reporting verb is in the present simple, present perfect or future?
2 What types of words do change?

6 Complete the text using the correct form of the words in brackets.

The prestigious Intel Science Talent Search has announced that this year's winner
[1] _____ (be) seventeen-year-old Sara Volz from Colorado, USA. She has won $100,000 in prize money for her work developing algae biofuel in the laboratory under her bed. This is great news for Sara, and also for the Research Science Institute (RSI) which has supported her in her research.

RSI is a six-week summer programme based in Boston, USA, for young people with a passion for technology, engineering and mathematics. It says that many of its students
[2] _____ (have) success in national science competitions over the years. Before this year's programme ended, I met some students and asked them [3] _____ (what / be / RSI) all about.

Sixteen-year-old Matt Coraccio from Utah explained that their programme [4] _____ (include) lectures from Nobel prize winners and other distinguished scientists, and its students
[5] _____ (must) conduct a significant amount of original research. He told me that he
[6] _____ (do) research into cancer treatment in a state-of-the-art university laboratory and
[7] _____ (can / ask) for help from experienced scientists whenever he wanted. He said that he [8] _____ (would / never / get) access to that kind of expertise without RSI.

Another student I spoke to was seventeen-year-old Marta Borowska from Poland. When I asked her if [9] _____ (there / be) many students from outside the USA on the programme, she replied that about 40% [10] _____ (come) from abroad. She said that more international students [11] _____ (should / apply), because the programme [12] _____ (will / give) them the opportunity to meet an amazing group of keen young scientists. She explained that the best eighty applicants from around the world [13] _____ (be selected) and [14] _____ (can / attend) the programme for free.

7 SPEAKING Work in pairs. Student A is one of the young scientists or inventors mentioned on pages 110 and 111. Student B is a news reporter. Conduct an interview. Then report your interview to another pair.

1 SPEAKING Read the newspaper article.
Do you think it was fair that Connor could
not work for Cisco? Why / why not?

TWEETED OUT OF A JOB

When twenty-two-year-old Connor Riley was offered a job at
tech company Cisco, her first instinct was to tweet about it.
Her Twitter message said, 'Now I have to weigh the utility of
a fatty pay cheque against the daily commute to San Jose and
hating the work.' A Cisco employee saw the message and told
the person that had hired her how Connor felt. The job offer was
withdrawn immediately.

2 ⊚ **2.22** Listen to a radio programme. What is a digital footprint?
What problems can it cause people?

3 ⊚ **2.22** Listen again and match the speakers, Donna (D), Mick (M) and Jenny (J),
to opinions 1–9. There are two opinions that you do not need.

1 If you wouldn't show something to your grandparents, you shouldn't put it online.
2 When people get in trouble because of their digital footprint, it's usually their own fault.
3 People shouldn't be punished just for 'liking' someone else's Facebook post.
4 It can be very difficult to control your digital footprint.
5 You should use your social media profile to show off your good points to universities and
employers.
6 Companies shouldn't be allowed to ask job applicants for their social media login details.
7 It's perfectly fair for universities to check your digital footprint during the selection process.
8 The bank worker who posted about her boss's salary shouldn't have lost her job.
9 It was fair that the crocodile wrestlers and the person with a headache got into trouble.

V Phrases with *under*

4 Complete the definitions with the words below.

■ attack ■ the radar ■ pressure ■ the weather ■ age ■ your belt ■ control ■ scrutiny

1 If people are looking carefully at something, it's **under** ....
2 If people are trying to destroy something, it's **under** ....
3 If you are dealing with something successfully, you've got it **under** ....
4 If you're feeling slightly ill, you're **under** ....
5 If you've acquired or experienced something useful, you've got it **under** ....
6 If you aren't old enough to do something, you're **under** ....
7 If someone is trying to make you do something, they're putting you **under** ....
8 If people haven't noticed something, it's **under** ....

5 Complete the sentences with the phrases in exercise 4.

1 This morning, Jack tweeted that he was feeling a bit .... He's staying in bed until he's
got his cold .... and doesn't need to blow his nose every five minutes!
2 My parents check my Facebook page every day. I hate being .... all the time, and now
they're putting me .... to delete my Facebook account, too. I feel as though my right
to free speech is ....
3 Muhammad Nizam, an Indian businessman, let his son drive his £127,000 Ferrari as a treat for
his ninth birthday, with no adults in the car. This .... driving might have slipped
.... of the police except for one thing – Nizam proudly posted a video of the event on
YouTube!
4 You've got some great work experience .... , but your tweets suggest that you are too
immature for a position in our company.

6 SPEAKING Work in pairs. Choose two opinions in exercise 3 and discuss them.

Vocabulary bank | Problems with technology page 142

Giving a presentation

7 **SPEAKING** Have you ever heard of an internet *cookie*? What is it? What does it do?

8 ⊙ **2.23** Listen to a presentation. What does the speaker want to ban? What three reasons does she give?

9 ⊙ **2.23** Complete the phrases from the presentation with the words below. Then listen again and check.

■ finish ■ happy ■ what ■ aim ■ point ■ questions ■ move ■ convinced

Stating the purpose of a presentation
In today's presentation, I'm going to talk about … .
The **1**............................ of my presentation is to … .
I'm here today to tell you about … .

Describing the structure of a presentation
First, I'm going to … . Then I'll … , followed by … .
I'll **2**............................ off with … .
There'll be some time for **3**............................ and answers once I've finished, so please hold any queries that you have until the end.

Moving between points
That's **4**............................ I'm going to talk about now.
I've just told you about … . Now I'm going to **5**............................ on to … .
I've got one final **6**............................ to make, and it regards … .
OK, that's all about … . I'd now like to look at … .

Concluding a presentation
To sum up, … .
In conclusion, … .
I hope my arguments have **7**............................ you that … .
Please feel free to ask any questions and I'll do my best to answer them.
If anyone has any questions, I'd be **8**............................ to answer them.

10 **SPEAKING** Plan a presentation about an aspect of technology that you would like to see banned. Include reasons to support your argument. Then give your presentation to the class.

1 SPEAKING Discuss the questions.

1 Which inventions have been most important in shaping the modern world? Agree on the top three.
2 Look at the planes in the photos. Which do you think could fly? Read the article and check.

2 Read the article. Then match statements 1–8 to planes A–C. There are two statements that you do not need.

1 It got a lot of attention before it flew.
2 Improvements were made to it after the inventor's death.
3 It spent many years outside its home country.
4 It made its inventor(s) rich.
5 It was designed by a government employee.
6 Its inventor(s) was/were also involved in another form of transport.
7 Its inventor(s) contributed to the construction of other planes.
8 It didn't survive long.

3 SPEAKING Work in pairs. Discuss the questions.

1 Do you think Whitehead will ever be widely recognized as the inventor of the plane? Why / why not?
2 Think of some famous inventors from your country. What have they achieved? Are they famous internationally? Why / why not?

V insight Adverbs with two forms

4 Match the highlighted adverbs in the article to meanings 1–10.

1 above the ground	7 near the end of a
2 to a high level	period of time
3 only	8 recently
4 fairly	9 near
5 with a lot of effort	10 very carefully
6 almost not	

5 Complete the text with the adverbs in exercise 4.

It's ¹......................... surprising that academics don't like the word 'inventor'. Most great inventions were possible because of previous, less famous inventions which, step by step, moved technology very ²......................... to that final breakthrough. And the person responsible for the last step is often impossible to identify, however ³......................... we try. Many of history's most famous inventors actually came up with their invention after someone else. The American Thomas Edison, for example, is known for inventing the electric light bulb ⁴......................... in the nineteenth century, but if you study his story ⁵........................., you'll find that the English scientist Humphry Davy created one seventy years earlier. Davy's invention wasn't terribly useful, however. The light burned out after ⁶......................... a few minutes, whereas Edison's could light a room for hours. So are we wrong to focus on 'firsts'? People say quite ⁷......................... that coming up with a concept for an important invention is a great achievement, but perhaps it's an even greater achievement to take a half-working concept and create something ⁸......................... useful with it.

The firsts and frauds of flight

For most of history, human flight was an impossible dream, but by the close of the 19th century, change was afoot. Several determined men were working hard on this emerging technology, and it was clear that
5 someone, somewhere, would soon develop a powered, controllable aircraft. Who would live on in history as the first to make this technological breakthrough? And would history reward the right man?

In the USA, the aviation inventor with the highest
10 profile was Samuel Pierpoint Langley. With financial support from the US government and the Smithsonian Institution – a group of museums and research centres founded in 1846 – he built the *Aerodrome*: a sixteen-metre plane with two pairs of wings, one behind the
15 other. On 7 October 1903, amid much fanfare, it was launched from a catapult on the Potomac River near Washington, D.C. It had hardly got airborne, however, before it crashed into the river and the pilot, Langley's assistant, was pulled – shaken but safe – from the
20 water. A second attempt, on 8 December 1903, ended with similar results.

A Langley's *Aerodrome*

Just nine days later, Orville and Wilbur Wright took their little biplane, the six-metre *Flyer* I, to Kitty Hawk Beach in North Carolina, USA. It soared above
25 the wind-swept sands, achieving a flight of fifty-nine seconds over a distance of 260 m. For the two brothers from Ohio, who had been quietly experimenting with flying machines in their bicycle shop for the last seven years, this was a proud moment.

30 But were they the first to achieve powered, controllable flight, as most history books say? Perhaps not. The rival to the crown is a German-born inventor called Gustave Whitehead (or Weisskopf). On 14 August 1901, more than two years before the Wright brothers' success,
35 Whitehead is thought to have flown his bat-like *Number 21* plane in Connecticut, USA. The flight, which went fifteen metres high and covered 800 m, included a turn to avoid some trees. ¹It was witnessed by the editor of the local newspaper, and articles around the
40 world soon congratulated Whitehead on inventing a successful aircraft.

B Whitehead's *Number 21*

So why are the Wright brothers highly respected inventors, and Whitehead a forgotten footnote in the annals of aviation history? The explanation is a sorry story of bad luck. ²Some people <u>criticized</u> Whitehead for not producing photographic evidence of his first flight, and <u>refused</u> to believe that it had really happened. ³They <u>advised</u> him to organize photos of his next flights, which took place close to New York in January 1902, but bad weather made the photos unusable. He had nowhere indoors to store his plane, and it was destroyed in the harsh winter. Then he ran into financial difficulties after a dispute with his business partner, and had to build engines for other people's aircraft to make ends meet. He returned to his own aviation designs too late: by then, the Wright brothers' achievement at Kitty Hawk had taken centre stage.

However, there is another, darker reason for Whitehead's obscurity. Fast-forward to 1914. Wilbur Wright was now dead, and so was Langley, who had failed to fly his *Aerodrome* despite the backing of the Smithsonian. The Smithsonian's director had been a long-time friend of Langley's and wanted him remembered with honour. He hired an engineer to reconstruct the *Aerodrome* and prove that it could really fly. After a lot of modifications to the machine, this was achieved, and Langley's aircraft was given pride of place in the Smithsonian's museum as the world's first successful plane.

Orville Wright was understandably furious at this misrepresentation of history. ⁴He <u>insisted</u> on exhibiting his own plane, *Flyer 1*, not at the Smithsonian but at the Science Museum in Britain. ⁵In 1948, after lengthy negotiations to bring *Flyer 1* home to the USA, the Smithsonian finally <u>admitted</u> making the changes to Langley's plane. ⁶They <u>agreed</u> by contract not to state that any aircraft prior to the Wright plane of 1903 had achieved controlled powered flight.

Lately, experts have looked closely at the evidence for Gustave Whitehead's flight of 1901. ⁷Many have concluded that his claims were genuine, but the Smithsonian <u>insists</u> that his flight never happened. It seems that the Wright brothers' place in history may not have been won justly, through the agreement of the scientific world, but by a lawyer's contract.

C The Wright brothers' *Flyer 1*

Verb patterns in reported speech

6 Study sentences 1–7 in the article. Then complete rules a–g below. Which verbs can be used in more than one of these structures?

We can use several different structures to report people's speech:

a verb + *that* + reported statement: *admit, agree, announce, apologize, boast, claim, confess, deny, explain, promise, say, ...*

b verb + object + *that* + reported statement: *remind, tell, warn*

c verb + infinitive with *to*: *demand, offer, promise, ..., ...*

d verb + object + infinitive with *to*: *ask, beg, encourage, forbid, invite, order, persuade, remind, tell, warn, ...*

e verb + gerund: *deny, recommend, suggest, ...*

f verb + preposition + gerund: *apologize for, boast of / about, confess to, ... on*

g verb + object + preposition + gerund: *accuse (someone) of, warn (someone) against, ... (someone) on, ... (someone) for*

| Reference and practice 9.2 | Workbook page 126 |

7 Rewrite the direct speech as reported speech using the most suitable reporting verb. There are two verbs that you do not need. Sometimes more than one pattern is possible.

■ deny ■ forbid ■ apologize ■ boast ■ order ■ suggest ■ invite ■ encourage ■ announce ■ refuse ■ agree ■ accuse

1 'We're creating a brilliant new social networking website,' said the Winklevoss twins, Cameron and Tyler.
2 'Let's talk to Mark Zuckerberg about this,' they said.
3 'Would you like to work for our tech start-up?' they said to Zuckerberg.
4 'OK, I'll write the code for your website,' said Zuckerberg.
5 'It would be great if you could do it quickly,' said the twins.
6 'I'm sorry that I'm taking a long time to finish the work,' said Zuckerberg.
7 'Zuckerberg has set up a social networking site called Facebook,' said the newspaper.
8 'You stole our idea, Zuckerberg,' said the twins.
9 'I didn't do anything wrong,' said Zuckerberg.
10 'Zuckerberg, give the Winklevoss twins $65 million in Facebook shares,' said the courts.

8 SPEAKING Work in pairs. Discuss the questions.
1 Are today's inventors recognized in the same way as the inventors of the past? Why / why not?
2 Is photographic evidence still the best way to prove that you've done what you say you've done? Why / why not?

1 SPEAKING Look at the photos. Which of these technologies are used in your school? Would you like to be able to use the other technologies in class? Why / why not?

2 Read the report and put paragraphs A–E in the correct order by matching them to the headings below.

1 Introduction
2 Current usage
3 Benefits
4 Drawbacks
5 Conclusions and recommendations

3 What similarities and / or differences are there between your school's use of tablet computers and Honeywick's?

STRATEGY

Ways of conducting research

There are several different ways to collect information for a report, and it is usually a good idea to use more than one technique.

a Interviews provide detailed information from key individuals. Prepare your questions before the interview, and during it, either take notes or make an audio recording that you can refer back to later.

b Focus groups bring together between three and ten people to discuss a topic. As with interviews, prepare your questions and keep a record of the discussion.

c Surveys are a good way to get information from large groups. Ask questions with multiple-choice or *yes / no* answers so that the results can be statistically analysed.

d Documents sometimes provide the information that you need. Ask about useful documents in your interviews or focus groups.

e Desk research can provide a wider context for your more specific research. Use books or the internet.

4 Read the strategy. Study phrases 1–6 in the report and match them to types of research a–e in the strategy.

V Evidence verbs

5 Study the highlighted verbs in the report. Then match them to definitions 1–5.

1 look carefully at something
2 make a true statement based on personal experience or on evidence
3 show that something is likely to be true
4 make a judgment about something after thinking carefully about it
5 show clearly that something is true (2 words)

6 Complete the sentences with the correct form of the verbs in exercise 5. Sometimes more than one answer is possible.

1 We've .... the arguments for using online tests, but we can't decide if they're a good idea for our school.

2 These survey results .... that a 3D printer in the technology lab would be beneficial, but more research is needed.

3 The students' wonderful songs .... that they can achieve a lot with the right recording equipment.

4 Several students .... to the fact that smartphone use in class improved behaviour.

5 The terrible exam results at Hillside School, where all students have their own tablet computer, ... that spending on technology is no guarantee of academic success.

6 We must .... the need for more computers before we spend any money.

A Unfortunately, the cost of tablets is high and their portability makes them more likely to be broken than desktop computers. [1]According to the ICT accounts, about 12% of the tablets need to be replaced each year. Teachers also testified to the unreliable Wi-fi in the school, which has occasionally forced them to abandon plans for tablet lessons at the last minute.

B [2]79% of student respondents said that they were more motivated to work hard when using tablets in class. [3]When discussing the issue, nine out of ten teachers with experience of whole-class tablet use agreed, and many also appreciated getting real-time feedback on students' understanding through interactive exercises.

C The purpose of this report is to examine closely the current usage of tablet computers at Honeywick Secondary School, assess their benefits and drawbacks as a learning tool using data from teacher focus groups and a student survey, and make conclusions and recommendations about their future role in the school.

D In conclusion, the highly positive response to tablets from both teachers and students demonstrates that their use should be encouraged in all subject areas. Since research has proved that they improve student motivation, the school should invest in more sets of tablets and a Wi-fi upgrade. Teachers and students need to work together to agree on measures that will reduce damage to tablets – [4]newspaper reports about other schools suggest that 6% is a realistic annual wastage rate.

E [5]According to the school's ICT Manager, Graham Davies, there are just three class sets of tablet computers in the school, which teachers have to book in advance. [6]Records show that the tablet computers have been used for an average of 5.6 hours in every six-hour school day this year, most frequently for music composition, art and maths (108, 81 and 52 lessons respectively) and less often for modern languages, science and PE (34, 20 and 18 lessons). The other subjects make hardly any use of tablet computers (just 5 lessons between them).

WRITING GUIDE

■ **Task** Choose an item of technology, research its use in your school, and write a report on your findings.

■ **Ideas** Think about your research:

1 Choose an item of technology to write about, either from the photos in exercise 1 or your own ideas.

2 Make a list of the information that you will need for your report.

3 For each item in your list, decide on the best way to get that information. Use the strategy to help you.

■ **Plan** Follow the plan:

1 Prepare your survey, focus group and / or interview questions.

2 Conduct your research.

3 Analyse your data.

4 Make notes under the headings in exercise 2.

■ **Write** Write your report. Use the headings in exercise 2 to help you.

■ **Check** Check the following points:

■ Have you explained the purpose of the report?

■ Have you included researched facts and figures?

■ Have you used a variety of phrases to introduce your findings?

■ Have you written a conclusion and a recommendation for the future?

■ Have you checked grammar, vocabulary, spelling and punctuation?

Vocabulary insight 9 Using a dictionary: adjectives and adverbs

1 Work in pairs. Read the two sentences from the unit. What part of speech are the highlighted words?

  1 Several determined men were working hard on this emerging technology … .

  2 She takes these new-born ideas in her arms, murmurs reassurances, and runs as fast as she can into the unknown.

> **STRATEGY**
>
> ### Adverbs and adjectives
> Most adverbs in English end in *-ly*, for example: *quietly*, *slowly*, *loudly*. However, some irregular adverbs have the same form as adjectives.
>
> *hard* as an adjective: *They were <u>hard</u> workers.*
> *hard* as an adverb: *They were working <u>hard</u>.*
>
> ■ If the word describes a **noun**, it is an adjective.
> ■ If the word describes an **activity**, it is an adverb.

2 Read the strategy above. Are the underlined words in sentences 1–8 adverbs or adjectives?

  1 In the future, we will have flying cars and will be able to fly <u>straight</u> to our destination.

  2 In the future, we will have flying cars and will be able to fly in a <u>straight</u> line to our destination.

  3 How <u>fast</u> was the Wright brothers' biplane *Flyer 1*?

  4 How <u>fast</u> did the Wright brothers' biplane *Flyer 1* fly?

  5 Whitehead's <u>hard</u> work led to the development of his *Number 21* plane.

  6 Whitehead worked <u>hard</u> to develop his *Number 21* plane.

  7 It can sometimes be difficult for planes to fly <u>low</u>.

  8 It can sometimes be difficult for planes to fly at a <u>low</u> height.

3 Put the words in the correct order to make sentences.

  1 nervous / get / when / high / I'm / above / I / ground / the

  2 high / the / it / airport / walls / has / around / all / got

  3 leaves / very / our / tomorrow / early / flight

  4 got / we've / tomorrow / flight / very / a / early

  5 instructions / are / for / games console / this / wrong / the

  6 playing / you're / this / wrong / game

4 Study the dictionary entries for *high* and *highly*. Which word, *high* or *highly*, would you use to express:

  1 something at the top or upper end of a musical scale?

  2 having a good opinion?

  3 being a long way above the surface of something?

  4 extremely?

  5 costing a large amount of money?

> **high** /haɪ/ *adj., noun, adv.*
> ■ *adv.* (high·er, high·est)
> ► FAR FROM GROUND/BOTTOM **1** at or to a position or level that is a long way up from the ground or from the bottom: *An eagle circled high overhead.* ◇ *I can't jump any higher.* ◇ *She never got very high in the company.* ◇ *His desk was* **piled high** *with papers.* ◇ *She's* **aiming high** *(= hoping to be very successful) in her exams.*
> ► VALUE/AMOUNT **2** at or to a large cost, value or amount: *Prices are expected to rise even higher this year.*
> ► SOUND **3** at a high PITCH: *I can't sing that high.* **OPP** **low**

> **high·ly** /ˈhaɪli/ *adv.*
> **1** very: *highly successful/skilled/intelligent* ◇ *highly competitive/critical/sensitive* ◇ *It is* **highly unlikely** *that she'll be late.* **2** at or to a high standard, level or amount: *highly trained/educated* ◇ *a highly paid job* **3** with admiration or praise: *His teachers* **think very highly of him** *(= have a very good opinion of him).* ◇ *She* **speaks highly of you.** ◇ *Her novels are very highly regarded.*

> **STRATEGY**
>
> ### Adverbs with two forms
> Some adverbs have two forms. One form is the same as the adjective and the other form ends in *-ly*. There is usually a difference in meaning between the two forms. Sometimes there is also a difference in the word order. For example:
> *He works hard.* (= He is a hard worker.)
> *He hardly works.* (= He doesn't work very much.)

5 Read the strategy above. Choose the correct answers. Use a dictionary to help you.

  1 She arrived **late / lately** at the technology conference.

  2 **Late / Lately** there have been some big developments in the mobile phone industry.

  3 I think it is **high / highly** unlikely that we will build houses on Mars in the future.

  4 The *SR-71 Blackbird* is a very powerful plane and can fly very **high / highly** in the sky.

  5 My computer was broken last week, but now it's working **fine / finely**.

  6 It's a **fine / finely** constructed piece of engineering.

6 Write example sentences to show the differences in meaning between these pairs of adverbs.

  ■ wide / widely ■ near / nearly ■ right / rightly
  ■ free / freely

Dictionary entries from *Oxford Advanced Learner's Dictionary* 8ᵉ, Oxford University Press 2010.

Vocabulary

1 Match the words below to definitions 1–7. There is one word that you do not need.

■ cord ■ earbuds ■ early adopters ■ headset ■ keypad
■ emerging technologies ■ handset ■ tech start-ups

1 Very small headphones that you wear in your ears.
2 A small set of buttons with numbers on.
3 New companies based on the internet.
4 Wire that connects electrical equipment to a power supply.
5 Those which are currently being developed.
6 Headphones with a microphone attached.
7 People who use a product as soon as it is available.

Marks .... / 7

2 Complete the text with the correct form of the verbs below. There are two words that you do not need.

■ bring ■ buy ■ dedicate ■ have ■ produce ■ launch
■ murmur ■ sink

A new product only ever reaches the market if a company thinks it ¹ .... legs. In some cases, products can be ² .... with a fanfare, but sales don't take off immediately. Only customers who are ³ .... to a certain brand will buy the product immediately. Those who are more cautious will wait to hear the sales staff ⁴ .... reassurances about its performance. Tech savvy friends are also good for ⁵ .... people up to speed on the latest models. Of course, those products that fail to arouse the consumer's interest eventually ⁶ .... into oblivion.

Marks .... / 6

3 Choose the correct answers.

Several technology companies are under ¹**attack / your belt / control** because of the poor working conditions in the factories that make their gadgets. Until now, these factories have been under ²**the weather / scrutiny / the radar** because observers have been denied access. Workers are often under ³**age / control / pressure** to work very long hours. They are rarely allowed to take sick leave even though they may be under ⁴**the radar / the weather / your belt**. Contractors have also been accused of employing under ⁵**pressure / age / scrutiny** workers. Company directors are being urged by human rights groups to keep their working conditions under ⁶**attack / the weather / control**.

Marks .... / 6

4 Match five of the adverbs to meanings 1–5.

■ close ■ closely ■ hard ■ hardly ■ high ■ highly ■ just
■ justly ■ late ■ lately

1 in recent times ....
2 fairly ....
3 not far ....
4 almost not ....
5 up from the ground ....

Marks .... / 5

Grammar

5 Report the quotes by famous people.

1 Thomas Edison: 'I never did anything by accident.'
Edison said ....
2 Orville Wright to his brother: 'No flying machine will ever fly from New York to Paris.'
Orvill Wright told ....
3 Film-maker H.M. Warner: 'Who wants to hear actors talk?'
H.M. Warner asked ....
4 French statesman Charles de Gaulle to a (male) journalist: 'What do you take me for?'
Charles de Gaulle asked ....
5 Alexander Fleming: 'One sometimes finds what one is not looking for.'
Fleming said ....

Marks .... / 10

6 Match the direct speech to gaps 1–11 in the text. Then complete the text with the sentences in reported speech.

A 'The Facebook team has ignored my warnings.'
B 'It allowed me to post on anybody's timeline.'
C 'All internet users should give money to a fund for Khalil.'
D 'I think you should fix the bug.'
E 'I have found a bug on your main site.'
F 'How did you hack Mark Zuckerberg's personal page?'
G 'Don't forget that there is a reward for finding bugs.'
H 'There isn't a bug on the site.'
I 'Yes, I hacked his account.'
J 'You tested the bug against another Facebook user.'
K 'I'm sorry that I broke your privacy.'

Last August, Khalil Shreateh contacted the Facebook security team.
First, he warned ¹ ....
Then, he explained ² ....
Finally, he suggested ³ ....
Instead of repairing the security breach, the team denied ⁴ ....

So Khalil went one step further and posted a message on the timeline of Mark Zuckerberg himself.
First, he apologized ⁵ ....
Then, he accused ⁶ ....
Finally, he begged Mr Zuckerberg to fix the bug.

Khalil's Facebook account was suspended within minutes and he received a call from a security officer on the Facebook team, who asked ⁷ ....
Khalil confessed to ⁸ ....
Then, he reminded ⁹ ....
The security officer accused ¹⁰ ....
He refused to give Khalil the reward.
When the head of an online security company heard about the incident, he encouraged ¹¹ ....
The campaign raised nearly $12,000 for the hacker.

Marks .... / 11

Total .... / 45

1 SPEAKING A utopia is an ideal society. How close to a utopia is the society you live in? Think about the issues below.

- political systems ■ distribution of wealth ■ education
- crime ■ gender roles

2 Read the article. In what ways are the two communities similar to or different from your own society?

3 Read the article again and choose the correct answers.

1 Why do people at Twin Oaks do several different jobs?
   a because there's a lot to do
   b because otherwise they have to leave Twin Oaks
   c because it's more interesting
   d because women prefer to do men's jobs

2 What doesn't the Twin Oaks community do?
   a attract new people to live there
   b allow residents to visit the outside world
   c keep all its residents happy all the time
   d reach decisions democratically

3 In Meghalaya, what can men do?
   a own their parents' property after they die
   b have a career in politics
   c give their surname to their children
   d give orders to their mother-in-law

4 What do many Meghalayan men have?
   a more difficulty than women in getting bank loans
   b a better education than their sisters
   c a lot to do
   d a successful business

5 What do most people in Meghalaya seem to want?
   a more equality between men and women
   b less knife crime
   c no change to their traditional way of life
   d a return to the lost traditions of the past

6 What is the purpose of the article?
   a to give examples of ideal societies
   b to persuade people to try a different lifestyle
   c to define what normal society is
   d to show how different other societies can be from our own

4 SPEAKING Work in pairs. Discuss the advantages and disadvantages of living in the communities described in the article. Would you like to live in either of them? Why / why not?

Different lives

We all have expectations of what a 'normal' society looks like: its gender roles, its political systems, its social classes. But society can take an infinite number of different forms, as these unusual examples demonstrate.

Communal living in the USA

A Imagine a society that needs no police for law enforcement, has no bosses to run the businesses, and rewards everyone's labour equally, whether they're washing dishes or writing software. Sounds crazy? Not according to the residents of Twin Oaks Community.

B For almost fifty years, a group of adults and their children – now about 100 in number – have lived together on two square kilometres of land in rural Virginia, USA, equally sharing their resources. Apart from bedrooms, all the rooms in their seven residential buildings are communal. Seventeen shared cars are at everyone's disposal, although they mostly rely on the communal bikes at Twin Oaks for local journeys. Even the clothes on their backs are borrowed from the community's well-stocked clothing library.

C There's no room for freeloaders, however. All adults work forty-two hours per week for the community, and persistent failure to do so would lead to expulsion. People are encouraged to choose a variety of tasks to keep boredom at bay, from farming, cooking and teaching the kids, to contributing to the community's hammock-making and tofu businesses, and a conscious effort to challenge traditional gender roles means that you'll often come across men on baby duty while women are wielding chainsaws in

Vocabulary: word analysis; society and citizenship; the electoral system; synonyms: global politics; giving examples and explanations
Grammar: defining and non-defining relative clauses; participle clauses; relative clauses: other structures

Speaking: a debate
Writing: a for and against essay

10A

The fight for men's rights

the woods. In return for their labour, everyone
30 is provided with housing, food, healthcare and a
little personal spending money so that they can
splash out on treats, such as luxury food items or
an occasional night out in town.

D With such an egalitarian distribution of
35 wealth, there have never been any problems with
crime, and decisions about the community are
made democratically, for the common good. 'Our
whole focus on equality means that we diversify
leadership. Everybody here is a manager of an
40 area and we have a committee that makes overall
decisions,' explains Keenan Dakota, who has
been living at Twin Oaks for twenty-six years.

E This way of life is not utopia. Complaints
range from other people's taste in loud music to
45 the fact that unpopular jobs like cleaning tend to
be neglected, and majority rule means that people
with views few residents share can feel powerless
and isolated. But despite its problems, the Twin
Oaks lifestyle is one that many more people would
50 like to embrace. There is a long waiting list of
potential new residents, and Twin Oaks members
have helped to set up several similar communities
elsewhere in the USA. They hope that the Twin
Oaks society can serve as a model for the wider
55 world, promoting greater social responsibility and
pointing the way to a fairer, more cooperative and
more sustainable future for all.

F In the Indian state of Meghalaya, it's the
women who wear the trousers. India is a country
of extreme ethnic diversity, and minority rights 60
and traditions are strongly defended by the
constitution. This allows Meghalaya to maintain
a custom unheard of elsewhere in India: property
and family names are matrilineal and so pass, not
from father to son, but from mother to daughter. 65
The youngest daughter inherits the family wealth,
accepting in return a duty to look after her parents
in their old age. Even in situations where there are
no daughters, a family has to adopt a girl to act as
the guardian of their wealth rather than leaving 70
property to a son.

G Although civic engagement is mostly a male
pursuit – only men are eligible for the role of village
elder and they make up 93% of state assembly
politicians – they have little say in domestic matters. 75
When they marry, they move into the home of their
mother-in-law and submit to her rule. In fact, they
have more authority over their sisters' children than
their own, as they have higher status in the home
where they grew up. Even in business, men are at 80
a disadvantage, as their lack of property means
they have nothing to use as collateral for a loan,
whereas women can borrow more easily and often
build successful companies. Because of the relative
importance of women in society, families tend to 85
prioritize the education of girls over boys, to the
extent that female university graduates commonly
have brothers who never finished high school. Men
often sit around for much of the day, with few
responsibilities to give their life purpose. 90

H A men's rights movement emerged about fifty
years ago, but lost momentum after hundreds
of women turned up at one of their meetings
brandishing knives. Recently, activists have
renewed the struggle for equal rights and equal 95
opportunities. Sixty-year-old Keith Pariat, leader of
the movement, explains that he and his colleagues
'do not want to bring women down. We just want
to bring the men up to where the women are.'
So far, however, the movement has gained little 100
support, despite the superior numbers of men in
the political arena. 'In most of Meghalaya, people
only know the old ways,' says Patricia Mukhim,
editor of the local paper, 'and they like the old ways
just fine.' It appears that, in this hilly corner of India, 105
the women will be wearing the trousers for some
time to come.

V insight Word analysis

5 Answer the questions, referring closely to the article.

1 Which phrase means that everyone can use something? Which adjective has a similar meaning? (B)

2 Which word means *people who take from other people and give nothing in return*? What happens to people like this at Twin Oaks? (C)

3 Which phrase means *to have a wider range of people in charge*? How is that achieved? (D)

4 Which metaphorical expression does the writer use to say that women are in charge? What would be an equivalent expression in your language? (F)

5 Which word means *the property that you agree to give someone if you can't pay back the money they lent you*? What type of property do you think the writer is referring to? (G)

6 Which phrase is a way of saying that something stopped developing or becoming more successful? What was the reason for this? (H)

V Society and citizenship

6 Study the highlighted phrases in the article and explain them in your own words. Then use them to complete the text below. There is one phrase that you do not need.

Plan your own utopia

1 How will you select your community's members, and how large will the community be? Too small and there may not be a sufficient range of skills, but too large and it's hard to agree on the .... – what is beneficial for everyone in the community.

2 What jobs will there be, and how will people be paid? Will there be an equal .... or a mix of rich and poor people?

3 Will there be strict gender roles, or a class system where only people from certain families can do certain jobs? Or will there be a policy of ....?

4 Will the community protect .... and prevent discrimination against people with disabilities or a different religion from the majority? How will it do this?

5 How will politics be organized? For example, will there be .... or another form of democracy, or will you be an authoritarian leader?

6 Will there be .... outside the community, for example involvement in the politics of the country where your community is based? Why / why not?

7 How will you encourage ...., so that people act in a way that doesn't cause problems for others and for the environment?

8 How will you deal with ....? Will community members be employed as police officers?

7 SPEAKING Work in groups. Plan your own utopia using the questions in exercise 6.

Vocabulary bank Politics and society page 143

1 SPEAKING Work in pairs. Discuss the questions.

1 'When money enters sport, corruption is sure to follow.' Do you agree?

2 What examples do you know of corruption in sport?

2 ◎ **2.24** Listen to the radio programme. How did Salt Lake City win their bid to host the Olympics?

3 ◎ **2.24** Listen again. Are the sentences true (T) or false (F)?

1 In 2002, no one knew the real reason <u>why Salt Lake City was hosting the Olympics</u>.

2 In the 1990s, there were some members of the IOC <u>that abused their power</u>.

3 Salt Lake City failed in their bid for the 1998 Olympics, <u>which taught the organizers some useful lessons</u>.

4 The Salt Lake City bidders paid toward the election campaign of the Chilean IOC member, <u>who was running for President</u>.

5 A woman <u>whose husband was an IOC member</u> had cosmetic surgery funded by Salt Lake City.

6 After newspapers wrote about the tactics <u>the bid committee had used</u>, the venue of the Olympics was changed.

Defining and non-defining relative clauses

4 Study the relative clauses underlined in exercise 3 and answer the questions.

1 Which four are examples of a defining relative clause, giving information that identifies the noun it is used with?

2 Which two are examples of a non-defining relative clause, giving extra information without which the sentence still makes good sense?

3 Which is an example of a sentence-relative clause, where the relative clause refers not to the noun before it but to the sentence as a whole? What relative pronoun is used?

4 In which type of relative clause can we use *that* instead of *which* and *who*?

5 In which relative clause can the relative pronoun be omitted? Why?

6 Which word introduces a relative clause about a reason?

7 What other words do you know that can introduce relative clauses?

Reference and practice 10.1 Workbook page 127

5 Join the sentences to make one sentence. Use a defining or non-defining relative clause, and a relative pronoun only if necessary.

1 The world's most-watched sport is football. It has 3.5 billion fans.
The world's most-watched sport is football ....

2 Sometimes, match results are arranged before the match. This is called 'match-fixing'.
Sometimes, match results are arranged before the match ....

3 Match-fixing has occurred in hundreds of recent matches. Gambling is the reason for this.
Gambling is the reason ....

4 There are thirty countries. Match-fixing has allegedly taken place there.
.... match-fixing has allegedly taken place.

5 Officials accepted bribes. The biggest bribes were $135,000.
The biggest bribes ....

6 Players in less famous teams also took bribes. Their salaries were not very high.
.... also took bribes.

Participle clauses

6 Study the participle clauses in sentences 1 and 2 from the recording. Rewrite them as relative clauses. Then choose the correct answers in rules a and b.

1 They bought luxury furnishings for the IOC member from Congo Republic, including doorknobs costing $673.

2 IOC members, bribed with more than $10 million from Salt Lake City, gave the US bid a landslide victory.

a We use the present participle (-ing form) to replace relative clauses containing **active / passive** verbs.

b We use the past participle to replace relative clauses containing **active / passive** verbs.

Reference and practice 10.2   Workbook page 127

7 Complete the text with the correct participle forms of the verbs below. There are two verbs that you do not need.

■ abandon ■ grow up ■ shout ■ commit ■ offer ■ play ■ look ■ borrow ■ invent ■ listen ■ take ■ think

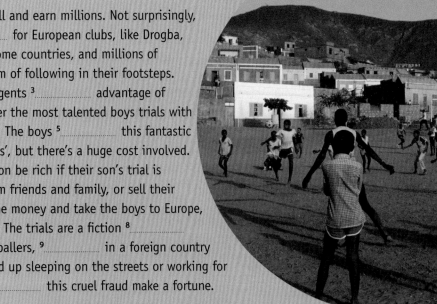

They go to Europe, play professional football and earn millions. Not surprisingly, celebrity West African footballers ¹............... for European clubs, like Drogba, Touré and Eto'o, are huge heroes in their home countries, and millions of young boys ²............... in West Africa dream of following in their footsteps. Unfortunately, there are lots of dishonest agents ³............... advantage of these boys with big dreams. The agents offer the most talented boys trials with European clubs ⁴............... for new players. The boys ⁵............... this fantastic opportunity are usually very keen to say 'yes', but there's a huge cost involved. Many parents, ⁶............... that they will soon be rich if their son's trial is successful, pay with money ⁷............... from friends and family, or sell their home to raise the funds. The agents take the money and take the boys to Europe, but then ... nothing. The agents disappear. The trials are a fiction ⁸............... to cheat the boys' families. The young footballers, ⁹............... in a foreign country without money or documentation, often end up sleeping on the streets or working for criminal gangs. Meanwhile, the agents ¹⁰............... this cruel fraud make a fortune.

8 SPEAKING Discuss the questions.

1 Which of the stories is most surprising? Which is most depressing? Why?

2 Which people are most at fault in these situations? Why?

3 Where, apart from sport, does corruption also occur? Give examples.

4 What could be done to limit the amount of corruption that goes on?

1 SPEAKING At what age can you vote in national elections in your country? Do most people who are entitled to vote do so? Why / why not?

STRATEGY

Identifying attitude

When you listen to people talking, it is useful to identify their attitude. Are they confident and assertive or submissive and hesitant? Do they feel strongly about the topic or are they neutral? Listen out for:

1 **Tone of voice:** Is it high-pitched or low-pitched? Is it quiet or loud?
2 **Speed:** Do they speak slowly or quickly?
3 **Language:** Do they use modals or language that implies uncertainty? Are they direct and assertive?
4 **Hesitation:** Does the speaker hesitate a lot?

2 ◉ **2.25** Read the strategy. For each of the attitudes below, answer questions 1–4 in the strategy. Then listen to a radio programme and match speakers A–D to the attitudes. There is one attitude that you do not need.

■ indecisive ■ outraged ■ enthusiastic ■ sympathetic ■ bitter

---

3 ◉ **2.25** Listen again and match the speakers to descriptions 1–9. There are two descriptions that you do not need.

1 This person holds extreme right-wing views.
2 This person is thinking of making a protest on election day.
3 This person tries to stop racism.
4 This person thinks that politicians lie to the people whose votes they want.
5 This person thinks politicians aren't interested in helping young people.
6 This person says that politicians have been paid money that they're not entitled to.
7 This person has a job in politics.
8 This person thinks the life experiences of politicians are too different from his / her own.
9 This person enjoys talking about politics.

V The electoral system

4 Study the words from the recording and explain their meaning in your own words. Then use the singular or plural form of the words to complete the text below.

■ general election ■ local election ■ constituency ■ polling stations ■ right-wing politics
■ left-wing politics ■ ballot paper ■ vote ■ candidate ■ electorate ■ turnout ■ manifesto

After weeks of political campaigning and debate about the contents of the parties' published
[1] ...., the big day is here at last. As well as the [2] .... to choose our next national government, there are also [3] .... to choose representatives for town and city councils across Britain. Early risers have already visited their [4] ...., which opened at 7 a.m., and the [5] .... will have until 10 p.m. tonight to complete their [6] .... Although [7] .... is expected to be low among younger people, who have not voted in large numbers in recent years, it will be much higher in [8] .... where there's a close contest between the two main parties. After officials have counted the [9] .... for each [10] .... hoping to win a seat in Parliament, the winners will be declared. Then, we will see whether [11] ...., with higher taxes and more help for the poor, or [12] ...., with lower taxes and less help for the poor, will dominate the running of our country for the next five years.

5 SPEAKING Discuss the quotes from the radio programme. Do you agree with the speakers' opinions? Why / why not?

1 'If I voted, I'd be giving my vote to the party that I hated the least, rather than the one I most wanted to lead the country.'
2 '(Politicians) don't really know or care about life in the real world.'
3 '(Politicians) never seem to care much about young people.'
4 'Political parties make all kinds of promises … , but they break half of them as soon as they get elected.'

A debate

6 🔊 **2.26 SPEAKING** Work in pairs. Look at the newspaper headlines and discuss your views on the debate question below. Then listen to the debate and compare your ideas.

> Should all politicians have a job outside politics before they can stand for election?

18-year-old wins town council election

Britain's finances run by politician with no business experience

7 🔊 **2.26** Listen again and complete the phrases from the debate. Then complete A–D with the headings below.

■ Interrupting ■ Chairing a debate ■ Getting your point across ■ Dealing with interruptions

A ....
Today's debate is on the ¹........................ of … .
Who would like to start us ²........................?
Thank you. Let's have some other
³........................ now.
I'd like to ⁴........................ on now to … .
Does anyone else have anything they'd like to
⁵........................?

B ....
Excuse me, can I just say … ?
Can I just ⁶........................ in here?
If I can ⁷........................ for a moment, … .

C ....
Hold on a minute, please.
If you could just let me ⁸........................, please,
I was going to say that … .
Sorry, but could you just ⁹........................ me out?

D ....
The main ¹⁰........................ here is … .
The other important ¹¹........................ is
whether … .
What's absolutely ¹²........................ is … .

8 SPEAKING Read the debate topic and make some notes. Then work in groups. Appoint one person as the chairman and have a debate.

> Should voting in national elections be compulsory for all adult citizens?

DVD extra Elections in the UK

1 SPEAKING Discuss the questions.

1 Think of famous politicians from the past. Why are they still famous today? Make a list of different reasons.

2 What do you know about US President John F. Kennedy? Do any of the reasons in your list apply to him?

2 Read the text about the Cold War. Which of the topics below do you think Kennedy talked about in his first speech as President, in 1961? Read his speech and compare your ideas. Then, in your own words, explain what he said about each topic.

■ the benefits of capitalism ■ NATO allies
■ the problems with communism ■ world poverty
■ the Soviet Union ■ nuclear weapons ■ space travel
■ World War II ■ spies

3 ⊚ 2.27 Listen to a lecture on the power of words in speeches. Make notes about the language devices below. Then find an example of each device in Kennedy's speech.

1 pathos ....
2 metaphor ....
3 alliteration ....
4 tricolon ....
5 antithesis ....
6 chiasmus ....

4 SPEAKING Did Kennedy succeed in making his speech powerful? Why / why not?

V insight Synonyms: global politics

5 Study the highlighted words in the speech. Then replace the words in italics in the text below with the correct form of the synonyms in the speech.

In 1959, Fidel Castro became the ruler of Cuba. His laws restricted important civil ¹*freedoms* (.....................) and he ²*got rid of* (..................... / ....) all political parties except the Communist Party. Many Cubans fled their ³*country* (.....................) and went to the USA, ⁴*promising* (..................... / ....) that they would one day remove Castro from power. With help from the American CIA they invaded Cuba at the Bay of Pigs in 1961, but they were quickly defeated. The Soviet leader, Nikita Khrushchev, sent Castro nuclear ⁵*weapons* (.....................) to help defend him from his ⁶*enemies* (..................... / ....), but when Kennedy found out about these weapons just 145 m from US soil, his military leaders advised him to attack Cuba in full force. Nuclear war with the Soviets seemed hours away, and it is thought that ⁷*the human population* (..................... / ....) has never been closer to total destruction. Luckily, Kennedy and Khrushchev managed to find a compromise and war was averted.

The Cold War

The Cold War (1947–1991) was a period of political and military tension between the capitalist United States and its NATO allies, predominantly in Western Europe, and the communist Soviet Union and its Warsaw Pact allies, mainly in Eastern Europe. ¹The Americans' rivalry with the Russians, with whom they had been allies in World War II, led to competitive space exploration, intense espionage, and wars in several regions of the world. ²Whenever it looked as though world war would break out, however, this was prevented by the knowledge that ³each side had nuclear weapons with which they could completely destroy the other.

President John F. Kennedy's inaugural speech, 1961

15 'We observe today not a victory of party, but a celebration of freedom – symbolizing an end, as well as a beginning – signifying renewal, as well as change. For I have sworn before you the same solemn oath our forebears prescribed nearly a
20 century and three-quarters ago.

'The world is very different now. For man holds in his mortal hands the power to abolish all forms of human poverty and all forms of human life. And yet the same revolutionary beliefs for which our
25 forebears fought are still at issue around the globe. Let the word go forth from this time and place, to friend and foe alike, that the torch has been passed to a new generation of Americans. Let every nation know, whether it wishes us well or ill, that we shall
30 pay any price, bear any burden, meet any hardship, support any friend, oppose any foe, to assure the survival and the success of liberty.

'This much we pledge – and more. To those old allies whose cultural and spiritual origins we share, we
35 pledge the loyalty of faithful friends.

'To those people in the huts and villages of half the globe struggling to break the bonds of mass misery, ⁴we pledge our best efforts to help them help themselves, for whatever period is required. If a free
40 society cannot help the many who are poor, it cannot save the few who are rich.

'Finally, to those nations who would make themselves our adversary, we offer not a pledge but a request: that both sides begin anew the quest
45 for peace, before the dark powers of destruction unleashed by science engulf all humanity in planned or accidental self-destruction.

'We dare not tempt them with weakness. For only when our arms are sufficient beyond doubt can we
50 be certain beyond doubt that they will never be

employed. But neither can two great and powerful groups of nations take comfort from our present course – both sides overburdened by the cost of modern weapons, both rightly alarmed by the steady
55 spread of the deadly atom, yet both racing to alter that uncertain balance of terror that stays the hand of mankind's final war.

'So let us begin anew – remembering on both sides that civility is not a sign of weakness, and sincerity is
60 always subject to proof. Let us never negotiate out of fear, but let us never fear to negotiate. Let both sides explore what problems unite us instead of belaboring those problems which divide us. Let both sides seek to invoke the wonders of science instead of its
65 terrors. Together let us explore the stars, conquer the deserts, eradicate disease, tap the ocean depths, and encourage the arts and commerce. And let both sides join in creating a new endeavor – not a new balance of power, but a new world of law – where
70 the strong are just, and the weak secure, and the peace preserved.

'Since this country was founded, each generation of Americans has been summoned to give testimony to its national loyalty. Now the trumpet summons us again –
75 not as a call to bear arms, though arms we need; not as a call to battle, though embattled we are; but a call to bear the burden of a long twilight struggle, year in and year out, against the common enemies of man: tyranny, poverty, disease, and war itself.
80 '⁵The energy, the faith, the devotion which we bring to this endeavor will light our country and all who serve it. And the glow from that fire can truly light the world.

'And so, my fellow Americans, ask not what your
85 country can do for you; ask what you can do for your country. My fellow citizens of the world, ask not what America will do for you, but what, together, we can do for the freedom of man.'

Relative clauses: other structures

6 **Match sentences 1–5 in the text about the Cold War and Kennedy's speech to rules a–c below.**

a As well as nouns, relative clauses can follow other words, including *anything, someone, that, those, much, many, some* and *all*: ....

b We can introduce relative clauses with *whatever, whichever, whoever, however, whenever* and *wherever*: ...., ...

c In relative clauses with prepositions, we can put the preposition:
- at the start of the relative clause: ...., ...
- at the end of the relative clause: *We'll be looking at the language (that) politicians depend on.*

Reference and practice 10.3 | Workbook page 128

7 **Rewrite the sentences so that they have a similar meaning. Change the underlined word(s) to the word(s) in brackets and make any other changes that are necessary.**

1 <u>Any time</u> that President Kennedy is mentioned, people think of his assassination in 1963. (whenever)

2 There is a lot of speculation about the circumstances <u>of his death</u>. (in / died)

3 The gun with <u>which</u> President Kennedy was shot was discovered in a nearby building. (that)

4 This was the building <u>that</u> Lee Harvey Oswald worked in. (which)

5 Oswald was arrested for Kennedy's murder, but there may have been other people <u>that he planned it with</u>. (whom)

6 <u>People</u> who were watching live TV two days later saw Oswald shot dead by nightclub owner Jack Ruby. (those)

7 <u>It doesn't matter who</u> planned the assassination. Kennedy is remembered today as one of the USA's greatest presidents. (whoever)

8 **SPEAKING** **Work in groups. Discuss the meaning of the quotes from Kennedy's speech. Are his ideas relevant to modern politics? Why / why not? Do you agree with them?**

1 'If a free society cannot help the many who are poor, it cannot save the few who are rich.'

2 'Civility is not a sign of weakness, and sincerity is always subject to proof.'

3 'Ask not what your country can do for you; ask what you can do for your country.'

Vocabulary bank | Idioms: politics page 143

1 **SPEAKING** Work in pairs. Do you have a right to free speech? What, if anything, are you not allowed to say in these different environments? Do you agree with any rules that are in place? Why / why not?

■ at school ■ at home ■ in society

2 Read the essay topic. Think of two reasons for restricting free speech and two reasons for keeping it unrestricted. Then read the essay and compare your ideas.

'Unrestricted freedom of speech is more dangerous to society than its suppression.' Discuss.

V Giving examples and explanations

3 Study the highlighted phrases in the essay and match them to category 1 or 2. Then match the phrases below to the categories.

■ to be more specific ■ such as ■ to illustrate this ■ like ■ for example ■ in particular ■ for instance ■ this can be illustrated by ■ by way of example ■ a case in point is

1 Giving examples: ....

2 Explaining: ....

4 Complete the sentences. Use a variety of the phrases in exercise 3 and your own ideas.

1 You can be arrested for things you write online ....

2 Political protests can be very successful ....

3 Newspapers sometimes publish secret information for the common good ....

4 Equal opportunity has still not been achieved ....

5 Life can be difficult in countries that don't have free speech ....

STRATEGY

Writing introductions

The first paragraph of an essay should motivate the reader to read to the end. It should be kept short and should include:

1 a hook to get the reader interested – this could be a thought-provoking fact, a quote, a rhetorical question or a paradox related to the essay topic.

2 whenever relevant, a definition of the key terms in the essay title.

3 a thesis statement – this is always the last sentence of the introduction. It tells the reader what is coming in the rest of the essay, briefly paraphrases the point of view given in the essay question and also states the opposite point of view.

5 Read the strategy. Then read the first paragraph of the essay and identify the different elements.

6 Match introductions a and b to two of the essay topics 1–3. Which is a better introduction? Rewrite the other one, using the strategy to help you. Then write an introduction for the remaining essay question.

1 'The advantages of nuclear arms far outweigh the disadvantages.' Discuss.

2 'An egalitarian society is an impossible dream.' Discuss.

3 'It should be a criminal offence for politicians to break manifesto pledges.' Discuss.

a Someone once said, 'Vote for the man who promises least; he'll be the least disappointing.' It often seems that broken pledges are an integral part of politics, but should we demand better? This essay assesses whether there should be legal consequences for politicians who break promises made to the electorate before an election, or whether they should be free to adapt their policies to the changing circumstances in which they govern.

b It depends what is meant by egalitarian. Communism was an attempt to make everyone equal, but the bureaucrats in the twentieth-century Soviet Union ended up with a much higher standard of living than ordinary citizens. I agree that an egalitarian society is an impossible dream.

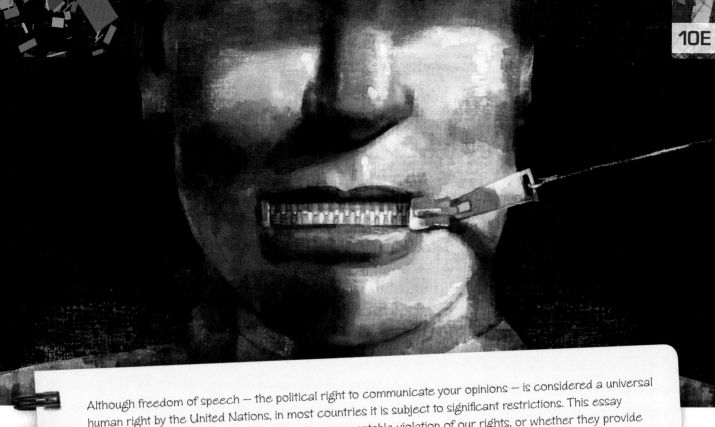

Although freedom of speech – the political right to communicate your opinions – is considered a universal human right by the United Nations, in most countries it is subject to significant restrictions. This essay assesses whether those restrictions are an unacceptable violation of our rights, or whether they provide a necessary protection against the dangers of free speech.

On the one hand, there are strong arguments for restricting free speech. Some people's words endanger lives, particularly in cases where they encourage others to act violently or where they reveal secrets about national security. It is argued that the right to safety outweighs the right to free speech. Another argument in support of restrictions is that they ensure a fair society. As an illustration, take lies that damage someone's reputation, which could cause unfair financial or psychological suffering.

On the other hand, opponents of free speech restrictions argue that they do more harm than good. Because speech which puts people at risk is very difficult to define, laws designed to protect people are sometimes used to prevent legitimate protest – an important aspect of democracy. Furthermore, it might seem worthwhile to put an end to views that offend people, but this can block scientific and social progress. A well-known example of this is the censorship of the theory that the Earth revolves around the Sun, which upset seventeenth-century religious groups, but later enabled important technological developments, specifically space exploration and satellite technology.

In conclusion, there are strong points to be made for both sides of the free speech argument. On balance, however, I feel that legal restrictions can be used in ways that damage society more seriously than having genuine, unrestricted freedom of speech.

WRITING GUIDE

■ **Task** Choose topic 1 or 2 in exercise 6 and write a for and against essay.

■ **Ideas** Make notes about:
- arguments in favour of the statement in the essay topic.
- arguments against the statement in the essay topic.
- examples to back up both sets of arguments.

■ **Plan** Follow the plan:

Paragraph 1: Write an introduction, including a definition if necessary, a hook and a thesis statement.

Paragraph 2: Present the arguments in favour of the statement in the essay topic.

Paragraph 3: Present the arguments against the statement in the essay topic.

Paragraph 4: Write a conclusion, giving your own, balanced opinion.

■ **Write** Write your essay. Use the paragraph plan to help you.

■ **Check** Check the following points:
- Have you written a clear, concise thesis statement?
- Have you used a range of suitable linking words?
- Have you checked grammar, vocabulary, spelling and punctuation?

1 Work in pairs. Make a list of ways of learning new vocabulary that you know. Then work with another pair. Compare your lists and agree on the five most effective ways of learning new vocabulary.

Extending vocabulary: making it personal

Think about the ways that you learn best and use these methods to extend your vocabulary. Personalizing your language learning will help you to become an active and independent learner.

You can **extend** your vocabulary by:
- reading widely and frequently and noting new words
- using a dictionary to find out about pronunciation, different meanings, synonyms, antonyms and collocations
- using the internet to find out more about topics that interest you
- rewriting your written work to include new vocabulary

You can **personalize** your learning by:
- making mind maps
- drawing pictures
- writing your own example sentences, stories and poems
- making audio recordings of sentences or texts
- annotating your dictionary with notes, pictures and other useful information

2 Read the strategy above and answer the questions.

  1 Which of the tips for extending vocabulary and personalizing your learning do you use?
  2 Which tips do you think are the most useful? Why?
  3 Which tips do you never use? Why not?

3 Practise using the tips in the strategy. Use a dictionary to help you.

  1 Find the word *citizen* in a dictionary. Write:
    a two different forms of the word.
    b a word that collocates with *citizen*.
  2 Make a mind map for the word *nation*.
  3 Choose six words from Unit 10 and write an example sentence for each word.
  4 Do some online research to find out more about the Twin Oaks Community. Make a note of any new vocabulary.
  5 Rewrite the sentence below to use some of the new vocabulary you have learned in the last month:
    I think it's important for all developed countries to look at the causes of poverty around the world and work together to make things better.
  6 Study the words which you have learned recently, choose your favourite six and use them in a sentence. Then make an audio recording of your sentence.

Extending vocabulary: using a diamante poem

A diamante poem is a poem in the shape of a diamond. It was developed by Iris Tiedt and is used to compare two subjects by writing synonyms and antonyms associated with these subjects. Creating these poems is another way of extending vocabulary and personalizing your learning.

4 Read the strategy above. Then study the poem and answer the questions.

democracy
egalitarian   popular
voting   campaigning   electing
minority   tyrant   responsibility   majority
ruling   restricting   obeying
authoritarian   powerful
dictatorship

  1 Look at the first word and the last word of the poem. Are they *synonyms* or *antonyms*?
  2 Look at the words *minority* and *tyrant* in line 4 of the poem. Do they relate to *democracy* (line 1) or *dictatorship* (line 7)?
  3 Look at the words *responsibility* and *majority* in line 4 of the poem. Do they relate to *democracy* (line 1) or *dictatorship* (line 7)?
  4 Which word, *democracy* or *dictatorship*, do the words in lines 2 and 3 relate to?
  5 Which word, *democracy* or *dictatorship*, do the words in lines 5 and 6 relate to?
  6 What parts of speech are the words in:
    a lines 2 and 6?   ....
    b lines 3 and 5?   ....
    c lines 1, 4 and 7?   ....

5 Choose one of the pairs of words from the list below and write a diamante poem beginning and ending with the words.

- freedom / slavery ■ power / weakness
- wealth / poverty ■ war / peace

Vocabulary

1 Complete the text with the words below. There is one word that you do not need.

■ collateral ■ communal ■ diversify leadership
■ freeloaders ■ lost momentum ■ shared equally
■ wear the trousers

A kibbutz is a small society that live on a **1**..............
farm in Israel. On a kibbutz, everything is **2**..............
between the members. Everyone has the same status,
and neither men nor women **3**.............. . The workload
is distributed between all the members, so there is no
room for **4**.............. who avoid responsibilities. There is
a system of rotation to **5**.............., so that everybody
takes a turn. The kibbutz movement was popular with
students in the 1960s and 70s, but it **6**.............. at the
end of the last century.

Marks .... / 6

2 Match the words in A to the words in B to make collocations.

A ■ common ■ distribution ■ equal ■ law ■ majority
■ minority

B ■ enforcement ■ good ■ of wealth ■ opportunities
■ rights ■ rule

1 ....   4 ....
2 ....   5 ....
3 ....   6 ....

Marks .... / 6

3 Complete the definitions with the words below. There is one word that you do not need.

■ ballot paper ■ candidate ■ constituency ■ electorate
■ manifesto ■ polling station ■ turnout

1 A .... elects its own representative to parliament.
2 A .... is where you mark who you are voting for.
3 The .... is the people who have the right to vote.
4 The .... is the number of people who vote in an election.
5 A .... is where a political party explains their beliefs.
6 A .... is where people go to vote.

Marks .... / 6

4 Choose the odd one out.

1 country / mankind / nation
2 abolish / diversity / eradicate
3 freedom / liberty / policy
4 pledge / vote / swear
5 tyranny / arms / weapons
6 adversary / enemy / politics

Marks .... / 6

Grammar

5 Complete sentence b so that it has a similar meaning to sentence a. Join the sentences to make one sentence. Omit the relative pronoun where possible.

1 a New Zealand gave women the vote. It was the first country to do so.
  b New Zealand ....
2 a Nelson Mandela is famous. The reason is because he helped get rid of apartheid.
  b The reason ....
3 a India has more than 700 million registered voters. It is the world's largest democracy.
  b India, ...
4 a The United Nations was founded in 1945. The Second World War ended then.
  b The United Nations ....
5 a Mahatma Gandhi was assassinated on 30th June, 1948. His supreme ideals were truth and love.
  b Mahatma Gandhi, ...
6 a Communism was introduced by Mark and Engels in 1848. This changed world politics forever.
  b Communism ....
7 a Kim Jong-il chose Kim Jong-un to be the next leader of North Korea. The man was his son.
  b The man Kim Jong-il chose ....

Marks .... / 7

6 Match the relative clauses to the gaps in the text. Then complete the text with participle clauses.

A which was written by investigative journalist Declan Hill
B which was played between Liverpool and AC Milan
C who claim to have fixed all kinds of football matches
D which is shared by many people
E which is remembered for two dubious penalties and a red card
F that faces modern sport
G who are investigating match-fixing

The respected French newspaper *Libération* has alleged
that the biggest threat **1**.............. is match-
fixing. The allegation was made in the review of a new
book called *The Fix* **2**.............. . In his
book, Mr Hill chronicles his experiences with gamblers
3.............. . *Libération* maintains that the
2005 Champions League Final, **4**..............,
was fixed. Mr Hill does not believe this particular claim,
although he knows of plenty of other cases. After one
German cup game, **5**..............,
a referee was sent to prison for trying to fix nine
matches. In the last ten years, hundreds of referees,
players and officials across Europe have been arrested
by police **6**.............. . Hill's opinion,
7.............., is that we can no longer
believe what we see these days.

Marks .... / 14

Total .... / 45

1 **2.28** Work in pairs. Discuss the questions. Then listen and compare your ideas.

1 What impact has technology had on politics?
2 How can technology help politicians?

2 **2.28** Listen again and choose the correct answers.

1 How has social media affected attitudes towards the news?
  a People always log onto news websites at the same time of day.
  b People choose not to find out about current affairs.
  c People are more selective now.
  d People no longer believe everything they are told.

2 What does Mr Woods compare the action of 'sharing' with?
  a a natural disaster
  b a marketing strategy
  c a government campaign
  d a social habit

3 What is Mr Woods's opinion of collecting feedback from social media?
  a It has some disadvantages.
  b It's very accurate.
  c There are better methods which are less expensive.
  d It isn't as quick as telephone research.

4 According to Mr Woods, how can social media be used best in political protests?
  a to check transport details
  b to look for volunteers to hand out leaflets
  c to change arrangements quickly
  d to organize venues

5 What is the final use of social media that Mr Woods mentions?
  a internet banking
  b fundraising
  c contacting large corporations
  d running a campaign

What makes a great speech?

The philosopher Cicero was the man who first laid down the rules for making a great speech. [1]............... It was Mark Antony who ordered his execution. Antony's wife, Fulvia, is thought to have pulled his famously fluent tongue out of his head once he was dead. She subsequently stabbed it several times with a hairpin, supposedly in revenge for everything he had said about them during his life.

A speech will only be truly great when it perfectly fits the times in which it is delivered. It is this that enables the speech to change the world. Take, for example, the wartime broadcasts of the French statesman Charles de Gaulle. [2]............... The result was that the French did not give in to the enemy and de Gaulle set off on his journey to being regarded as the saviour of France. Likewise, the towering personality of 1980s Britain was only established once Margaret Thatcher stood up and insisted that, despite rocketing unemployment, 'the lady's not for turning'.

If historical circumstance is the most important factor in any great speech, the choice of the right words for the occasion is another essential part of the mix. A detailed study of speeches through the centuries will reveal some tricks of the trade, many known to orators since Cicero's time, that tend to crop up time and time again. [3]............... Once again, it is de Gaulle who gives us the perfect example. Instead of calling on men who have served in 'any of France's armed forces', he issued his summons in sequence to men of the army, navy and air forces. The rhythm reinforces the entreaty for everyone to do their bit.

Speaking

3 Work in pairs. Your school has received some money to spend on technology. Look at the photos. Which technology would you choose and why? Which would you not choose and why?

4 You are going to present your chosen technology to the school board to convince them to choose this one. Prepare a plan of your presentation. Deliver your presentation to the rest of the class.

A

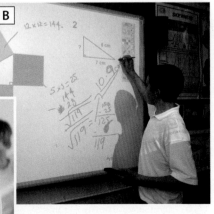

B

C

Literature insight 5 Workbook page 92

Great speeches are often those that contain a sound bite – a short phrase that is considered to be particularly effective or appropriate. Creating ³⁵ linguistic expressions that encapsulate a message has always been an essential part of these speeches. Yet even the best sound bites rely on very old tricks. ⁴............... Margaret Thatcher, for example, wheeled out the then well-worn phrase about Labour's 'winter ⁴⁰ of discontent,' but then held out in its place the promise of 'an autumn of understanding' and 'a winter of common sense'.

Today, audience expectation has changed and so great speech-makers have had to adapt. Public ⁴⁵ meetings no longer attract the interest that they once did, and – in an increasingly distracting world – attention spans have declined. ⁵............... What is more, technology has had a huge effect. In the past, a momentous speech would reach most people as ⁵⁰ newsprint; but first radio, then TV and now the internet have changed that. Today, it is delivery that propels a speech into greatness. The best example of a speaker who possessed this skill is, of course, Martin Luther King. It cannot be denied that speech-making has ⁵⁵ changed over the centuries, but it appears that the power of the spoken word will last forever.

Reading

5 Complete the article *What makes a great speech?* with extracts A–E.

A These were made after the invasion of 1940, when the country could potentially have been on its knees. However, the three speeches were made in such a way that they rallied the people and gave them hope.

B No modern political leader writes a speech running to tens of thousands of words, as they did in the past. Those were the days when audiences were expected to sit still and listen for hours at a time.

C One is phrase reversal, for example John F. Kennedy's use of 'Ask not what your country can do for you, but what you can do for your country.' Another is taking an established cliché and adapting it.

D Renowned for having a sharp tongue, he used it to attain high office, win court cases and secure changes to governing policy. Tragically, it could not protect him in the struggle for supremacy with his rival.

E One of the most basic is the 'rule of three'. No one quite knows why, but speakers have always found that by grouping things together in threes they can hammer home their message.

Grammar and vocabulary

6 Complete the text with the words below. There are two words that you do not need.

■ did ■ for ■ made ■ must ■ in ■ it ■ on ■ was
■ were ■ who ■ whom ■ would

Emmeline Pankhurst is a person to ¹............... all British women should be grateful. ²............... was under her leadership that liberal women known as suffragettes fought for their right to vote in the late nineteenth and early twentieth centuries. The fight began in 1889 when the Women's Franchise League ³............... founded by Emmeline and her daughters. At this stage, Emmeline insisted ⁴............... using peaceful protest among her followers. Later, she helped to found a more militant organization called the Women's Social and Political Union. The new group was criticized ⁵............... its methods, and members ⁶............... often arrested. In protest, the women ⁷............... go on hunger strike, but the wardens ⁸............... them eat by force-feeding them. The suffragettes succeeded ⁹............... gaining the vote for women over thirty in 1918, but it wasn't until 1928 that they were granted equal rights with men, ¹⁰............... could vote at the age of twenty-one.

Writing

7 Write an opinion essay on the topic below.

Politicians today have lost the art of making good speeches. Discuss.

Ways of looking

1 Match the highlighted verbs in sentences 1–8 to definitions a–h.

1 She glanced at her watch for a second to check the time.
2 My brother glared at me for revealing his secret.
3 Everybody is squinting in that photo because of the sun.
4 Sharon spends hours gazing at her new baby as he sleeps.
5 We glimpsed the sun before it disappeared behind the clouds.
6 The children gaped in astonishment when they saw how much food there was.
7 Don't peek at your presents before your birthday.
8 Lots of drivers slowed down to gawp at the accident.

a to look at something for a long time with your mouth open because you are shocked, surprised, etc.
b to look at something for a long time in a stupid or rude way
c to look steadily for a long time either with love or surprise or because you are thinking of something else
d to look quickly at something or somebody
e to look at somebody in a very angry way
f to see something for a moment, but not very clearly
g to look at something quickly and secretly
h to look at something with your eyes almost closed in order to keep out bright light or to see better

2 Choose the correct answers.

1 We **gawped / glimpsed / peeked / squinted** at my aunt when we saw what she was wearing!
2 The teacher **glared / glimpsed / peeked / squinted** at me when I said I hadn't done the homework.
3 They are in love, so they spend hours **gaping / gawping / gazing / glaring** into each other's eyes.
4 He **glanced / glimpsed / peeked / squinted** as he came out of the dark room into the light.
5 I **gaped / glanced / glared / glimpsed** at the headlines because I didn't have time to read the whole paper.
6 She **gaped / glared / glimpsed / glanced** at him in surprise when he told her she had got the job.
7 I **gazed / glimpsed / peeked / squinted** my friend when I walked past her classroom.
8 They **glimpsed / glared / peeked / squinted** at their sister's wedding dress a week before the big day.

3 SPEAKING Work in pairs. Look at the verbs in exercise 1 and think of another situation in which you could use each one.

You glance around a room to see who is there.

Qualities of a hero

1 Complete the table with the noun forms.

noun	adjective	noun	adjective
1	compassionate	2	humble
3	courageous	4	inspirational
5	dedicated	6	persistent
7	determined	8	resourceful
9	dignified	10	willing

2 Complete the definitions with the adjectives in exercise 1.

If someone is

1 ...., they have firmly decided to succeed, even if it is difficult.
2 ...., they don't think that they are more important than other people.
3 ...., they behave in a calm and serious way that makes other people respect them.
4 ...., they are able to control their fear in the face of danger.
5 ...., they are happy to do something.
6 ...., they make others want to do things.
7 ...., they make a lot of effort for things they believe are important.
8 ...., they are good at finding ways of doing things.
9 ...., they feel pity for others who are suffering.
10 ...., they continue doing something even though other people say they cannot do it.

3 Choose the correct answers.

One of the most [1]**compassion / inspirational / willing** women in history is the founder of modern nursing, Florence Nightingale. Many women have entered the profession because of her. Florence was born on 12 May 1820, and when she grew up, she was [2]**courageous / determined / resourceful** to become a nurse. Her wealthy family opposed her decision, but her [3]**humble / humility / persistence** eventually paid off and in 1851 she went to train in Germany. When the Crimean War broke out in 1853, Florence said she was [4]**inspirational / persistent / willing** to oversee the military hospitals in Turkey. Conditions in the hospitals were desperate, and Florence used her [5]**resourcefulness / dignified / humility** to write articles to publicize the situation in the press back home. This resulted in increased funds and a newly-designed hospital. Florence showed great [6]**courage / dedication / inspiration** to her job by working very long hours. Her patients were grateful for the [7]**compassion / determined / resourcefulness** she showed them and many of them wrote home mentioning the woman who made her rounds late at night. She soon became known as 'the Lady with the Lamp'. Florence has gone down in history as the [8]**courageous / compassion / willingness** woman who tended the wounds of the injured during the Crimean War.

The natural world and outer space

1 **Label the photos with the words below.**

■ bay ■ estuary ■ glacier ■ grassland ■ ice floe ■ stream ■ mountain range ■ peninsula ■ plain ■ pond ■ swamp ■ tundra

1 .... 2 .... 3 ....

4 .... 5 .... 6 ....

7 .... 8 .... 9 ....

10 .... 11 .... 12 ....

2 **Match the words below to definitions 1–10.**

■ asteroid ■ constellation ■ galaxy ■ meteorite ■ moon ■ planet ■ solar system ■ star ■ sun ■ universe

1 A very large round object which moves around a sun or a star, e.g. Mars.
2 The star that shines during the day and gives the Earth light and heat.
3 The whole of space and everything in it.
4 A rock from space which hits the Earth.
5 A ball of burning gas in space. At night we see these as spots of light in the sky.
6 A group of stars which form a pattern and have a name.
7 A group of planets which move around the same star or sun.
8 A large group of stars and planets. The Earth is part of the Milky Way.
9 Something which moves around another planet.
10 A large rock or small planet.

3 **SPEAKING** Put the words in exercise 2 in order of size starting with the smallest.

Urban landscape

1 **Match the compound nouns below to definitions 1–8.**

■ bus shelter ■ cycle path ■ high-rise building ■ road sign ■ industrial estate ■ parking meter ■ pedestrian crossing ■ speed bump

1 a raised area across a road that is put there to make drivers go slower
2 a machine where you put money when you leave your car in the road
3 a piece of metal near the road with a picture or writing that gives information and instructions to drivers
4 a structure with a roof where people wait for public transport
5 a special part of the road that allows people to reach the other side safely
6 an area on the edge of town that is especially for factories
7 a very tall structure with a lot of floors
8 a part of the road or pavement that is only for two-wheeled vehicles

2 **Complete the text with the correct singular or plural form of the words in exercise 1.**

Milton Keynes is the largest new town in the UK. Its design is based on grid squares, which are separated by a distance of one kilometre so that residents are all within walking distance of a ¹ .... if they wish to use public transport. A network of footpaths and ² .... called the 'redways' separates pedestrians and cyclists from the fast moving traffic, and underpasses have been built under the major roads so that cars do not have to stop at ³ .... In some of the quieter housing estates, there are ⁴ .... across the roads which slow the cars down. There is a height limit to the buildings in Milton Keynes, so ⁵ .... are found only in the central business district. Because the town has not been given city status, ⁶ .... indicate the 'centre of Milton Keynes' instead of the 'city centre'. In the centre itself, drivers have to use different coloured ⁷ .... , depending on how long they want to leave their cars. The town has several ⁸ .... where many of the residents are employed.

3 **Which of the adjectives below are positive and which are negative? Use a dictionary to help you.**

■ boarded-up ■ crumbling ■ derelict ■ flourishing ■ prosperous ■ refurbished ■ robust ■ shabby

4 **SPEAKING** Work in pairs. Look at the words in exercise 1. Describe things near to where you live using the adjectives in exercise 3.

There's a flourishing industrial estate on the edge of town.

British vs American English

1 Complete the definitions with the British English words below. Then match them to their American English equivalents.

British English

■ chest of drawers ■ cooker ■ curtains ■ dustbin ■ flat
■ garden ■ lift ■ tap ■ torch ■ wardrobe

American English

■ apartment ■ closet ■ drapes ■ dresser ■ elevator
■ faucet ■ flashlight ■ stove ■ trash can ■ yard

1 a .... is a machine used for carrying people from one floor to another
2 a .... is a large container outside your house where you throw things away
3 a .... is a set of rooms used as a home
4 a .... is a type of handle that you turn to let water out of a pipe
5 a .... is a piece of furniture with drawers that is used for storing clothes
6 .... are pieces of cloth that you can move to cover a window
7 a .... is a large piece of kitchen equipment used for making meals
8 a .... is a piece of land next to a house where flowers and vegetables can be grown
9 a .... is a cupboard where you can hang your clothes
10 a .... is a small light that you carry in your hand

2 Complete the sentences with the American English words in exercise 1.

1 Shall we walk up the stairs or take the ....?
2 The kids are outside playing in the ....
3 They live in an .... on 42nd Street.
4 The sun's really bright today; let's close the ....
5 When is the .... emptied? It's starting to smell.
6 The .... is leaking, so we'd better get a plumber in.
7 Your watch is probably on the ...., where you left it.
8 Do you have a ....? I can't see a thing.
9 Don't leave the kitchen if there's a pan on the ....
10 Please hang your clean clothes in your ....

3 Use a dictionary to find the American English equivalents of the words below.

■ block of flats ■ clothes peg ■ high street ■ pavement
■ rubbish ■ tea towel

Objects in a museum

1 Label the photos with the words below.

■ coins ■ helmet ■ jewels ■ mask ■ mummy ■ pottery
■ sculpture ■ statue ■ tablet ■ tools ■ vase ■ weapons

1 .... 2 .... 3 ....

4 .... 5 .... 6 ....

7 .... 8 .... 9 ....

10 .... 11 .... 12 ....

2 Match the comments made by visitors to a museum to the objects in exercise 1.

1 'You can see the veins standing out on his hand.'
2 'Do you think they used to put flowers in it?'
3 'I guess a soldier wore it to protect his head.'
4 'They probably used them to make things.'
5 'It's huge, but I've no idea what it's supposed to be.'
6 'Which army used those, do you suppose?'
7 'They might have kept oil and vinegar in it.'
8 'What do you think it says?'
9 'How many different precious stones can you see?'
10 'What did they buy with them?'
11 'Do we know how old he was when he died?'
12 'Do you think the person who wore it could breathe?'

3 SPEAKING Work in pairs. Look at the photos in exercise 1. Which of the objects have you seen and where? What was your impression of them?

I saw a mummy at the Bristol Museum. It was much smaller than I expected.

Phrases with *mind*

1 Match the highlighted phrases in sentences 1–10 to definitions a–j.

1 I'm sorry, your birthday completely slipped my mind!
2 It crossed my mind that I was doing the wrong job.
3 I gave him a piece of my mind about eating my chocolates.
4 I almost went out of my mind when I couldn't find my smartphone!
5 I can't study because I have something on my mind.
6 I'm in two minds about studying abroad. I'd enjoy the experience, but I'd also miss my family.
7 I was upset about my exam results, but I went out with some friends to take my mind off it.
8 I kept in mind my mother's advice for the future.
9 I can't make up my mind which universities to apply to.
10 I've changed my mind – I don't want a laptop for my birthday; I want a tablet.

a become crazy or very worried
b be forgotten
c come into your thoughts
d decide
e decide something different
f be unable to decide between two things
g have a problem that is worrying you
h help somebody forget about something unpleasant
i remember
j speak to somebody angrily because of something they have done

2 Complete the sentences with the correct form of the highlighted phrases in exercise 1. Sometimes more than one answer is possible.

1 My parents will .... if my little sister doesn't come home.
2 I'm not going to .... about the party. I don't want to go.
3 My mother will .... if I'm late for dinner.
4 I couldn't .... whether to order the chicken or the fish.
5 It's difficult to study if you ....
6 Does it ever .... that you ought to get up earlier?
7 My sister often goes for a long walk to .... her studies.
8 Don't spend all your money at once. .... that it has to last you all month.
9 I sometimes have so much to do that the most important things .... and I forget them.
10 I suppose you must .... about going to university. It'll be a great experience, but you won't have any money!

3 SPEAKING Work in pairs. Compare your answers in exercise 2. Explain any differences in meaning where you have more than one answer.

Body parts

1 Match the body parts below to definitions 1–12.

▪ artery ▪ (thigh) bone ▪ brain ▪ heart ▪ liver ▪ lungs ▪ ribs ▪ skin ▪ skull ▪ spine ▪ stomach ▪ vein

1 the organ inside your chest that sends blood around your body
2 one of the hard parts inside the body that make up its frame
3 the part of your body that cleans your blood
4 a tube which takes blood from the heart to other parts of the body
5 the curved bones that go around your chest
6 the organs inside your chest that are used for breathing
7 the row of bones that are connected together down the middle of your back
8 a tube that takes blood from all parts of your body to your heart
9 the bone structure of the head
10 the part of your body that controls your thoughts, feelings and movement
11 the organ where food goes when you have eaten it
12 the natural outer layer that covers the body

2 Label body parts 1–12 with the words in exercise 1.

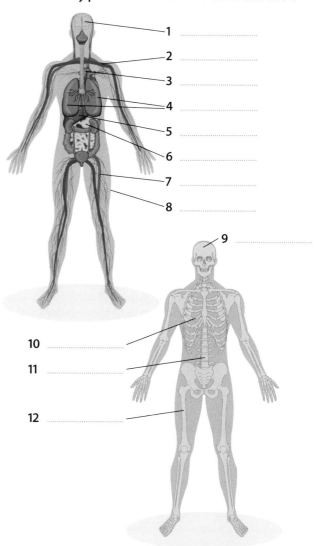

1 ....
2 ....
3 ....
4 ....
5 ....
6 ....
7 ....
8 ....
9 ....
10 ....
11 ....
12 ....

Acronyms

1 Match the acronyms 1–12 in the text messages to their meanings a–l.

1	2	3	4
fyi last train is 23.55	btw it's Anna's birthday	fwiw Monday is a holiday	need Tom's number tia

5	6	7	8
imho new film is cool	idk what to do	tmi about doctors visit!	call me asap

9	10	11	12
paid 100 euros for concert tickets yolo	love the hat lol	afaik party starts at 9	must go bfn

a as far as I know
b as soon as possible
c bye for now
d by the way
e for what it's worth
f for your information
g I don't know
h in my humble opinion
i laughing out loud
j thanks in advance
k too much information
l you only live once

2 Write the acronyms from exercise 1.

Which acronym is used

1 when you tell someone something you think they should know?
2 when someone tells you something you don't want to know?
3 when you tell someone what you think of something?
4 when you want to say something that is not the main point of the conversation?
5 when you have no idea about something?
6 when you are not completely certain that something is true?
7 when you do something a little bit crazy?
8 when you think something is very funny?
9 when you want something to happen quickly?
10 when you want someone to do something for you?
11 when you give information and you don't know if it's useful or not?
12 when you want to end a message?

3 **SPEAKING** Work in pairs. What are the meanings of the acronyms below? Use the internet to help you.

■ brb ■ glhf ■ lmk ■ nagi ■ rofl ■ ttyl

Book structure

1 Study the words below and answer the questions. Use a dictionary to help you.

■ back cover ■ bibliography ■ contents page ■ glossary ■ dust jacket ■ front cover ■ hardback ■ index ■ imprint page ■ paperback ■ spine ■ title page

1 Which two words are types of books?
2 Which words are things you can find inside a book?
3 Which words are things you can find on the outside of a book?

2 Complete the text with the singular or plural forms of the words in exercise 1.

Books can be classified into two types. [1]................... have a thick cover which helps maintain the book's shape. They often have a(n) [2]................... which keeps the book clean. [3]................... do not have this protection and are less expensive. The design of the outside of the book is usually the same in both cases. The [4]................... often has an illustration with the title and the author printed on top. This information is also included in a line down the [5]..................., along with the name of the publisher and the publisher's logo. The [6]................... often contains a summary or description of the book and possibly some quotes from other sources praising it. Inside the book, the first section is called the front matter. The first page is usually the [7]..................., which repeats the information on the cover. Details about the publisher can be found on the [8]................... which is either on the back of this page or on the last page of the book. After that, there is a(n) [9]................... which lists all the different sections in the book and where they start. The largest section is usually the body matter, which is followed by the back matter. This sometimes includes a(n) [10]................... of words of importance used in the work, together with their definitions. There may also be a(n) [11]..................., where the author lists other works he or she has consulted. In non-fiction books, there is often a(n) [12]................... of terms used in the text, accompanied by the page number where the term can be found.

3 **SPEAKING** Work in pairs. Take a book and discuss the different parts you can identify.

Headlines

1 **Match the highlighted words in the headlines to their synonyms 1–10.**

Riddle of missing schoolgirl solved

Valuable gems stolen from millionaire's home

Head teachers to ban soft drinks from schools

Royal couple in privacy plea

Athlete succeeds in world record bid

Manager to quit at end of season

EXILED PRESIDENT VOWS TO RETURN

Government to axe 5,000 jobs

ENERGY SECRETARY BACKS REACTOR PLANS

Minister announces measures to curb inflation

1 attempt ....
2 control ....
3 cut ....
4 jewels ....
5 mystery ....
6 promises ....
7 prohibit ....
8 request ....
9 resign ....
10 supports ....

2 **Complete the headlines with the highlighted words.**

1 Rapper .... President's re-election campaign
2 Police chief .... to put fear in the minds of criminals
3 England fails in .... to host competition
4 Wife's desperate .... to husband
5 Broadcaster to .... new reality show
6 Protesters call to .... politicians' pay rises
7 Film director to .... in the middle of filming
8 .... get their chance to shine
9 Senator to .... smartphone app
10 .... of the seas. Is there a monster?

3 **SPEAKING Work in pairs. Look at today's headlines and translate five of them from your own language into English.**

Film-making

1 **Match the words below to definitions 1–12.**

■ audio engineer ■ boom ■ costume designer ■ prop ■ lighting ■ location ■ screenplay ■ scriptwriter ■ storyboard artist ■ storyline ■ stuntman ■ voice-over

1 the basic plot in a film
2 a person who makes drawings of the clothes to be worn by actors
3 the words for a film and the instructions on how it should be acted
4 a person who does dangerous things in a film instead of an actor
5 comments in a film that are given by a person who is not seen on the screen
6 a long pole that carries a microphone
7 a person who produces the words for a film
8 the arrangement ensuring that a scene is not too dark
9 a person who creates a series of drawings showing the outline of the story in a film
10 a place outside a studio where scenes of a film are made
11 a person who is responsible for recording all the sounds for a film
12 a small object used by actors in a film

2 **Complete the text with the singular or plural forms of the words in exercise 1.**

The first stage in the film-making process is when the ideas for the film are created. The producer contracts a [1] ...., who develops the [2] .... of the film. Successful [3] .... are given the green light by a film studio and a production company is created. The producer hires a crew which includes the director and the heads of all the different departments. There is a [4] .... who prepares all the actors' clothes; a 'scout' who looks for the [5] .... where the scenes will be shot; and a person who is in charge of any [6] .... the actors might need. There is also a [7] .... who is responsible for producing the visual images the director might need to communicate instructions to the actors. During production, an [8] .... records all the audio material using a [9] .... which must not be visible on the screen. An engineer looks after the [10] .... so that the right atmosphere is created for the action to take place. At the end of each day, the cast and the [11] .... receive the shooting schedule for the next day. During post-production, the [12] .... is added, if there is one, and finally, the film is released to the cinemas.

Vocabulary bank 7

Phrases with *time*

1 Match the highlighted phrases in sentences 1–12 to definitions a–l.

1 Sometimes our classes finish ahead of time.
2 My parents tell me to tidy my room all the time.
3 My marks are never very high at the best of times.
4 I'm not very good at doing two things at the same time.
5 At one time, I thought I knew what I wanted to study, but now I'm not so sure.
6 Disco music was popular before my time.
7 My parents are a bit behind the times.
8 I'm quite happy at school for the time being.
9 I wish I lived somewhere different from time to time.
10 This term will be over in next to no time.
11 I'm sure I'll get married in the course of time.
12 I got home last night in the nick of time.

a at the moment, but not permanently
b just in time before something bad happens
c earlier than was expected
d at one time; together
e even when the circumstances are very good
f before you were born or before you can remember
g old-fashioned in ideas and habits
h very often, repeatedly
i occasionally, but not regularly
j in the past, but not now
k when enough time has passed
l so quickly that it is surprising

2 Complete the sentences with the highlighted phrases in exercise 1. Sometimes more than one answer is possible. Explain any difference in meaning.

1 Stop complaining .... – it's really annoying!
2 The ambulance arrived ....
3 The holidays will be here ....
4 My grandparents are really .... – they don't even have a colour television.
5 ...., my cousin wanted to be a professional footballer, but it's a bit late now.
6 My flight landed fifteen minutes ...., so I had to wait to be picked up.
7 It's possible that they'll find a cure for cancer ....
8 They've just moved to Paris and they're renting a flat ....
9 I didn't bother listening because everybody was talking ....
10 I don't remember the fall of the Berlin Wall – it was ....
11 He looks a mess ...., so a new suit won't make any difference.
12 Kate is a nurse, so she has to work nights ....

3 SPEAKING Are the sentences in exercise 1 true for you? Discuss with a partner.

Generation gap

1 Read comments 1–6. Were they made by the older generation (O) or the younger generation (Y)?

1 'They get up to all sorts of things that we never dreamed of doing. What's more, they always seem to get away with it!'

2 'They're always going on about how things were better in their day. I wish they would just leave us alone.'

3 'I usually feel at ease with them, because I don't have to try and impress them like I do my friends. I guess it's easier to be yourself when you're that age.'

4 'Nowadays, their parents give in to them too much. Even the little ones get their own way!'

5 'Most of them are set in their ways, which makes them a bit narrow-minded. It also means that they're out of touch with all the new developments in technology.'

6 'They appear to be incapable of standing on their own two feet. Most of them stay at home living off their parents until they're in their thirties.'

2 Match the highlighted phrases in exercise 1 to definitions 1–12.

1 act naturally
2 be comfortable and relaxed
3 stop fighting or arguing and accept that you can't win
4 be busy with something secret or bad
5 not know what is happening in a particular subject
6 do what you want when somebody has tried to stop you
7 have habits and opinions that you do not want to change
8 talk about something for a long time in an annoying way
9 be independent and able to care for yourself
10 receive money from somebody else because you do not have any yourself
11 do something bad and not be punished for it
12 not annoy or speak to somebody

3 SPEAKING Work in pairs. Discuss your relationship with the older generation. Use the phrases in exercise 1.

Environmental threats and protection

1 Match the words in A to the words in B to make collocations related to the environment. Use a dictionary to help you.

A	B
ban	an imbalance
cause	nature
conserve	harmful practices
maintain	an impact
have	resources
overexploit	an ecosystem
prevent	a species
reduce	fires
threaten	carbon emissions
destroy	toxic waste
produce	animals
protect	a habitat

2 **SPEAKING** Work in pairs. Look at the collocations in exercise 1. Which ones are threats to the environment and which are ways of protecting it? Use a dictionary to help you.

3 Complete the text with the collocations in exercise 1.

The aim of the World Wide Fund for Nature (WWF) is to
¹.. so that future generations may
enjoy it. Much of its work is based around the conservation
of different biomes. In Indian rainforests, several activities
occur that may ².. as magnificent
as the Bengal tiger, for example. Loggers tend to
³.. by cutting down too many trees,
and farmers burn the land to make room for their crops.
By doing this, they ⁴.. which is home to
many different birds and mammals. The goal of the WWF is
to ⁵.. in the area by ensuring that they
have a safe place to live. The organization wants to stop
deforestation and ⁶.. from burning
trees in an attempt to save the rainforest. It would also like
to ⁷.., such as hunting endangered
animals for their skin.

The WWF is also concerned about the ways that different
industries ⁸.. on the environment.
It wants factories to ⁹.. in an effort to
slow climate change. It is also working with companies
that ¹⁰.. which pollutes the world's
rivers. The danger here is that the poisonous substances
can ¹¹.. in the food chain. If the fish
die, then so do the birds and mammals that feed on them.
The WWF insists that we need to ¹²..
so that the living things continue working together in the
way they always have.

Ways of cooking

1 Match the words below to definitions 1–12.

■ bake ■ barbecue ■ boil ■ fry ■ grill ■ poach ■ roast
■ scramble ■ steam ■ stew ■ stir-fry ■ toast

1 cook in a pan with hot fat or oil
2 cook in an oven with a little fat or oil
3 cook in water heated to 100 °C
4 mix together and heat (eggs)
5 cook in an oven with no extra fat
6 cook something slowly in liquid in a closed dish
7 cook on a metal frame outdoors over an open fire
8 cook gently in a small amount of liquid
9 make something go brown by putting it close to heat
10 cook under or over a very strong heat in the oven
11 cook quickly in a pan in very hot oil
12 cook over boiling water

> The past participle (-ed form) of most cooking verbs
> can be used with an item of food:
> a **boiled** egg, **stir-fried** chicken BUT **roast** potatoes

2 Look at the photos. What are the people going to eat? Complete the phrases with adjectives formed from the verbs in exercise 1.

1 .... eggs
2 .... vegetables
3 a .... chicken
4 .... broccoli
5 .... carrots
6 .... potatoes
7 .... mackerel
8 .... bacon
9 .... rice
10 a .... sandwich
11 a .... steak
12 .... fruit

3 **SPEAKING** Work in pairs. What is your favourite food? How is it cooked? Tell your partner.

I love lasagne. First of all, you have to fry the meat ...

Describing gadgets

1 Complete the definitions with the adjectives below.

■ bulky ■ cutting-edge ■ handy ■ hard-wearing ■ pricey ■ sleek

1 .... gadgets are smooth and shiny and look modern.
2 .... devices are easy to use and don't cause any problems.
3 .... items are very expensive.
4 .... objects are too big and difficult to carry.
5 .... technology has all the newest features.
6 .... machines last for a long time.

2 Read the comments about gadgets and complete the table with the highlighted synonyms and antonyms.

1 That's exorbitant! There's no way I could afford it. Mine was a bit more reasonable.
2 That one looks a bit fragile. I need a more resilient one that won't break if I drop it.
3 It's too cumbersome. I'd prefer something lightweight that I can slip into my pocket.
4 This model is smaller and more elegant than the last. The previous one was very plain.
5 The first model is obsolete now. The latest has an innovative design that hasn't been seen before.
6 My old one was useless. This one is much more convenient and it's so easy to use.

	synonym	antonym
bulky	1	2
cutting edge	3	4
handy	5	6
hard-wearing	7	8
pricey	9	10
sleek	11	12

3 Choose the correct answers.

Technology has changed so much. Take the mobile phone, for instance. The first model was nicknamed 'the brick' because of its [1]**bulky / elegant / sleek** design. It weighed over a kilo, but its size made it strong and [2]**hard-wearing / fragile / lightweight**. 'The brick' was rather [3]**resilient / pricey / reasonable** – it cost $3,995!

Today's mobiles are [4]**obsolete / convenient / useless** gadgets with many different functions. Despite their complexity, many different [5]**plain / cumbersome / lightweight** models are available. Of course, the first mobile phone is now [6]**cutting edge / innovative / obsolete**.

4 SPEAKING Work in pairs. Describe the gadgets you own to your partner.

Problems with technology

1 Match the nouns below to definitions 1–12.

■ backup ■ bug ■ cookie ■ data ■ firewall ■ spam ■ spyware ■ Trojan ■ update ■ virus

1 an improvement or a fix for software
2 an error in a computer program
3 information that is stored on a computer
4 a copy of a file that can be used if the original is lost or damaged
5 a small program designed to spread from one computer to another and destroy the drive
6 a software program that can collect secret information like usernames and passwords
7 a software program that seems to be helpful but that is, in fact, designed to destroy data
8 a system that prevents unauthorized users gaining access to a private computer network
9 data sent to a computer by a web server that records a user's actions on a certain website
10 advertising material sent by email to people who have not asked for it

2 Complete the text with the singular or plural form of the words in exercise 1.

The internet can be a dangerous place, but there are steps you can take to keep your computer safe. Firstly, you should install a [1]................................ to protect your machine from other network users. You should also have a filter on your inbox which should stop you receiving [2]................................, offering you services you did not ask about. Unfortunately, there are all kinds of things that can reach your machine in spite of this protection. [3]................................ are used to gather details about your browsing habits, not to mention [4]................................, which is on the lookout for more important information, like your credit card number. A [5]................................ can cause chaos on your hard drive by deleting important files. A [6]................................ might appear to be a computer game, but once you double-click it, it starts writing over your files. A good antivirus system will help here, but the problems can often be avoided by taking proper care of your machine. By installing the latest [7]................................ of the software that your computer uses, you can avoid being affected by any [8]................................ the programs may contain. More importantly, if you do a monthly [9]................................ of everything, you will not lose your [10]................................. This can help to save you from just about any disaster, including security issues.

3 SPEAKING Work in pairs. Look at the words in exercise 1. Talk about your own experience of problems with technology and the experiences of other people that you know.

My laptop got a Trojan last week, but my antivirus system got rid of it.

Politics and society

1 Match the words below to definitions 1–6.

■ communal ■ egalitarian ■ extreme ■ mainstream
■ reactionary ■ secular

1 shared by a number of people
2 considered normal and accepted by most people
3 not connected to religious matters
4 far from what most people consider reasonable
5 based on the belief that everyone should have the same rights
6 opposed to political and social change

2 Match the words below to their antonyms in exercise 1.

1 alternative ....
2 class-based ....
3 moderate ....
4 private ....
5 radical ....
6 spiritual ....

3 Choose the correct answers.

Despite recent changes, the USA is still [1]**a class-based / an egalitarian** society, with different groups having greater or lesser opportunities. Occasionally, some of the more [2]**radical / reactionary** groups protest in favour of a change in the system, but the vast majority have [3]**extreme / moderate** views and are willing to conform. The government is a [4]**secular / spiritual** institution, which aims to separate religion from the state. However, there are still a number of [5]**secular / spiritual** groups in the country which support one religion or another. One of the most famous is the Amish, a group which leads [6]**an alternative / a mainstream** lifestyle, very different from the average American's. The Amish live outside [7]**alternative / mainstream** society and are recognized for their [8]**radical / reactionary** attitude to modern technology, which they refuse to accept. Families have their own [9]**communal / private** houses, but caring for the children is often a [10]**communal / private** activity, and mothers spend time with other families as well as their own. The Amish live in [11]**a class-based / an egalitarian** society regarding social groups, as no particular group receives special privileges. However, the gender roles are different, and it is the men who are responsible for keeping order. The most [12]**extreme / moderate** punishment is expulsion from the community.

4 SPEAKING Work in pairs. Use the words in exercises 1 and 2 to describe the society you live in.

Idioms: politics

1 Match the highlighted phrases in sentences 1–10 to definitions a–j.

1 He didn't tell any lies, but he was definitely being economical with the truth.
2 We avoided saying anything about his appearance because we were being politically correct.
3 The opposition leader was quick off the mark when she answered the Prime Minister.
4 What it all boils down to is money, or the lack of it.
5 The party capitalized on their popularity.
6 The health minister has come under fire for closing down several hospitals.
7 I just plucked the figure of $1,000 out of the air and asked if that would be enough.
8 The Foreign Secretary called a press conference to set the record straight about the negotiations.
9 They talked up the latest opinion poll figures to make it look as if they were more popular.
10 The ministers agreed that they would toe the line to give the appearance of stability.

a have as a main or basic point
b say a name or number without thinking about it
c describe something in a way that makes it sound better or more important than it is
d do what somebody in authority tells you to do, even if you do not want to
e be fast in reacting to a situation
f avoid causing offence to a particular group of people
g give people the correct information about something
h not give important information to disguise the facts
i be criticized severely for something you have done
j take advantage of something

2 Complete the sentences with the idioms in exercise 1. Sometimes more than one answer is possible.

1 They .... the latest unemployment figures so that they sounded better than they were.
2 He had no idea of the price of a carton of milk, so he just .... a number ....
3 We thought that our company was doing well, but we discovered that the boss had ....
4 Members of the party have said they will .... so as not to lose their jobs.
5 The police were .... to blame rioters for the accident.
6 Ministers have .... for the amount of money they claim on expenses.
7 Finding a job these days .... luck.
8 The company director .... after the wrong figures had been published.
9 Don't talk about a person's age if you want to ....
10 The new government .... its election victory to increase taxes.

3 SPEAKING Work in pairs. Compare your answers to exercise 2. Explain any differences in meaning where you have more than one answer.

OXFORD
UNIVERSITY PRESS

Great Clarendon Street, Oxford, OX2 6DP, United Kingdom

Oxford University Press is a department of the University of Oxford.
It furthers the University's objective of excellence in research, scholarship,
and education by publishing worldwide. Oxford is a registered trade
mark of Oxford University Press in the UK and in certain other countries

© Oxford University Press 2014

The moral rights of the author have been asserted

First published in 2014

2018 2017 2016 2015 2014

10 9 8 7 6 5 4 3 2 1

ISBN: 978 0 19 401109 9

Printed in Portugal by Grafica Maiadouro S. A.

This book is printed on paper from certified and well-managed sources

ACKNOWLEDGEMENTS

The authors and the publisher would like to thank Jane Hudson and Kath Stannett for the material they contributed to this book.

The authors and the publisher would also like to thank the many teachers who contributed to the development of the course by commenting on the manuscript, taking part in lesson observations, focus groups and online questionnaires.

The publisher would like to thank the following for their permission to reproduce photographs:
Alamy Images pp.8 (subway/Tomas Abad), 9 (pilot/Blend Images), 9 (patient/Radius Images), 9 (father & daughter/Inmagine), 9 (brothers/Blend Images), 10 (Nelson Mandela/Gallo Images), 13 (Pakistan girls school/imagebroker), 18 (Kilauea lava flow/ Neil Fraser), 18 (plane/Thierry Grun-Aero), 18 (sunset/Gary Doak), 19 (Kilauea volcano/Corey Ford), 21 (Polaris Building, Fairbanks/Sam Harrel/Fairbanks Daily News-Miner/ZUMAPRESS.com), 21 (mural/Jim West), 22 (Aboriginal art/Bill Bachman), 22 (Aboriginal cave paintings/Susanna Bennett), 22 (Aboriginal Dreamtime art/Robert Harding Picture Library Ltd), 25 (The Pink Road House Oodnadatta/David Wall), 28 (forest fire/Design Pics Inc.), 28 (tornado/Deco), 28 (blizzard/Derek Croucher), 31 (squalid bathroom/Caro), 31 (untidy bedroom/ Fotomatador), 35 (Olive oil/Brian Yarvin), 35 (fan/Ken Welsh), 36 (The Rosetta Stone, British Museum/Richard Osbourne), 37 (*Elgin Marbles*,British Museum/Steve Vidler), 37 (British Museum/Tony French), 42 (digital child/age fotostock), 44 (Hugh Laurie/AF Archive), 49 (industrial town/Interfoto), 54 (fast food/Cultura Creative (RF)), 54 (tired student/OJO Images Ltd), 56 (reading/Image Source), 57 (Scrabble/David Taylor Photography), 59 (walking dog/Onoky-Photononstop), 60 (telephone box library/ Iowefoto), 60 (students/PhotoStock-Israel), 62 (books/Nathan Benn), 63 (The Globe Theatre/Robert Harding Picture Library Ltd), 69 (demonstration/Jay Shaw-Baker), 80 (reading newspaper/David J. Green), 80 (presenter/Image Source), 80 (tablet/ Pixellover RM 8), 80 (smartphone/Anatolii Babii), 82 (model/RGB Ventures LLC dba SuperStock), 83 (steps/Blackout Concepts), 86 (senior woman/Image Source), 86 (young woman/Ashley Cameron), 87 (helping hands/amana images inc.), 90 (carer/Golden Pixels LLC), 96 (Imperial scorpion/age fotostock), 97 (iPhone/Alex Segre), 98 (fried insects/Mar Photographics), 101 (Brighton Pier/Eyebyte), 106 (supermarket shelves/Jeff Greenberg), 106 (fruit stall/Images & Stories), 106 (allotment/i love images), 107 (grilled insects/Forget Patrick/SAGAPHOTO.com), 107 (grub meal/David Hancock), 112 (using tablet/Pixellover RM 9), 113 (class/Radius Images), 116 (whiteboard/Bob Daemmrich), 122 (running cartoon/dieKleinert), 124 (ballot box/Rob Wilkinson), 124 (election poster/Jeff Morgan 12), 124 (election poster/Jeff Morgan 14), 132 (class with tablets/Tetra Images), 132 (interactive whiteboard/Patrick Eden), 133 (Emmeline Pankhurst/Archive Pics), 134 (Florence Nightingale/Pictorial Press Ltd), 135 (Lutak Inlet, Alaska/Alaska Stock), 135 (ice floe/ Radius Images), 135 (Autumn in the tundra/blickwinkel), 135 (icebergs/Don Paulson), 135 (Virgin Islands/Steve Murray), 135 (arctic tundra/Accent Alaska.com), 135 (map/Peter Noyce LC), 136 (Egyptian mummy/SuperStock), 136 (Roman coins/ Rob Bartee), 136 (Roman statue/Peter Adams Photography Ltd), 136 (Ming dynasty vase/UK Alan King), 136 (*Cuenca*, Museo de Arte Abstracto Espanol, Abesti Gogora 1960-1964/Bildarchiv Monheim GmbH), 136 (Imperial Cross/Insadco Photography), 136 (pots/Stockconcepts), 136 (Maasai mask/Brian Perry), 138 (back cover blurb/ Henry Westheim Photography), 141 (scrambled eggs/Viktor Fischer), 141 (mackerel/ Food and Drink Photos), 141 (carrots boiling/Craig Yates), 141 (baked potatoes/MBI), 141 (roast chicken/fStop), 141 (bacon/scphoto), 141 (toast/PhotoEdit), 141 (stew/ Catherine Higgins), 143 (Amish buggy/Jeff Greenberg); Central European News p.84 (Frano Selak holding lottery tickets/Europics); Candy Chang p.20 ('I Wish This Was…' project); Corbis pp.7 (kids playing on rubbish/Anna Kari/In Pictures), 10 (Mandela family/Gideon Mendel), 11 (Nelson Mandela/Louise Grubb/Corbis Saba), 12 (Malala Yousafzai/Brendan McDermid/Reuters), 13 (Malala Day/Masroor/Xinhua Press), 16 (Yupik fishing/Kevin Smith/Design Pics), 18 (fisherman/Monty Rakusen/ Cultura), 28 (Richat Structure in Mauritania/George Steinmetz), 28 (Spotted Lake

near Osoyoos, BC/Ernst Kucklich/First Light), 29 (Lanzhou mountains/Imaginechina), 30 (hoarding/Sandy Huffaker), 32 (shark, bath miniature/Martin Gallagher), 33 (beach litter/Ashley Cooper), 34 (*Trash People*/HA Schult/Kirsten Neumann/ Reuters), 35 (litter/PhotoAlto), 54 (The frozen woolly mammoth Yuka/Kiyoshi Ota/ EPA), 55 ('The Frozen Woolly Mammoth Yuka from Siberian Permafrost'/Kiyoshi Ota/ EPA), 62 (Shakespeare's Henry VIII/Luke Macgregor/Reuters), 87 (helping/Dann Tardif/ LWA), 87 (learning to ride/Jose Luis Pelaez Inc/Blend Images), 97 (boys/fStop), 98 (rice fields/Justin Guariglia), 100 (fish and chips/Image Source), 114 (Langley Aerodrome No. 5/Bettmann), 115 (Gustave Whitehead), 116 (students with tablets/Ariel Skelley/ Blend Images), 121 (Khasi wedding/Reuters), 123 (kids football/Bernard Annebicque/ Sygma), 129 (*Lips Zipped Shut*/Todd Davidson/Images.com), 133 (Charles de Gaulle/ Raymond Darolle/Europress/Sygma), 135 (Alaskan Peninsula/NASA), 135 (Ingleton waterfalls/Chris Hepburn/Robert Harding World Imagery), 135 (meadow/Ocean), 135 (swamp/Theo Allofs/Minden Pictures); Duval Guillaume p.71 ('Push To Add Drama' button/TNT 'Your Daily Dose of Drama' campaign); Getty Images pp.6 (We Day/Adam Bettcher), 9 (female footballer/Jade/Blend Images), 10 (Nelson Mandela's cell/Hoberman Collection/UIG), 12 (Malala Yousafzai & family/Queen Elizabeth Hospital Birmingham), 17 (Inupiat people/Luciana Whitaker), 17 (Togiak/Ernest Manewal), 24 (Sydney/Harvey Lloyd), 28 (Giant's Causeway/Patrick Swan/Design Pics), 34 (Ha Schult with his '*trash people*'/Norbert Schiller), 35 ('*Life as we know it*' by artist Slinkachu/Leon Neal/AFP), 35 (mask/Inigo Aspirez/Flickr), 35 (Christopher Columbus portrait/British Library/Robana), 46 (female injection/Peter Dazeley), 46 (male injection/Peter Dazeley), 47 (Vietnamese girl/Hoang Dinh Nam/AFP), 54 (tanning/Francisco Orellana), 59 (man with tablet/Anna Bryukhanova), 60 (DVD's/ Jill Ferry/Flickr), 63 (Shakespeare statue/Jupiterimages), 68 (reporters/Robert Daly), 72 (Falcon Heene/John Moore), 81 (David Attenborough/Popperfoto), 89 (Robert Frost & family/Lofman/Pix Inc./Time & Life Pictures), 90 (joggers/Mark Bowden), 94 (shark fishermen/Jeff Rotman), 95 (dried shark fins/Randy Olson/National Geographic), 95 (shark fins/Sankei), 95 (sharks/Secret Sea Visions), 96 (diver/Carrie Vonderhaar/ Ocean Futures Society/National Geographic), 97 (burger/Lauri Patterson/Vetta), 97 (water bottle/Chris Stein), 97 (coffee beans/Adam Gault/OJO Images), 97 (satchel/ Catherine Farrell/FilmMagic), 101 (fish and chips van/General Photographic Agency), 110 (Kelvin Doe/John Lamparski/WireImage), 115 (The Wright Brothers 1902/SSPL), 116 (recording studio/Chris Schmidt), 120 (gardening/Norm Shafer/The Washington Post), 125 (George Osborne/Matt Cardy), 132 (computer class/sturti), 133 (Margaret Thatcher/William Lovelace), 136 (swords/Javier Larrea), 136 (Stone Age tools/DEA/G. Dagli Orti/De Agostini Picture Library), 140 (family portrait/skynesher), 141 (stir fry/ Foodcollection RF), 141 (broccoli/Philippe Desnerck), Kobal Collection pp.43 (*Gattaca* 1997/Columbia), 44 (*Grey's Anatomy*/ABC-TV), 49 (*Frankenstein* 1931/Universal), 75 (*Fahrenheit 9/11*/Dog Eat Dog/Miramax); Oxford University Press p.35 (football/ Photodisc), 61 (book covers), 65 (*The Great Gatsby* book cover); Peter Menzel Photography pp.99 (Jeff Devine, What I Eat: Around the World in 80 Diets/Peter Menzel), 99 (Alamin Hasan/What I Eat: Around the World in 80 Diets/Peter Menzel), 99 (Mestilde Shigwedha, What I Eat: Around the World in 80 Diets/Peter Menzel), 99 (Riccardo Casagrande, What I Eat: Around the World in 80 Diets/Peter Menzel); Press Association Images p.98 (cultured beef/David Parry/PA Wire); Rex Features pp.39 (The Lost Collection: Art Left on London Transport, London - 13 May 2011/KK Outlet), 44 (Albert Einstein/Roger-Viollet), 74 (*Nanook of the North* 1922/Moviestore Collection), 81 (Sir David Attenborough), 125 (Tom Bletsoe/Geoffrey Robinson), 127 (John F Kennedy/Sipa Press), 136 (Administrative tablet of clay:Mesopotamian/ Sumerian 3100-2900 BC/Universal History Archive/Universal Images Group); Seawater Greenhouse Ltd p.98 (Seawater greenhouses); Science Photo Library p.111 (Algal research/Pascal Goetgheluck); Shutterstock pp.35 (seashells/Ed Samuel), 35 (Sunglasses/Aaron Amat), 35 (Moroccan tile/Tawin Mukdharakosa), 39 (underground/Samot), 43 (DNA/Yang Nan), 57 (text/Cerbi), 59 (female with headphones/Spectral-Design), 60 (knitting/littleny), 88 (forest road/CWB), 96 (technology/Oleksiy Mark), 109 (futuristic glasses/Syda Productions), 109 (touch screen/italianestro), 127 (American flag/xtock), 135 (lilypads/Ethan Daniels), 135 (estuary/MartinsL), 136 (armour/Sibrikov Valery), 137 (human anatomy/ Vectomart), 141 (wok/SergeBertasiusPhotography), 141 (barbecue/Brian Holm); The Advertising Archives pp.70 (*The Guardian* TV advert 1986), 70 (*The Guardian* TV advert 1986), 70 (*The Guardian* TV advert 1986), 70 (*The Guardian* TV advert 1986); TravelEyes pp.4 (Traveleyes tourists), 5 (TravelEyes tourists), 5 (Amar Latif).

The authors and publisher are grateful to those who have given permission to reproduce the following extracts and adaptations of copyright material: p.10 Adapted extract from *Long Walk To Freedom* by Nelson Mandela. Copyright © 1994, 1995 by Nelson Rolihlahla Mandela. By permission of Little, Brown and Company. All rights reserved; p.16 Adapted extract from 'In Remote Alaskan Villages, Teachers Struggle to Make School Meaningful' by Sarah Garland. © 2013. The Atlantic Media Co., as first published in The Atlantic Magazine. All rights reserved. Distributed by Tribune Media Services; p.42 Adapted extract from "Gattaca at 15" by Daniel Allott, http://spectator.org 24 October 2012. Reproduced by permission of The American Spectator; p.88 "The Road Not Taken" from the book *The Poetry of Robert Frost* Edited by Edward Connery Lathem. Copyright © 1944, 1969 by Henry Holt and Company, copyright © 1944 by Robert Frost. Used by Permission of Henry Holt and Company, LLC.; p.108 Adapted extract from 'I grew up in the future' by Veronique Greenwood, www. aeonmagazine.com 18 March 2013. Reproduced by permission of Aeon Magazine (@ aeonmag); pp.14, 26, 40, 66, 9, 104, 118 Definitions from *Oxford Advanced Learner's Dictionary 8th Edition*, Oxford University Press 2010; pp.14, 78 Definitions from *Oxford Collocations Dictionary for students of English 2nd Edition*, Oxford University Press 2009; p.14 Definitions from *Oxford Idioms Dictionary for learners of English 2nd Edition*, Oxford University Press 2006; pp.14, 40 Definitions from *Oxford Phrasal Verbs Dictionary for learners of English*, Oxford University Press 2006; p.14 Definitions from *Oxford Learner's Thesaurus*, Oxford University Press 2008; p.14 Definitions from *Oxford Wordpower słownik angielsko-polski polsko-angielski*, Oxford University Press 2007.

Although every effort has been made to trace and contact copyright holders before publication, this has not been possible in some cases. We apologise for any apparent infringement of copyright and, if notified, the publisher will be pleased to rectify any errors or omissions at the earliest possible opportunity.